The Computerized Society

Living and Working in an Electronic Age

Selections from THE FUTURIST

Edited by Edward Cornish

World Future Society
4916 St. Elmo Avenue
Bethesda, MD 20814
U.S.A

The Futurist's Library

The purpose of the Futurist's Library is to make available in a convenient form a selection of articles from THE FUTURIST magazine bearing on a single theme. Volumes that have appeared to date include:

1999: The World of Tomorrow. Edited by Edward Cornish (1978).

Education and the Future. Edited by Lane Jennings and Sally Cornish (1980).

Communications Tomorrow: The Coming of the Information Society. Edited by Edward Cornish (1982).

Careers Tomorrow: The Outlook for Work in a Changing World. Edited by Edward Cornish (1983).

The Great Transformation: Alternative Futures for Global Society. Edited by Edward Cornish (1983).

Global Solutions: Innovative Approaches to World Problems. Edited by Edward Cornish (1984).

Habitats Tomorrow: Homes and Communities in an Exciting New Era. Edited by Edward Cornish (1984).

(These volumes are available from the World Future Society at $6.95 each.)

Editorial Coordination: Ulla Bogdan, Sarah Warner
Production Manager: Jefferson Cornish
Front Cover: Painting by John Porter

Published by:
    World Future Society
    4916 St. Elmo Avenue
    Bethesda, Maryland 20814-5089
    U.S.A.

International Standard Book Number: 0-930242-24-6

Printed in the United States of America

The Futurist's Library consists of collections of articles from THE FUTURIST magazine. Most of the articles are of recent vintage but a few older articles have been chosen. These articles have stood the test of time in terms of their significance and lasting interest, but they contain details reflecting the time at which they were first published. Readers should bear in mind the original publication dates.

Contents

Introduction

The Thinking Machine

The computer is perhaps the greatest surprise of the twentieth century.

Futurists and science-fiction writers long anticipated the airplane, television, and space travel. But the development and triumph of the computer seem to have surprised everyone.

Even after the computer had been invented, no one seems to have foreseen its eventual importance. A survey indicated that there was virtually no use for the contraption aside from perhaps a few very large government agencies. IBM initially refused to manufacture computers and changed its mind only after other companies had entered the business. George Orwell wrote his brilliant novel about the future *Nineteen Eighty-four* without ever mentioning computers, though they had been operational for years before he wrote his book.

But the computer advanced anyway, constantly surprising even its enthusiasts. Initially, computers were large, stupid, and very expensive, and they could be understood and operated only by an elite group of high priests. But the computers got steadily smaller, smarter, cheaper, and easier to use. By the mid-1970s, the microcomputer had appeared as well as the portable terminal and the "modem" to connect computers to each other through ordinary telephone lines. Computer technology proliferated in every direction. Long-time computer enthusiasts rubbed their eyes at how much computer power could be packed into a cheap, modest-sized appliance that could sit on anybody's desk. Edward Steinmuller, a Stanford economist, once remarked, "If the airliners had progressed as rapidly as this technology, the Concorde would be carrying half a million passengers at 20 million miles an hour for less than a penny apiece."

Now huge data banks are putting at our fingertips incredible quantities of information about almost anything from house prices to trademarks, from airplane schedules to stock quotations. A single computer terminal now is the window through which one may inspect the contents of thousands of "yellow pages" or virtually all the scholarly books ever written about the poet Dante.

The intellectual power of a huge computer from the 1960s can now be compressed into a silicon wafer no bigger than a baby's fingernail. Yet that may seem only a modest accomplishment 20 years from now. Already, technologists are talking about new devices to make computers still smarter and to miniaturize them still further. Fantastic amounts of data may be compressed into tiny magnetic areas that go round and round like chains of bubbles deep inside an electronic chip.

Now the race is on to build "supercomputers" with the power to solve problems beyond the capability of hundreds of ordinary mortals. Near panic seems to have seized certain U.S. scientists who fear that the Japanese with their crash program to develop "Fifth Generation" computers will outstrip American efforts, thus leaving the United States disadvantaged both militarily and economically.

There is talk of "biochips" no bigger than large molecules. These could lead to another breakthrough in the effort to miniaturize the computer's capabilities, raising the hope—or specter—of tiny microrobots that might perform a wide variety of tasks that we today have some difficulty even imagining. One possible example might be microrobots that could be introduced into a person's circulatory system to make emergency repairs on a defective artery, clean up a blood clot, or chop away at a cancer. Conceivably, miniaturization might reach the point where a microrobot could enter a living human cell and destroy a virus or perhaps remove a harmful gene. Though still little more than a gleam in the eyes of computer enthusiasts, biochips might make it possible to pack almost incredible amounts of information into a tiny space. Three-dimensional arrays of data would imitate the complexity of the human brain. Lewis Branscomb, IBM's vice president for research, has projected that a computer in the twenty-first century may have the power of 16,000 human brains— and even that awesome projection could fall short of future reality.

Biochips could also hasten the day when human brains are physically linked together, thereby creating a new race of superintelligent cyborgs. Possibly there will be a way to hook our brains into a computer so that we acquire its memory. This man-machine symbiosis might lead to an entirely new form of human experience and a tremendous increase in human capabilities.

Already, experiments are under way to use computers and robots to replace the functions of defective body organs. Paraplegics, for instance, may use voice commands to direct robots that can prepare a meal, remove a tray, or provide a drink.

People will find it increasingly easy to speak to computers in ordinary language and ask them to solve the most abstruse scholarly or mathematical problems. The computer's awesome capabilities may both thrill and frighten us. If computers can do so much, will there be any need for people in the future? Is the computer a humble and faithful servant or a new God? A loyal friend and worthy colleague, or an evil force that is now devouring our humanity like an electronic cancer?

The Computer As Colleague and Rival

The computer was touted initially as merely a mechanical device that could perform huge amounts of arithmetic drudgery. Computers were really very stupid, computerists assured us. They couldn't "think"; all they could do was plod along doing simple-minded things that would bore human beings.

Computers went to work on humble clerical tasks—keeping track of social security and tax records for government agencies, maintaining indexes for major libraries, and doing huge amounts of mindless "number crunching" for college professors who could not interest bright graduate students in such a tiresome task.

So long as computers were expensive—and not very bright—they were not widely viewed as potential replacements for human labor. But by the 1970s, computers had reached the point where it was clear that they could replace human workers for many purposes. With the advent of rising unemployment, the computer came to be viewed as a potential threat to human workers.

No longer was there any question that computers could increase human productivity, sometimes by prodigious amounts. Applied to word processing, the computer might enable a single typist to produce as much work as two or three equipped only with typewriters. To make matters "worse," a secretary's boss might take over the computer and do the job without any help at all.

By the 1980s, microcomputers were proliferating everywhere in society, taking over one job after another. The displacement of human labor did not, however, appear to be as big a problem as some feared, for several reasons. First, most people had plenty of other work to do even after a computer took over part of their job. Second, the computer was often used to improve the quality of the product rather than simply to produce the same product more cheaply: A document that once might have been corrected in ink now was sent back to be done again.

Still, there was little doubt that computers were enabling human workers to become far more productive and the potential for a major displacement of human workers remained. Just as blue-collar workers worried that robots would take over the assembly lines, white-collar and professional workers saw the possibility that they, too, might be automated out of their jobs.

Human translators saw, for example, that computers could take over much of their work. A computer makes a rough translation of a Russian text into English; then a human translator corrects the text, removing errors and making sentences more idiomatic. Result: A human translator plus a computer can do about the same amount of work as two human translators, suggesting the possibility that 50% of translators would lose their jobs—and even more as computers improve. Actually, of course, the picture is much more complicated: The improved productivity of translators equipped with computers will lower the cost of translation, and that may greatly expand the market. Many more books, reports, and other materials can be translated and the demand for translators may actually grow, thanks to computers doing much of the work.

The Computer As Teacher

For educators, the computer may prove the most significant technology since the book.

Educators have long sensed the power of the computer to revolutionize their profession but generally have not been overly enthusiastic about it. The book had a similarly cool reception from academia when writing was the new technology. The philosopher Socrates warned his students: "The discovery of the alphabet will create forgetfulness in the learners' souls, and cause them to lose their memories."

Practicing what he preached, Socrates never wrote a line and would be forgotten today if his admirers had not disregarded his strictures against writing. Perhaps some of today's professors who find little use for computers will be remembered in the future only because their books and papers are accessible through computerized data banks.

But computers are slowly winning over the educators, just as writing did. Some colleges now routinely issue a computer to every student. Others won't let students graduate without proving thier skill with a computer.

The computer's progress in elementary and secondary schools has been slower, but the growing number of teaching programs for computers plus the increasing power of computers and their declining costs suggest that more and more children—even toddlers—will find computers in their schools in the years ahead.

Like the book, the computer promises to make education more convenient, more pleasant, faster, and cheaper. Everyone stands to benefit: Young people will find it easier to master mathematics, spelling, and other subjects that cause them much trouble today, because the computer can patiently tutor them until they have gained mastery. Teachers will escape many dull tasks and gain salary raises because of their improved productivity. Parents will find their youngsters learning to read faster. And school boards may be willing to pay teachers more when the taxpayers see that their money is being spent cost-effectively.

The results of computerizing the educational system could be astounding. But even more surprising may be how much children learn before they enter school. Three-year-olds may learn to read on their home computers, having picked up the skill with only a little nudging from their parents. "Computers appear to be unique in their ability to motivate and captivate students," says Tom Rich of Prince Edward Island's Department of Education.

Learning how to read may become a game, going something like this: The child placed at a computer keyboard starts hitting the keys more or less at random. Ordinarily that would quickly get boring, but the computer begins talking:

"B," says the computer. "B. . .B. . .B. . .F. . .F. . . F. . .H. . .H. . . ."

The child soon discovers that he can control what the computer says by selecting the keys. Now he is ready to write his name, especially if he gets a suggestion from an adult that he might try to get the computer to say his name.

What joy when the computer finally says "Billy"!

From then on, the child can go on to writing whole sentences saying things like "Billy wants a bike for Christmas."

Perfectly average children may be reading and writing at age three or four if they have access to a computer and are given a few minutes of instruction.

It will be easy for youngsters to write Grandma a thank-you letter for her Christmas present: A difficult chore for a youngster using paper and pen becomes simplicity itself with a computer hooked up to an electronic network. And because electronic mail is so easy, the youngster may write to Grandma quite often and tell her a great deal. People who write letters on computers typically find themselves writing far more than they would otherwise because the writing is so easy.

The youngster may also start keeping a diary because it will be so much fun. The diary will be useful for all kinds of purposes in later life, but in the early years it will be a splendid tool to help a young person develop intellectually and emotionally.

Computers will also make it relatively easy for youngsters to learn arithmetic, spelling, science, and other subjects before entering school, which will raise the question: How will schools deal with youngsters who have mastered most of the curriculum of the local elementary school before entering first grade? One provisional solution may be to allow them to continue working on computers, advancing to high-school subjects while still in elementary school. More likely, the entire curriculum will be advanced so that in the future the average youngster finishing elementary school will know as much as a high-school graduate today. A Canadian study suggests that students may go through the traditional school curriculum in only 7 years rather than 13. Assuming they start school at age 6, they could apply for college at age 12.

Business and government are using computers to train their employees, with impressive results: British Columbia Telephone reports that a computerized course reduced the time required to learn material by nearly half. Meanwhile, many parents are buying computers for their children. Already, some people are worried that children in poor families will suffer irretrievably because their families may not be able to afford to give them a computer.

The Computer As Expert

Computers are likely to become the "world's greatest experts" in a growing number of fields. Expert systems—computer programs that can answer questions on a subject better than most human experts—now constitute one of the hottest areas in the race for artificial intelligence.

To develop expert systems, a new field—"knowledge engineering"—is now developing rapidly. A knowledge engineer interrogates experts to determine how they make their judgments and then puts their answers into the computer in the form of a series of "IF—, THEN—" statements. (IF the car won't start, THEN the battery may be dead; IF the battery is dead, THEN a new battery may be needed.) Once the statements are in the computer, the computer can answer questions like an expert.

By picking the brains of a number of experts and merging their collective wisdom, the computer may actually outperform any single human expert. Unlike the human experts, the computer does not forget any of the rules, once they are programmed into it.

The power of an expert system was demonstrated a few years ago when a system called PROSPECTOR succeeded in locating a rich deposit of molybdenum that human geologists and miners had sought in vain for many years. PROSPECTOR, developed at SRI International in Menlo Park, California, called attention to a small area that had been neglected, though miners had sunk shafts all around it.

Knowledge engineers now are using "shell" programs—into which specialized knowledge from many different fields can be entered. A "shell" program greatly speeds up the process of preparing an expert system since it is, in effect, an "empty" expert and all that is required is to place into it the special knowledge required to make it an expert on a particular subject.

Shell programs originated at Stanford University after Edward Feigenbaum, a pioneer in artificial intelligence, developed a program called MYCIN to deal with determining what parasitic disease a patient might have. To develop other medical programs, Feigenbaum and his associates stripped away the portion of the MYCIN program that related specifically to parasitic diseases. What was left constituted a "shell" into which other specialized bodies of knowledge could then be fitted.

Expert systems may be expected to proliferate in fields ranging from law to car repair. People will use them much as they now use a book. The creation of expert systems has revealed that many textbooks today are quite inexact and unintelligible. Thus expert systems may lead to better textbooks in the future and also better teachers.

Physicians are beginning to use computerized "medical experts" to make sure that they have considered all possible causes of a patient's problem. In the future, patients may have the option of consulting computers about their symptoms just as many now consult books. Sensing devices connected to a computer could take the patient's temperature, perform blood and other tests, and then use the latest medical knowledge to offer a diagnosis. Experiments indicate that many patients prefer to deal with a computer—especially when discussing private matters like sex. However, patients would still need a human physician to prescribe medicine, perform surgery, and carry out other tasks.

The Computer As Friend

We may not be able to take a computer to lunch, but increasingly the computer is functioning as a friend.

A computer operated by the telephone company

politely tells us that we have reached the wrong number and to please check the number we are calling. A computer in an automobile may remind us that we have left the key in the ignition or forgotten to close the door.

As computers become more humanlike, they will increasingly function as companions. Psychologist Philip R. Harris has speculated in THE FUTURIST magazine that space colonists may become emotionally attached to their robots, It will cost too much to ship food for dogs and cats, so robots will become substitute pets.

Automobile owners often give their cars human names, and this seems to be particularly true for cars that talk. Sometimes, however, the computer may become a kind of invisible friend: at least, that is the case with a saleswoman in Bethesda, Maryland. She likes the fact that her car's voice reminds her of things—and thinks of it as an invisible companion called Sarah, who travels with her and constantly looks after her.

In the future, we may find that computers are increasingly becoming artificial friends—providing us with helpful reminders about what we need to do, remembering addresses for us, playing music for us that we have indicated we like, etc.

The possibility for people to find a form of friendship in their computers may seem curious, but people do become friends with dogs, cats, horses, and other nonhumans. Computers have the potential of becoming far more intelligent and perhaps more satisfactory as friends than animals, especially if the computer seems human in its voice or appearance.

The Computer As Home

In the future, we may find ourselves living in a computerized environment. A home may have a central computer that will serve as its brain. Once installed, the computer will run the house, summoning plumbers and electricians as needed, turning down the light, alerting the police to unauthorized entry, and exchanging information with the computers of neighboring houses. ("Can we borrow a cup of sugar? . . . Do you know a good babysitter? . . . ")

The home computer may also order up music to suit our moods, along with appropriate fragrances and video scenes. When we come home after a hard day at the office, it may give us soft music, sunset scenes, and perhaps the smell of a sea breeze.

Computers will prepare our meals, perhaps with the help of robots. Very likely, much of the "intelligence" will be decentralized—placed in appliances like refrigerators, microwave ovens, etc., rather than centralized in a single master computer, but the effect will be that of living within an intelligent environment—one that is very friendly and sensitive to all our whims.

The Computer As Superior

There seems little doubt today that computers may eventually prove superior to human beings in many ways. There is no reason, however, to think that they will necessarily be our masters or that they will be in any way malicious. Thousands of years ago, man tamed horses and cattle, beasts that are far bigger and more powerful than he is. In the future, we may develop similar friendly relationships with computers without their dominating us.

Computers will help us solve many of our human problems—and thus make life much better for us. Conceivably, there will be great networks of super-computers that will tackle world problems that now lie beyond the power of human experts. Little by little, we may be able to construct electronic experts in peacemaking that would help prevent the outbreak of future wars. We can only speculate on how that could be accomplished, but it now seems clear that computers can, in some ways at least, develop greater intelligence than we ourselves have.

George Bugliarello, president of the Polytechnic Institute of New York, believes that we are at the dawning of an era of "hyperintelligence," the result of computers working in collaboration with thousands of human brains and social organizations.

"A network of millions of nodes turned to problem-solving represents a large quantum step in the problem-solving ability of our species," says Bugliarello. "If we are willing and able to pursue the opportunities that the emergence of global computer networks offers us, then we can truly expect that hyperintelligence and a new and higher form of human society will emerge."

—Edward Cornish

TOM CHALKLEY

Fred Best

Technology and the Changing World of Work

The United States and other industrial nations are now experiencing wave after wave of innovations that bring profound changes in our personal and occupational lives. At the core of these changes is the computer. More than 3 million Americans purchased home and personal computers during 1982, with that figure doubling to 6 million in 1983. If the cost of purchased or rented computer time continues to decline at its historical rate of 50% every two and one-half years, and if the complexity of utilization is reduced by "user-friendly" software, computers and allied technologies will soon be assimilated into every aspect of our lives.

The impacts of such technological change on the economy, the world of work, and our personal lives will be phenomenal. These innovations are likely to alter the nature of work activities within all economic sectors, dramatically affect the growth and location of employment opportunities, and shift the relationships between our jobs and personal lives.

Changing Skill Requirements

Up to 45% of existing U.S. jobs will be significantly altered by technological changes over the next

Computers and other technological innovations are changing the nature of work and the balance between our jobs and our personal lives. Here, an expert on the impacts of new technologies offers some long-term speculations on the future of work.

20 years, many through an upgrading of skills.

The historical trend toward mechanization is becoming increasingly sophisticated as robots and computer-coordinated operations take over routine and dangerous tasks now performed by workers. For example, the installation of robots in the United States has been growing by 30% per year, increasing from 200 in 1970 to 3,500 in 1980. Moderate estimates indicate that there will be 35,000 installed robots in America by 1990 and that applications will skyrocket during the last decade of the twentieth century.

Small computers, sophisticated sensors and servo-mechanisms, and design and control instruments that are easier to understand and use are moving us rapidly toward the "cybernetic promise" of highly integrated and flexible production systems. For example, the growing application of CAD/CAM systems (computer-assisted design/computer-assisted manufacturing) now allows industrial planners to design products on computer screens and then reformat machinery on the shop floor to produce products by centralized programming. The implications for increased productivity and product diversity are spellbinding.

Many workers will have to be reassigned to new tasks. While some of these new tasks might not require greater skill, many necessitate an understanding of new and more complex technologies. For example, General Motors Corporation predicts that 50% of its work force in the year 2000 will be categorized as skilled tradespersons (technicians, inspectors, monitors, etc.), compared with 16% in 1980. Thus, there will be a need for more highly trained personnel such as engineers, technicians, computer specialists, and managers with basic technical skills.

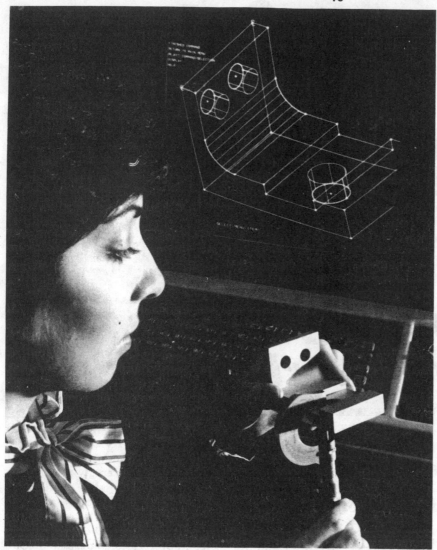

SPERRY CORPORATION

Applications analyst compares computer-generated drawing with finished bracket produced by computer-assisted design and manufacturing system. Innovations such as this CAD/CAM system are increasing demand in manufacturing sectors for computer specialists, engineers, technicians, and managers with basic technical skills.

because of productivity gains from using microelectronic rather than mechanical parts. The General Motors plant in Lordstown, Ohio, reduced its work force by 10% after increasing productivity 20% through the introduction of welding robots. In Providence, Rhode Island, the *Journal Bulletin* cut its printing staff from 242 workers in 1970 to 98 in 1978 as a result of new typesetting technology. These examples underscore the fact that workers have indeed been displaced by technology; however, the question remains as to how extensive such displacement will be in coming years.

Concern over job loss due to the higher productivity of machines has historical roots, beginning with Luddite resistance to industrial mechanization in early-nineteenth-century England. However, despite isolated cases of worker dislocation, most experts believe that technological advances have generally fostered economic and job growth by increasing the quality and quantity of products while lowering the costs.

Because costs are lower, producers can afford to sell at lower prices, which in turn commonly causes consumers to buy more. As a result of increased demand, producers generally employ as many or more workers than before technological innovation began to increase output. When this process occurs throughout the economy, the result is economic growth, with higher real wages and an increase of employment.

Two historic examples illustrate this process. First, during the early stages of the Industrial Revolution, the introduction of the Hargreaves jenny in 1770 ultimately allowed one worker to produce as much as 200 spinners could without the jenny. Yet employment in Britain's textile industry increased from less than 100,000 in 1770 to about 350,000 in 1800 because productivity allowed major reductions in price, leading to even more dramatic increases in market demand for textiles.

A second example is the introduction of the assembly line by Henry Ford. As a result of this combination of machinery and in-

Technological innovations will also profoundly affect the nature of work in both office and service occupations. Just as we have moved from manual typewriters and carbon copies to memory typewriters and photocopy machines over the last few decades, newer technologies will vastly increase the efficiency and output of information processing.

Dramatic reductions in the cost of computers, the development of user-friendly software, and the availability of high-speed printers and telecommunication systems will create a fundamental shift from paper to electronics as the main medium of operation. Typewriters, file cabinets, and mail systems will increasingly be replaced by word processors, computerized data retrieval systems, and video transmissions between computer terminals.

As in the case of manufacturing and material processing, many jobs will become unnecessary. Demand will gradually disappear for mail deliverers, file clerks, stenographers, and other workers. Familiarity and skill with computers will become essential to all office workers, from manager to secretary.

Displacement and Realignment

National Cash Register reduced its U.S. work force from 37,000 to 18,000 between 1970 and 1975

The Evolution of Work

The social, institutional, and human roles associated with work have changed dramatically as human civilization has evolved. The work of antiquity was essentially direct physical toil, required for immediate survival. For primitive peoples, "work" and "leisure" were almost completely integrated. As civilization developed, work and nonwork activities continued to be integrated within families and tribes.

With the emergence of agriculture, economic surpluses, and culturally transferable knowledge, work became easier and more distinct as a social activity. Specialization and individual roles and responsibilities began to emerge as key elements of human existence.

As economic surplus, development of productive tools, and specialization continued to grow, the goals and conditions of work continued to change. Work became increasingly oriented toward the improvement of the human condition rather than bare survival. The resulting surpluses gave rise to increasingly productive tools, and ultimately machinery, which correspondingly allowed and required further refinement of skills and increased specialization.

While work dominated life, the concept of "leisure" as distinct from "work" began to crystallize. Industrial society was a natural outgrowth of these trends. As machinery became increasingly important and sophisticated, work became progressively specialized and oriented toward the use of tools and capital within the context of complex human organizations.

Organizational interdependence and division of labor gave rise to the ultimate predominance of employment. While productive human activity continued to be performed outside the context of employment, work became commonly viewed as an activity performed by "holding a job."

These dramatic shifts have caused a near inversion of the concepts of "work" and "leisure." As defined by classical philosophers, leisure was restricted to reflection and the fine arts; it was commonly viewed as nonmanual activities within preindustrial societies. Commerce, science, politics, writing, and all arts came to be viewed as the freely chosen "leisurely" pursuits of the elites.

Today, as progressively larger proportions of the work forces in advanced industrial societies become employed in "white-collar" jobs doing "knowledge work," the work activities of today are increasingly like the "leisure" activities of the past. While contemporary work conditions are commonly far from utopian, today's jobs tend to require more autonomy, creativity, freedom of expression, and skill than that required during the pre-industrial and early industrial eras.

While the work of the foreseeable future is likely to resemble much of what we do today, historical perspective suggests the importance of keeping an open mind to the possibility of radical changes in the medium- and long-range future. Just as the all-encompassing struggle for physical survival that commonly epitomized primitive humanity has little resemblance to "jobholding" within the offices of today, the nature of work in the future may take on new dimensions that we can scarcely perceive.

—Fred Best

---

dustrial organization, it took 56% fewer hours to produce the average car in 1920 than it did in 1910, leading to a 62% reduction in the real dollar price of an automobile. Consumers who previously could not afford a car began to make purchases, sales increased tenfold, and Ford employment rose from 37,000 to 206,000 in just 10 years. Workers may have been shifted to new assignments, but there was no overall loss of jobs.

From the standpoint of preserving and creating jobs, there appear to be few alternatives to technological innovation. While these changes are likely to cause considerable displacement and reassignment of workers, failure to modernize will cause affected industries to lose pace with national and international competition and ultimately cause even greater loss of employment and economic growth.

Technology and Non-Job Work

There are increasing signs that technological change may also alter the balance between job activities and our personal lives. If we define work as "productive human activity," it is clear that work has never been confined to "holding a job." There have always been people who are self-employed, who build their own houses, raise children, provide voluntary social services, and perform countless other productive actions outside the context of employment. The balance of productive activity inside and outside the workplace has undergone many changes in recent years and will probably change considerably in the future.

Just as the development of heavy machinery drew work out of the home and into factories and offices during the Industrial Revolution, new technologies may cause households and neighborhood groups to become more self-sustaining and to abandon institutional settings for many productive activities. Harbingers of such realignments are suggested by the emerging uses of many new technologies:

• **Home and personal computers.** The potential of home and personal computers, which didn't exist 10 years ago but now are an increasingly common new "home appliance," has scarcely been explored. This technology, which is greatly expanding in power and diminishing in price, is already being used for home entertainment centers, long-distance communication and mail systems, cookbooks, medical advisors, high-speed typewriters, portable offices, family business and tax filing systems, art and graphics devices, educational tutors, library reference services, financial planning, and control of other household appliances. Countless new uses, many of which are integrated with other new technologies, are being developed daily.

• **Video recorders.** Like home and personal computers, video recorders and disc players have emerged from nowhere in the course of only a few years. As archives of television and motion picture entertainment are rapidly transferred to video tapes and discs, a progressively larger portion of entertainment is likely to be pulled back into the home. The use of video recorders as substitutes for home movie cameras also affects the entire film development and processing industry.

• **Decentralized energy production and conservation.** A variety of new, improved, and rediscovered technologies are being developed as alternatives to centralized energy sources. Photovoltaics, solar heating, windmill generation, a variety of conservation measures, and other energy-related technologies are replacing or reducing dependence on central energy sources. These devices are likely to become more attractive as prices decline and the costs of central energy increase.

• **Decentralized medical care.** A number of affordable devices and services are being developed that provide patient-utilized and home-based medical care. For example, new technologies make it both desirable and less expensive to undertake sophisticated "do-it-yourself" medical treatments such as kidney dialysis, cancer chemotherapy, and intravenous feeding.

• **Decentralized and interactive communication systems.** Home-linked and controlled communication technologies are being developed that greatly expand the choice of information and provide options

COURTESY OF DIGITAL EQUIPMENT CORPORATION

Computer terminal and telephone allow office work to be done at home. Individuals can move work activities out of formal organizations and create new balances between their jobs and personal lives.

for interaction and local control. Cable and satellite television greatly enhance viewer choice, provide the potential for two-way communication, and open the option of local and neighborhood stations. Teleconferencing expands the concept of conference calls on the telephone to include visual communication. Satellite and microwave transmission greatly reduce the cost and difficulty of long-distance communication. When these communication systems are used with other technologies such as personal computers, work tasks that formerly had to be located and coordinated at a central location can be decentralized.

While the ultimate impact of these and other technologies is uncertain, their utilization will dramatically change the activities and skill required for work. They might significantly alter the timing, location, and organizational context of work in the future. These same technologies will increase self-sufficiency, open new options for individual business ventures, and generally reduce the need for "holding a job."

An Exploratory Scenario: Toward a Home-Based Economy?

Many novel developments are emerging that might make it desirable, efficient, and necessary to reduce traditional jobholding as the focus of "purposeful and productive human activity." High unemployment and growing job instability suggest the need for individuals to find backup modes of activity that are economically and psychologically rewarding.

The emergence of relatively inexpensive and user-friendly technologies may make it economically efficient and personally rewarding to move both job and non-job work activities out of formal work organizations. Greater flexibility in work arrangements could allow many individuals and groups to meet personal and economic needs through a better balance of job-linked work and other productive efforts.

There are already countless jobholders with computer-based home businesses and flexible worktime and workplace arrangements that allow them to perform job responsibilities without having to be "at work" in the usual sense of the term.

If such conditions become more prevalent, the average worker of tomorrow might work "full time" for six or seven years within a traditional work environment. Then, in order to better handle family responsibilities, the worker might arrange to perform most job responsibilities at home using information technologies. He or she might then reduce worktime given to employment and develop an auxiliary business enterprise, perhaps to increase home-based self-sufficiency. Ultimately, the worker might return to work on a part-time or part-year basis while retraining for new skills.

Without doubt, such arrangements would pose some costs and dangers to individuals, employers, and the economy. For example, the worker might worry about being able to return to suitable employment after an extended period away from an organization. Organizations might have trouble de-emphasizing and re-emphasizing the roles of individual workers. There might also be concern with the loss of social-professional networks, problems of maintaining income during de-emphasis of employment, and discontinuance or reduction of fringe benefits.

Certainly such a system would entail individual responsibility, initiative, and accountability. However, more people might be willing to confront the costs and dangers

Couple tries out program on home computer. About 6 million Americans bought home and personal computers in 1983—twice as many as the year before. The impact of computers and other new technologies will be felt in every aspect of our personal and working lives, says author Best.

if recurrent unemployment and job insecurity make it necessary, if individual preferences for more autonomy within work settings increase, and if institutional and social policies provide the necessary options and resources.

While new balances between household- and employment-based economies may emerge primarily via individual initiative, they could be encouraged by a number of institutional and social policies. Policies that might support such developments include:

• Tax incentives to defer use of earnings for utilization during periods of de-emphasized employment.

• Guaranteed credit and loans.

• Individually vested retraining vouchers.

• Guidelines for job-return rights.

• Subsidies and tax incentives for the purchase and use of home-based technologies.

• Options for flexible worktime arrangements.

• Financial incentives to encourage use of homes as offices and to reduce job-related travel.

• Standardization of selected information technologies.

• Options for selecting and continuing fringe benefits during de-emphasized employment.

• Options for using income maintenance payments to start small business enterprises.

The costs of such policies are not likely to be undertaken unless private and public expenditures for other policies such as income

maintenance, retraining, public transportation, public service employment, and general social services are reduced. Clearly, the political consensus for such a tradeoff is not likely to emerge until a significant number of individuals have developed nontraditional home-job work patterns on their own.

Although jobholding will probably continue as the prevalent pattern of work for the immediate future, ongoing transitional instability, shifting human preferences toward work, and new technologies may foster continued growth of hybrid balances between job and household activities. We can only speculate on whether such patterns will develop into a major trend or prevalent pattern; however, private and public policy makers must begin now to think about the implications, costs, and benefits.

About the Author

Fred Best, president of Pacific Management and Research Associates (1208 Seventh Avenue, Sacramento, California 95818), has written extensively on management and human resources, economic development, and the impacts of new technologies. His books include *The Future of Work, Flexible Life Scheduling*, and *Work Sharing*. This article is excerpted from his report *The Future of Work: A View from the United States*, prepared for the Swedish Secretariat for Future Studies.

Eight Scenarios for Work in the Future

by Martin Morf

Work in the future may be challenging and profitable—if you can get it and if you can do it. Changes in society and technology could bring a broad variety of possible futures, as these eight scenarios of the world of work show.

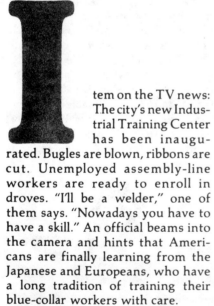

Item on the TV news: The city's new Industrial Training Center has been inaugurated. Bugles are blown, ribbons are cut. Unemployed assembly-line workers are ready to enroll in droves. "I'll be a welder," one of them says. "Nowadays you have to have a skill." An official beams into the camera and hints that Americans are finally learning from the Japanese and Europeans, who have a long tradition of training their blue-collar workers with care.

A few days later, the news features an expert on robotics. "Anyone now in a training program for welders is learning an obsolete set of skills," he says. "Robots can and will weld much faster and better than human operators."

Who is right? More generally, what will the world of work—Daniel Bell's "techno-economic struc-ture" and Karl Marx's "sphere of necessity"—look like 10 or 20 years from now?

Several issues will shape the future world of work, including: the rate of growth of technology, the degree to which future technology can be operated by the average worker, the amount of work generated by the economy, the kind of work (challenging or routine) generated by the economy, the degree to which workers are rewarded, the fairness with which work is distributed, the amount of make-work invented by the politicians, and the amount of informal work generated by personal needs that cannot be met with money from paying jobs.

We don't know the exact direction these issues will take, but we can use assumptions about them to create scenarios of what work might be like in the future. Some of these issues are closely related. For example, if the technological growth rate remains high, the economy might generate fewer jobs. Similarly, if the economy generates fewer jobs, the need for politically inspired make-work projects should increase. Be-cause these issues affect each other, they generate a relatively small and manageable set of scenarios. The future may bring not one, but a combination of the scenarios explored here.

More Technology, Less Work

Among the more widely accepted scenarios of the future of work are those based on the assumption that technology will continue to grow exponentially. It has often been said, mainly to soothe nervous workers in the increasingly automated manufacturing sector, that technology creates as many jobs as it abolishes. But neither the empirical evidence nor common sense suggests that this is the case at present.

Unemployment is up in part because technology reduces the need for the kind of work most people do, and it is hard to imagine that the typical American manager will eagerly invest scarce capital in new machinery that will not save money on wages and salaries. What can we expect if technology continues to progress and to reduce the number of available jobs?

Scenario 1: Extreme Taylorism.

Shortening the workweek has been the dream of utopians for ages. Work, after all, constitutes Marx's enslaving and alienating "sphere of necessity." Ironically, the capitalist Americans have been more successful in reducing the necessity for work than the communist societies. In 1881, American engineer Frederick Taylor timed and analyzed the motions of workers in Pittsburgh's Midvale Steel Plant, starting a quest for "scientific management" and efficiency that was considered uniquely American until the Europeans and Japanese caught on with a vengeance in the 1960s and 1970s.

Taylorism reduces work to machine-tending that requires little training and effort and that maximizes productivity. It has two faces. We see its ugly face when it serves as the tool of short-sighted employers who replace motivated, proud, and self-respecting craftsmen with docile human robots, ignoring social costs such as unemployment and unbearably monotonous work. We see its attractive face in the work of Taylor himself. He saw scientific management as the means to increase productivity while reducing effort—the means to have one's cake and eat it, too.

To those who see Taylor's scientific management from the optimistic perspective, the extreme Taylorism scenario looks like the road to salvation and universal contentedness. Increased productivity makes most work superfluous and brings the 10-hour workweek within reach. Everyone serves on the economic front a few hours each day and everyone is entitled to a living wage.

Workers are liberated by machines, computers, and robots and can work less and live more; they spend their free time in productive pursuits in their vegetable patches, pursuing a liberal education, fixing their cars, helping their kids with the homework, traveling, and so on.

This scenario thus assumes that technology is user-friendly and that

The world of work in the classic film *Modern Times* is a factory where Charlie Chaplin tends massive machinery. How the world of work will look in the future will depend on a broad range of issues, including the growth rate of technology. For example, if robots take over the operation of factories, human workers of the future may never know the kind of work depicted in *Modern Times*.

the economy generates less work, which is considered a mildly annoying duty one has to perform to be eligible for funds that society provides to those who have done their share. A basic income is assured and there is no need for make-work projects or for informal underground work activities on the fringes of the formal economy. Work is evenly distributed since most people have no desire to do more than their share.

But there is one telling objection to a future of extreme Taylorism, as French author Simone Weil writes: "No one would accept to be a slave for two hours a day." Indeed, if we spent all but two hours each day in the comfortable "sphere of liberty," we might find it difficult to change gears and adopt the values of punc-

"If we spent all but two hours each day in the comfortable 'sphere of liberty'. . . the prospect of doing chores at all might incite us to revolution."

BRADFORD F. HERZOG/COURTESY OF WELLESLEY COLLEGE

Students enjoy the afternoon sunshine on the Wellesley College campus. In the late 1960s, universities provided agreeable environments that kept restless youths off the street and out of the job market. If future work can be performed only by a technological elite, a similar system may be needed to occupy the idle majority.

tuality, reliability, and diligence demanded by work. The prospect of doing chores at all might incite us to revolution.

Perhaps a more workable option is the three-and-a-half-day workweek suggested by author James Martin. A system of work shifts lasting eight hours on three days and four hours on the fourth would allow continuous operation of factories and offices. This system could be both efficient and beneficial to our quality of life as consumers of services. Such a solution would exploit fully the large capital investment in the complex technology that may characterize the workplace of the future, and it would provide services around the clock.

Scenario 2: Feudal unions. The news that available work may melt

away like butter in the hot pan of technology is not greeted with joy by those who see work, or at least job-holding, as a desirable activity. Less work, or fewer jobs, raises the question of how work can be distributed among the many who, for one reason or another, want to do it.

One way would be to rely on powerful unions. In a bitter struggle against often greedy and brutal employers over the past century, labor has acquired a certain control over much of the work that needs to be done. Union leaders sometimes see themselves as entitled to distribute work, i.e., to decide who will work and for whom. They are also prepared to defend their turf vigorously, not only against employers and their technology but also against the unorganized work force, against other unions, and against politicians who venture into make-work projects that could, even indirectly, reduce the need for unionized workers. Thus in one jurisdiction the members of the school janitors' union may not fasten loose and dangerous seats to the floor because

only the members of the carpenters' union may use the sacred instrument called the "screwdriver."

In a scenario of even greater union power, some current problems worsen. One problem is the effect of uncontestable job security on work motivation. When some grumpy bureaucrat barks at you, you know that he knows that next to nothing can separate him from his job.

A second problem is runaway wage rates. In the past, unions used strikes and the threat of strikes often and vigorously to extract an ever-larger piece from the economic pie. Wages outran productivity, a development that has already materially contributed to the present weak competitive position of the United States. With even greater union power, runaway wage rates may be unbearable.

A final problem is unemployed youth. Seniority rather than skill or merit determines who will work, and one prospect facing many workers is that they will not be employed in the future unless they have supported the right union faithfully for a long time. This work allotment system shuts out the young from the job market to such an extent that many of them restlessly roam the streets, creating new jobs for themselves as drug dealers, hustlers, pimps, prostitutes, and muggers.

Scenario 3: Underground work. The feudal union scenario is thus quite compatible with an "underground work" scenario in which ever-greater segments of the work force operate outside the formal economy. High wages, complex jurisdictional rules, expensive fringe benefits, and the iron law of seniority encourage managers to operate with the smallest possible number of employees. The result is higher unemployment. But union-management contracts are only one factor among several that force many workers out into the cold where they are left to their own devices.

Government regulations reduce participation in the formal economy, no matter how good the intentions may be. For example, unfair or confusing income tax laws and excessively costly labor legislation spur workers to operate outside them and reinforce the tendency of managers to invest more in technology and less in people.

The complexity of technology can also contribute to this problem. In this scenario, technology is so complex that it can only be operated and serviced by highly trained workers. The requirement of union membership for job-holding is reinforced by qualifications beyond the grasp of many. Furthermore, the economy generates challenging jobs; intrinsically desirable work, added to a secure income, makes the lucky minority of job-holders even more eager to hang on to their jobs and to keep others from encroaching on them. The privileged job-holders, or even job-owners, are separated by an uncrossable chasm from the jobless. The jobless, with no "legitimate" income and little help from government, must look elsewhere—join the underground economy—to support themselves.

Scenario 4: Work coupons. The salient shared characteristic of the feudal union and underground work scenarios is an uneven distribution of the scarce, but essential and possibly interesting, commodity called a job. Both are depressing scenarios, with a large section of the population left to its own devices, and both go against the grain of American egalitarianism.

However, an equitable means of distributing work could be devised. Just as food was a scarce and essential commodity in many countries during the two world wars, work could be the most sought-after commodity of the future. Governments proved to be ingenious in devising systems based on ration coupons to distribute food, usually with reasonable fairness. A future

"A future of rationed 'work coupons' could assure a fair distribution of limited employment opportunities to unlimited numbers of citizens eager to seize them."

of rationed "work coupons" could assure a fair distribution of limited employment opportunities to unlimited numbers of citizens eager to seize them.

More Technology, More Work

The scenarios sketched so far assume that more technology means less work. But even if technology expands, there may be more work in the future than many people think.

New products and new services tend to create new needs, which in turn require new effort. The dishwashing machine may fulfill a housewife's dream, but it creates new needs for special soaps, water softeners, plumbers' services, and so on.

Even more important is the tendency of service work to increase exponentially with the number of people in a group or society. Whenever two people live on adjacent plots of land, some work is required to coordinate their activities. Today, huge office towers hum with the activity of millions of workers and managers checking, controlling, supervising, coordinating, expediting, and informing. The natural environment is also likely to require more work; nations will have to increase efforts to conserve and even rebuild the environment if populations continue to grow.

Scenario 5: Gods and clods. If the technology that society develops is impenetrable rather than accessible to the average person, there could arise, to an extent even more marked than today, a society made up of an extremely busy elite of professionals and a useless majority unable to manipulate the words and

mathematical symbols of the information society: an elite of gods doing the work and a majority of clods merely getting in the way.

There might be much work, but few people would be qualified to do it. Managing the complex technology would require a high level of competence and long hours of work each day. The expert managers would have to work extremely hard, not only to meet the demand for their services but also to develop their skills and update their knowledge.

This gods and clods scenario raises the problem of how to keep the majority of the population occupied. The elite, the high priests of technology, would have a soft and a hard option for dealing with it.

The soft option might resemble the universities of the late 1960s, which were often described as "holding tanks," permissive and generally agreeable environments to keep restless and rebellious youths off the streets and away from crowded job markets. The soft option thus implies a liberal attitude toward sex and narcissistic self-expression, since both are time-consuming and mildly gratifying pursuits that keep the populace in a reasonably unrevolutionary state of mind.

But abundant leisure spent surfing, reading *Playboy*, and building tans may not be enough to prevent unrest. Thus, the hard option would make the majority work no matter what, either by selectively withholding technology or by creating make-work projects.

Straightforward make-work projects are not unknown today, but the form they might assume in the future is perhaps best depicted in Kurt Vonnegut's novel *Player Piano*. Vonnegut depicts a society of gods with Ph.D.'s in engineering and clods who have either joined the army or the "Reeks and Wrecks" (Reconstruction and Reclamation Corps). In the former, they stomp around in accordance with a sergeant's bellows; in the latter, they dig ditches and fill them up again.

Scenario 6: Shadow work. Even without formally created make-work, the future may bring more "shadow work." The phrase *shadow work*, coined by Ivan Illich, refers to activity that does not contribute to subsistence but is a necessary complement to the production of goods and services in an industrial society. Much of this activity will be necessary (for example, children will probably continue to be raised in the home). But much of it might not be necessary; much of it could be make-work informally created by "the system."

Consider the time spent getting to and from work. The average person commutes by car; usually there is no alternative. This means that a car must be maintained, and this car generates the ample unpaid work of taking it to the garage and back and learning enough about how it works so that we can vaguely follow the mechanic's scribbles on our substantial bills. It also means fighting traffic into and out of the city and, when there are accidents, visits to hospitals and insurance companies.

Much of this make-work will be generated by unnecessary service consumption. We need the services of accountants to follow the regulations of the Internal Revenue Service and to straighten out its errors. We need lawyers to defend us against nuisance suits and to help us buy a house.

Productive technology may well increase such informally created make-work in the future. "By the end of the century," Ivan Illich writes, "the productive worker will be the exception." Rising productivity will generate unemployment and an "increasing need to diagnose ever more people for shadow work."

In the future foreseen by Illich, most people work as hard as ever—but not in traditional jobs. They are engaged in shadow work generated

"In the future foreseen by [Ivan] Illich, most people will work as hard as ever—but not in traditional jobs. They will be engaged in shadow work generated inadvertently by a highly technologized environment that gives rise to many artificial personal needs that must be attended to."

inadvertently by a highly technologized environment that gives rise to many artificial personal needs that must be attended to.

In this scenario, there is no need for formal make-work projects. The shadow work is distributed unfairly: The rich and powerful hire agents to stand in line for them and to fly them to the workplace.

Technology is mystifying; effort and time are required to locate someone who knows what is going on, who can press the right buttons and call the right programs to find the missing file. The lucky minority employed in the formal economy may find their work unchallenging, but since these people are powerful, they see to it that they are well paid.

Scenario 7: The electronic cottage. Two decades ago, only the specially trained worked with computers, which were demanding, unforgiving, and temperamental beasts with flashing lights and rumbling moving parts. Today, home computers grace many a den, and high-level programming languages, essentially simple and standardized combinations of basic English and elementary mathematics, have already placed the awesome potential of computers at the fingertips of the office worker and the hobbyist.

In the "electronic cottage" future, technology is pervasive and accessible to all. The high economic growth rate generates challenging and profitable work, and the work is distributed fairly. Electronic networking replaces the need for much informal and shadow work, such as doing the shopping, standing in line at the bank, waiting in the doctor's office

to ask a question, or fulfilling other personal needs.

In this scenario, there is plenty of work for home workers engaged in both routine tasks and highly creative and specialized ones. Workers are needed to create and update data banks containing vast amounts of standardized and easily accessed legal, medical, economic, and scientific information. Specialists write counseling programs that generate diagnostic questions to assess the needs of people inquiring about medical symptoms and psychological problems.

Working in the electronic cottage could bridge the gap between the world of work and the culture in which we live—that sphere of liberty encompassing everything from disco dancing and banal commercial TV entertainment to family relations and obligations, higher education, and hobbies. Futurist Alvin Toffler even surmises that the shift from the central workplace to the home could revive the nuclear family and bring about a future of more closely knit relationships contrasting sharply with our present cold society of apathetic bystanders.

Working with Less Technology

Scenario 8: Subsistence work: While all eight scenarios in this article are presented as heuristic tools designed to stimulate thought on the future of work, the subsistence work scenario plays a particularly important role because it challenges a basic assumption of the other seven: the assumption that the future will bring more of the same as far as technology is concerned.

But the future is not necessarily

more of the same. Not only are people consuming available resources voraciously, but society is also only as rich as its most limited vital resources permit it to be. If, for example, new supplies of cheap fossil fuels were to become available in the United States, the country might be poorer than before because vigorous energy and industrial production would accelerate the depletion of the really limited resources: clean air, clean water, and clean land. It is thus by no means clear that the technology-intensive scenarios are more plausible than the view that the future may bring less wealth-producing machinery.

Resource limits mean that people will have to lower their expectations. The attitudes and optimistic hopes of the resource-rich ages of colonization and industrial expansion are not likely to serve us well in the future. Terms like "expectations" and "attitudes" suggest that people should approach work not only from the economic but also from the psychological point of view. Perhaps Americans are beginning to question the creation of artificial needs by relentless advertising and to examine which needs are real and worthwhile.

This radical scenario demands a reversal of our ulcer-producing path toward ever-greater consumption, material wealth, and physical comfort, back to earlier methods of production that are more labor intensive and more clearly linked to the important and meaningful business of subsistence.

According to this scenario, the future could bring a society in which more people roller-skate, cycle, and jog to productive jobs and live in smaller houses, apartments, and niches, compensating for crowdedness and thinner walls by being considerate enough to turn down the volume on electronic boom boxes and TV sets. Lowered demands reduce the importance of productivity and transform work from a large-scale campaign against nature to what Illich calls "subsistence work."

Americans may not become meditating and fasting Buddhist monks living on a daily glass of spring water or a properly peeled orange, but they may cease to be hogs rummaging through supermarket aisles loading their carts with mountains of junk food. Workers may learn to execute with care and competence the meaningful work required for subsistence.

This scenario suggests that the quality of life may be higher in the future even in case of economic decline. The quality of life has much to do with the balance between what people need and want and what their environment can provide. Lower expectations could thus increase satisfaction with the quality of life.

The quality of life depends on the quality of work done by the many people around us on whom we depend. The technical meaning of "quality of work" is good or bad working conditions, the degree to which workers can use their skills and develop new ones, the degree to which they find their work meaningful and are in a position to make decisions about how it should be executed. Few people seem to use the term *quality of work* in the more obvious sense of the superb, adequate, or poor way in which work has been done. The notion that workers can be competent on the job and do work of high quality is deemed outdated in an age of complex work organizations that consist not only of people but also of machinery, regulations, plans, and goals. But it may have been discarded too soon. The individual may matter once again in a resource-poor future trying to optimize the quality of life.

Demise of Work Greatly Exaggerated

The future may bring more work than most people think. The immediate environments of individuals are likely to generate as much work as ever. People will always feel a need to repair their houses and to pull weeds from their flower beds. They will always farm out some of this work to the neighbor's kids and to small entrepreneurs offering specialized services. Perhaps communal work will increase as the bureaucracies of governments and multinational corporations grow more immense, more distant, and more ineffective. There may be more cooperative efforts to maintain neighborhoods, to look after the very old and the very young, and to provide training programs tailored to local needs.

Under some conditions, the amount of work generated by the formal economy may decrease. But under most conditions it is likely to stay at present levels. If technology is severely constrained by the lack of natural resources, the economy could even produce more work than it does now. Labor-intensive methods of getting things done might replace capital-intensive ones.

Even if technology continues to grow at a rapid rate, there need not be a dearth of formal work. It seems premature to think of a 10-hour workweek while inner cities need large-scale refurbishing, while the buses run only sporadically, and while many freeways are deteriorating and sport dangerous potholes.

As we saw earlier, a growing population makes social relationships ever more complex, requiring greater efforts of coordination and regulation. A few dozen settlers in the Old West were able to function with a marshal, a station master, and a preacher; a thousand urbanites today require hundreds of workers providing essential services ranging from pest control to heart transplants.

There will probably be work not only for an elite of the technologically astute, but also for the average person. Microcomputers have already become user-friendly and raise the possibility of a thriving electronic cottage industry. And if we stop looking only at quantitative economic indices, we see that the quality of life depends as much on character, patience, and motivation as it does on exceptional brains. In fact, the helpful cab driver, the caring and knowledgeable gardener, and the dutiful train conductor may have a more direct impact than the technological elite on the quality of daily life.

About the Author

Martin Morf is an associate professor of psychology who teaches courses in industrial psychology. His address is Department of Psychology, University of Windsor, Windsor, Ontario, Canada N9B 3P4.

Getting Ready for the Jobs of the Future

by Marvin J. Cetron

The same technologies that are eliminating many jobs are creating lots of new ones. But workers need to be retrained if they are to be able to fill the new jobs.

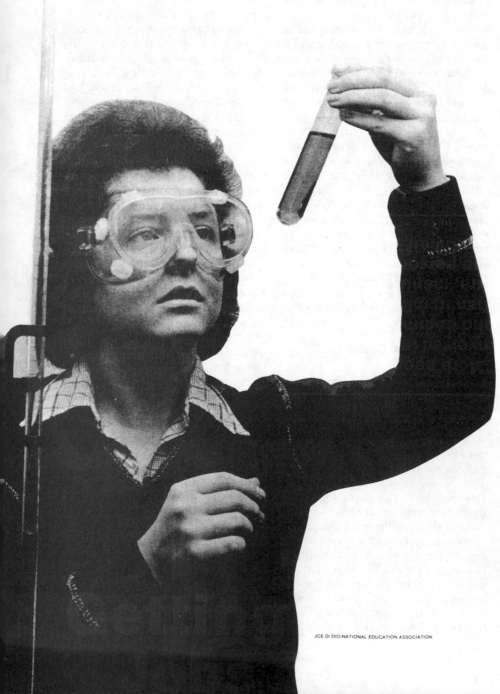

JOE DI DIO/NATIONAL EDUCATION ASSOCIATION

One thing is certain about tomorrow's job markets: dramatic shifts will occur in employment patterns. These changes are going to affect how we work and how we are educated and trained for jobs.

Major shifts in the job market won't necessarily mean major changes in the numbers of people employed. What the changes do mean is that many of the old jobs will disappear—and not just because of robots and computers. Manufacturing will provide only 11% of the jobs in the year 2000, down from 28% in 1980. Jobs related to agriculture will drop from 4% to 3%. The turn of the century will find the remaining 86% of the work force in the service sector, up from 68% in 1980. Of the service-sector jobs, half will relate to information collection, management, and dissemination.

Unemployment will be an ongoing problem. If the current recession were to end tomorrow, probably 1.2 million of the more than 11 million unemployed in the United States today would never be able to return to their old jobs in the automobile, steel, textile, rubber, or railroad industries. This loss of jobs is called structural unemployment.

Foreign competition in low-wage countries will eliminate about one-sixth of the 1.2 million jobs; another

High-school chemist examines results of her classroom experiment. To retain its technological edge over other countries, America must place more emphasis on science and math education and encourage its youth—especially girls—to be proud of their skills, says author Marvin Cetron.

one-sixth will disappear because of the nationalization of many major industries in other countries that results in "dumping" of products on the U.S. market and undercutting American prices. "Computamation" (robotics, numerically-controlled equipment, CAD/CAM [computer-aided design and computer-aided manufacturing], and flexible manufacturing) will assist in the demise of the remaining two-thirds of the jobs eliminated.

As this technological transition takes place, productivity will increase. For example, the use of a robot or a CAD/CAM system in the automotive industry can replace up to six workers if operated around the clock. Quality control increases fourfold, and scrap is reduced from 15% to less than 1%.

Japan already uses some of these new jobs and technology. It had no choice. Currently, it imports 96% of its energy. By the year 2000, that will rise to 98%. Eighty-seven percent of all of Japan's resources come from the outside. These statistics contributed to the decision to go robotic. But the essence of Japan's problem is that, between 1985 and 1990, 20% of the entire work force will retire at 80% of their base pay for the rest of their lives. Japan was forced to go robotic to remain competitive. The United States, too, will be filling many of today's blue-collar jobs with robots. The displaced workers will have to learn the new skills necessary to build and maintain the robots.

White-collar workers in the office of the future will also see some dramatic changes in their jobs. Currently, about 6,000 word lexicons—machines that type directly from speech—are in use. After a person dictates into the machine, a word lexicon types up to 97% of what was said. In addition, it can translate the material into nine languages, including Hebrew, which it types backwards, and Japanese kanji symbols, which it types sideways and the user reads down the columns. Machines such as this will eliminate 50% of all clerical and stenographic jobs. But instead of going to an unemployment line, many of these workers may find jobs controlling the robots in factories using word-processing equipment.

TED SPIEGEL © 1982/OFFICE OF TECHNOLOGY ASSESSMENT, U.S. CONGRESS

Teachers at Oxford High School in Massachusetts review books and computer software for use in a summer workshop for computer educators. Teachers will require continual retraining through in-service or summer programs to keep up with the demands of preparing students for a changing world.

> **"Currently, a 4.5% unemployment rate is considered full employment. But by 1990, 8.5% unemployment will be considered full employment."**

As the types of jobs change, so will the definition of full employment. Currently, a 4.5% unemployment rate is considered full employment. But by 1990, 8.5% unemployment will be considered full employment. This figure is not as disturbing as it first appears, for at any given time 3.5% of the work force will be in training and education programs preparing for new jobs.

Workers will be able to take time out for retraining, in part, because of the shift in job patterns. In 1980, 45% of American households had two people working. In 1990, this proportion will increase to 65%, and in 2000, 75% of family units will have two incomes. This shift will allow easier transitions from the work force to training programs and back to the work force. Forecasts estimate that every four or five years one of the spouses or partners will leave the ranks of the employed to receive the additional knowledge and skills demanded by changes in technology and the workplace.

With these changes already taking place, workers must learn to do new jobs now and in the future. Vocational educators and trainers must gear up to provide this vital education and training to the work force of the next two decades—jobs related to robots, lasers, computers, energy and battery technology, geriatric social work, hazardous-waste management, and biomedical electronics. (See table for some of the jobs that are disappearing and others that are growing in the shifting job market.)

New Occupations for the 1990s

The following occupations are among those that we can expect to become increasingly important:

Energy Technician (650,000 jobs) jobs will increase dramatically as new energy sources become marketable.

Housing Rehabilitation Technician (500,000 jobs). Intensifying housing demand will be met by mass production of prefabricated modular housing, using radically new construction techniques and materials.

Hazardous Waste Management Technician (300,000 jobs). Many years and billions of dollars may be required to clean up air, land, and water. New industries will add to the demand with new wastes.

Industrial Laser Process Technician (600,000 jobs). Laser manufacturing equipment and processes, including robotic factories, will replace much of today's machine and foundry tools and equipment.

Industrial Robot Production Technician (800,000 jobs). Extensive use of robots to perform computer-directed "physical" and "mental" functions will displace hundreds of thousands of workers. But new workers will be needed to insure fail-proof operations of row after row of production robots.

Materials Utilization Technicians (400,000 jobs) must be trained to work with new materials being engineered and created to replace metals, synthetics, and other production substances unsuited for advanced manufacturing technologies.

Genetic Engineering Technician (250,000 jobs). Genetically engineered materials will be used extensively in three general fields: industrial products, pharmaceuticals, and agricultural products. New and modified substances will be produced under laboratory-like conditions in industrial mass-production quantities.

Holographic Inspection Specialist (200,000 jobs). Completely automated factories that use optical fibers for sensing light, temperature, pressure, and dimensions will transmit this information to optical computers to compare this data with stored holographic, three-dimensional images.

Bionic-Medical Technician (200,000 jobs). Mechanics will be needed to manufacture bionic appendages while other specialists work on highly sophisticated extensions of sensory and mental functions (seeing, hearing, feeling, speaking).

Automotive Fuel Cell (Battery) Technicians (250,000 jobs) will perform tests and services for new fuel cells and batteries used in vehicles and stationary operation, including residences.

On-Line Emergency Medical Technician (400,000 jobs). Needs for paramedics will increase directly with the growth of the population and its aging. In forthcoming megalopolises and high-density residences, emergency medical treatment will be administered on the spot, aided by televised diagnoses and instruction from remote emergency medical centers.

Geriatric Social Workers (700,000 jobs) will be essential for the mental and social care of the nation's aging population.

Energy Auditors (180,000 jobs) will use the latest infrared devices and computer-based energy monitoring to work with architects, product engineers, and marketing staffs in the production, sales, and operation of energy conservation and control systems for housing, industrial plants, and machinery.

Nuclear Medicine Technologists (75,000 jobs) will work with medicines and serums using radioisotopes. As the isotopes are absorbed in tissues and muscles, diagnosticians can observe functions of normal and/or damaged tissues and organs and can determine treatment needs and responses to medication, thus reducing the need for surgery.

Dialysis Technologists (30,000 jobs) will operate new portable dialysis machines and the expected greater number of hospital dialysis machines.

Computer Axial Tomography (CAT) Technologist/Technician (45,000 jobs). Though more than a decade has passed since development of this technique for using X rays with computer technology to give sectional views of internal body structures, the supply of qualified technicians has not kept pace with the growth of the technology. Jobs for technicians to install, maintain,

The Shifting Job Market
Some jobs that will be disappearing by 1990:

Occupation	% Decline in Employment
Linotype operator	−40.0
Elevator operator	30.0
Shoemaking machine operators	19.2
Farm laborers	19.0
Railroad car repairers	17.9
Farm managers	17.1
Graduate assistants	16.7
Housekeepers, private household	14.9
Childcare workers, private household	14.8
Maids and servants, private household	14.7
Farm supervisors	14.3
Farm owners and tenants	13.7
Timber cutting and logging workers	13.6
Secondary school teachers	13.1

Some jobs that will be growing until 1990:

Occupation	% Growth in Employment
Data processing machine mechanics	+157.1
Paralegal personnel	143.0
Computer systems analysts	112.4
Midwives	110.0
Computer operators	91.7
Office machine service technicians	86.7
Tax preparers	77.9
Computer programmers	77.2
Aero-astronautic engineers	74.8
Employment interviewers	72.0
Fast food restaurant workers	69.4
Childcare attendants	66.5
Veterinarians	66.1
Chefs	55.0

Dying Factory Gets New Lease on Life

GENERAL ELECTRIC COMPANY

A view from the control booth of GE's "factory with a future," where just two workers can do in 16 hours what it once took 70 workers 16 days to do.

An electronic "heart transplant" has been given to an aging factory in an industry and in a region that many had given up for dead.

The General Electric Company is investing $316 million over the next three years to revitalize its locomotive plant in Erie, Pennsylvania. When all of the robots, computerized machine tools, and other automation systems are in place, the Erie "factory with a future" will have increased its production capacity by one-third.

One of the first automation projects to come on line is a $16-million flexible machining system for traction motor frames. With this system, two workers operating nine machine tools can do in 16 hours what used to take 70 workers 16 days to do using 29 aging machine tools.

But increased productivity through automation means more rather than fewer jobs, says Carl J. Schlemmer, vice president and general manager of GE's Transportation Systems and Business Operations, who predicts that the higher level of production will require a 10% increase in employment in the Erie plant.

Although current employment there is down almost 30% since 1980, much of the decline is attributed to the nationwide recession; GE already has announced plans to recall about 900 laid-off workers by the end of the year.

"There may be some initial dislocations, but long-term automation is going to have a positive effect on the employment situation here," Schlemmer says. "We're confident that the growth we've projected, coupled with the competitive edge derived from productivity improvements, will serve to provide *growth* in jobs—not *loss* in jobs."

GE is expecting a strong upsurge in the locomotive market once the current recession eases. "The U.S. railroad industry, our major customer, is going through a strong renaissance," says Schlemmer. "The anticipated growth in rail traffic, plus the need to replace an aging fleet, should create demand significant-

ly higher than the average market of the 1970s."

Work in the automated factory will be different. Sophisticated, highly automated factories need skilled labor to run them. To train its workers in the newly-required skills, GE has built a $6 million Learning and Communications Center, which opened last October.

The learning center has four fully equipped classrooms; a high-technology laboratory for training in machine tool control and system applications; laboratories for computer study, diesel engine maintenance, and rotating electrical machinery; and a high-bay lab that can accommodate an entire locomotive for hands-on maintenance training.

But there is more at stake than just this factory: GE is not only automating its own plants but is also helping other companies automate—with GE equipment.

For further information, contact: News Bureau, General Electric Co., Box 5900, Norwalk, Connecticut 06856.

and operate CAT scanning systems and assist in the analysis of these scans will offer attractive employment for thousands of qualified people.

Positron Emission Tomography (PET) Technician/Technologist (165,000 jobs). PET scanners are used for diagnoses of disorders of the brain. The need for qualified workers in this field will increase with advances in and the growing use of this technology.

Computer-Assisted Design (CAD) Technician (300,000 jobs). The computer can do more, better, and faster than traditional design methods. Whether designing modes of transportation, dwellings, or other products, CAD will affect education, employment, and ways of work more than any other single technology.

Computer-Assisted Graphics (CAG) Technician (150,000 jobs). Rapid growth of computer-assisted graphics will affect the education, training, and employment of all graphics technicians as no other event in graphics history. Demands for artists and technicians will increase tenfold, in large part due to an increase in demand for new forms and dimensions of graphics to portray objects, schemes, and scenarios before they are actually produced.

Computer-Assisted Manufacturing (CAM) Specialist (300,000 jobs). CAM systems will permit all the design, development, specification, and logistics data to be pulled out of CAD and CAG data bases and reprogrammed into computer-assisted manufacturing programs, which will then operate most of the production facility. This permits the attainment of flexible manufacturing cells in which every step of producing a product is determined and programmed sequentially for accomplishment without (or with minimal) human intervention.

Computerized Vocational Training (CVT) Technicians (300,000 jobs) will be employed to develop educational and training materials to use in programs at all levels in public and private educational institutions. Utilizing the demonstration capabilities and versatility of CAD software in conjunction with computer graphics, educators and train-

ers will be able to depict any object and any action with a vividness and dynamism that will produce higher learning benefits than any mode ever employed. Students will be able to assemble or disassemble the most complex mechanisms, construct the most artistic forms, and design dwellings and structures without ever leaving their computer terminals. While "hands-on training" will remain an essential part of vocational training, terminology and work sequencing will be learned at the CRT. Textbooks, lengthy lectures, and dissertations will become passé in the coming decades of learning by doing at the computer terminal. Up to 75% of all instruction will be acquired at the computer console, allowing teachers to spend much more time helping students learn actual on-the-job work skills with actual products and processes.

Most of these new jobs will require some kind of postsecondary vocational or technical training—training that is for the most part not now available.

"Competent teachers in vocational education, math, and science can earn 50-60% more in the private sector."

Attracting Competent Teachers

To ensure that the vocational education system provides the education and training needed by the labor force of the future, competent teachers must be attracted to the field.

Currently, competent teachers are not attracted to the profession due to low salaries and low status. Competent teachers in vocational education, math, and science can earn 50-60% more in the private sector. The decline in competent teaching of these subjects must and can be stopped.

Over the years, teacher education programs have encountered declining enrollments due, in part, to low salaries, to oversupplies during baby-boom years, and to the high status of working in the private sector. To counteract the declining enrollments, teacher training programs lowered their standards for entry,

which resulted in attracting a lower caliber of student. The programs became a curriculum of last resort for students failing in other areas.

To reverse this trend, long- and short-term strategies must be instituted in the United States. Teaching can be made more attractive through the support of administrators and by raising the salaries of teachers, especially in those areas of high demand, i.e., vocational education, math, and science. Raising the salaries by 20% across the board and by an additional 20% in those areas of high demand will attract teachers back from the private sector and encourage a higher caliber of student to enter undergraduate teacher preparation programs. The law of supply and demand will work if other constraints, such as inflexible pay scales and tenure laws, are lifted; but standards must not be lowered.

For long-term solutions to assuring a supply of competent teachers, a series of three hurdles must be instituted by teacher preparation programs and departments of education:

● For acceptance into a teacher education program, students must score at least 850 combined total on their SATs and pass a proficiency test in reading, writing, and computational skills.

● To continue in a teacher education program, students must maintain above-average grades (3.0 GPA or the equivalent) for the first two years of undergraduate work.

● Before receiving permanent certification, a teacher must pass a competency examination and receive positive evaluations from supervisors, administrators, and peers.

These are not new suggestions; each has been implemented successfully in several states already. The implementation of these standards will not happen without controversy. Witness the furor caused by Penn State's Joe Paterno and the NCAA when they decided to require a total of 700 on the SATs before accepting college athletes. But for the sake of the teaching profession, these standards must be initiated and maintained.

Requiring each prospective teacher to overcome these hurdles will

TED SPIEGEL © 1982/OFFICE OF TECHNOLOGY ASSESSMENT, U.S. CONGRESS

High-school students in Oxford, Massachusetts, work with a learning aid that familiarizes them with electrical and electronics wiring. This vocational education will help them prepare for work in the state's burgeoning electronics industry. To prepare America's youth for the more technical jobs of the next two decades, schools must be equipped to provide vital vocational education and training.

tighten the profession's standards and limit those entering to the best. The resulting shortage of teachers will raise salaries and attract more from other places. The downward spiral in teacher competence will be reversed and the status of the teacher will rise, along with the salaries and the level of competence. If the trend is not reversed, America may be forced to use teachers from foreign countries, similar to the medical profession's solution to maintaining medical services in rural areas.

To relieve the short-term lack of math, science, and vocational teachers, rather than tolerate less than the best, the best retired teachers or business people in these fields could take a 1-2 month refresher course and return to the classroom for a year or two. To further alleviate the shortage, corporations could be encouraged to make available some of their skilled technical people to provide some teaching.

Higher salaries and other benefits to attract good teachers will raise flags with the cost-conscious and bankrupt some states and school districts. That is why cooperation between the public and private sectors is imperative in the academic arena. High-technology companies have the equipment and personnel to assist schools and teachers during this transition time.

Along with limiting entrants into the profession to the best, schools must continually retrain their good teachers. For example, computer literacy for every high-school student and every teacher must be required. In-service programs provided by school districts or departments of education should be available and every teacher should be able to pass a computer literacy test within four years.

Some colleges and universities have planted the seed of computer literacy with good results already. Hamline University in St. Paul, Minnesota, has a computer literacy requirement comparable to other required courses such as English and beginning mathematics. No student may successfully leave Hamline without computer proficiency. Now several other private schools in the Minneapolis-St. Paul area are joining the literacy network.

Union Plans Strategy for the Future

A union whose members face some of the most dramatic changes during the transition from an industrial to an information society is now making a concerted effort to look ahead.

The Communications Workers of America, which represents 675,000 telecommunications workers, created a Committee on the Future in 1981 and assigned it the task of assessing the tremendous changes occurring in the industry and in the world of work.

At a special conference in March 1983, the committee made its recommendations for how the union can best achieve its fundamental goal of employment security for its members.

In an age of tremendous technological change, the key to employment security is training and retraining, which requires the cooperation of employers and government with the union, "for we cannot do the job alone," the committee said. "While we cannot lay aside our powerful confrontational skills, there is no way we can achieve employment security through training and retraining if we and our employers get bogged down in the old ways. Careful new initiatives in bargaining, political action, joint consultation, and public relations will be necessary," said the committee's report.

The committee also told the special conference that CWA must become strategy-driven rather than reactive in its method of dealing with external events. It identified some of the major outside forces affecting the union:

• Technological changes that will affect job opportunities.

• Structural changes in the telecommunications/data processing industry, such as the divestiture of AT&T, the union's primary employer.

• Changes in the composition, life-styles, needs, and interests of the work force.

• Power shifts in business and politics, especially toward ultra-conservative and anti-union groups.

• Economic turbulence and uncertainty.

The committee, led by union president Glenn E. Watts, told the union that these forces are threatening only if CWA fails to deal with them strategically. "The key to bringing off a successful CWA strategy that links together bargaining, organizing, political action, education, and other vital union activities lies in the formation of a number of 'strategy centers' within CWA," the committee said in its report.

Each strategy center would concentrate on a major objective. For example, one would address the "new" AT&T; another would deal with independent telephone system companies and the new Bell Operating Companies (BOCs); another would be concerned with the problems of the union's public-sector workers. These centers would be formed or disbanded according to the union's changing needs.

To succeed, the committee stressed, the union must overcome its natural resistance to change. The committee recognized that nearly all CWA members will feel tremendous jolts and disturbances as the union restructures itself to ride with the forces of the future. "But we can take this, because the prize—employment security—is worth it," the committee concluded. "And because the alternative is to watch thousands of our members become victims of America's move into the Information Age and the global economy."

If teachers do not fill the gap in their skills, they should be phased out for failing to keep current with the requirements of their profession. To win the salaries and esteem that the profession deserves, schools cannot keep deadwood on their faculties.

Changing Attitudes Toward Education, Training, and Technology

Across the board, the gap is closing between the highest and lowest students. Special programs help the lower students come up to their capacities; however, few programs help the truly brilliant students perform at theirs. Teachers who could teach brilliant students are going into other occupations and are being replaced by less adequate teachers, so students with great potential are not getting the necessary support.

The National Commission on Excellence in Education recently issued a report saying, "If an unfriendly foreign power had attempted to impose on America the mediocre educational performance that exists today, we might well have viewed it as an act of war. As it stands, we have allowed this to happen to ourselves." The commission recommended increased support for math and science and stiffer math, science, and computer literacy requirements in high school. The commission also recommends increasing the length of the school day from six hours to seven or eight hours and the length of the school year from 180 to 210 days. These revisions are vital if the United States is to maintain the lead in technology that it now enjoys, especially since other countries are rushing to close the gap. For example, Russia requires seven years to America's two-and-one-half years of these subjects in high school, while Japanese students go to school 240 days a year.

America must encourage its youth, especially girls, to be proud of their skills in science, math, and vocational subjects. Traditional funding sources, as well as parent/teacher groups, booster clubs, etc., should be encouraged to make money and give funds to "mathletes" and "chemletes" as well as athletes. Students should be awarded letters in math, physics, chemistry, and vocationally related extracurricular activities, similar to athletic letters. Finally, schools should be pouring dollars into computers rather than stadiums.

Education must equip people to change. As important as math, science, and vocational skills are, they are not enough. As society changes, so will the skills and knowledge needed to be productive and satisfied. The higher levels of cognitive skills must be learned as early as possible. People must be taught skills in decision-making, problem-solving, creativity, communication, critical thinking, evaluation, analysis, synthesis, and the structuring of problems to understand what the results ought to be. We must make people think and also make them communicate. Already, well-educated chief executives, who should and do know better, depend on industry lingo to communicate their ideas. The day of the simple sentence—using real words, not jargon—must dawn again, or the gap between buyer and seller, maker and user will never be filled.

Updating Teaching Methods

Keeping vocational-education programs up to date always has been a problem. The rapid pace of technological change accentuates and widens the gap between programs and the cutting edge of knowledge. Budget cutbacks make the problem even greater. The same problem has hit industry. Consequently, businesses are turning to computerized training to lessen the cost and, at the same time, maintain or improve the quality of their programs. At the forefront of this nationwide trend is the PLATO computer-assisted instruction system developed by Control Data Corporation.

The applications for PLATO are as limitless as the range of business and industry itself. Such diverse industries as manufacturing, petroleum, banking, real estate, finance, aviation, and emergency medicine find PLATO indispensable. Individual companies and associations training with PLATO include American Airlines, General Motors, General Mills, Shell, DuPont, Federal Express, National Association of Securities Dealers, Bank Administration Institute, Con Edison, and Merck, Sharp, and Dohme.

Computer-assisted instruction (CAI) is easily adaptable for short-term training. Many of the unemployed need two or three months of training for a job that will exist. CAI is practical and effective; the infor-

mation is up to date.

If this or similar programs were implemented in vocational-technical schools, every teacher and every student would have immediate access to the most recent information available. Students could learn theory and related content on the computer. Teachers could then work individually with students for the hands-on training that is so vital in vocational education. This method requires a different kind of thinking by teachers. Insecure teachers will feel threatened by the computer if they have not yet become computer literate. But the computer is a tool to make teaching more efficient and more effective—not a replacement for the teacher.

This fear is dissipating somewhat as microcomputers march into the classroom, mainly due to the efforts of businesses that sell them. Control Data, for example, has spent much time helping educators incorporate the technology into the class-

"Training dollars must go only for jobs that exist or will exist in the near future."

room in such a way that everyone—students, teachers, taxpayers—receives the maximum benefits from it.

And as teachers realize the power they can exert through the computer—introducing and updating courses, record-keeping, administrative functions—the teacher-replacement issue will fade.

Maintaining a skilled work force will take an enormous expenditure of resources. Operating training programs in vocational, technical, and industrial facilities 24 hours a day will eliminate much of the need for duplicating expensive equipment.

Even more importantly, training dollars must go only for jobs that exist or will exist in the near future. In the past, the training programs sponsored by CETA (Comprehensive Education and Training Act) did not give Americans what was promised. Sixty percent of the money was used for administration; the remaining 40% went into training. Only 3% of the trainees actually obtained

jobs. The people were trained for jobs that did not exist and will not exist. For example, up until 1979 people were still being trained to be linotype and elevator operators, even though a need for these skills had not been identified for the preceding 10 years. In fact, linotype equipment had not been manufactured for 15 years preceding 1979.

The new Job Partnership Training Act has tried to correct this by requiring that 70% of the funds go to actual training programs and limiting administration to 15%. The remaining 15% is designated for basic literacy education and child-care services for trainees.

The jobs of the future are changing in nature. America needs to make short- and long-term changes to avoid disastrous consequences. The first step is to begin to encourage the unemployed to upgrade their skills and take lower-paying jobs as temporary solutions. The next step is to get the education system back on track to produce educated minds that accept the challenges of the future and want to learn more. Strong emphasis on education is necessary; however, it is not sufficient. Training for the occupations of tomorrow is also needed. Finally, Americans must admit past mistakes and do what it takes to make the country strong and stable in the future.

About the Author

Marvin J. Cetron, a pioneer and expert in the areas of technological forecasting and technological assessment, is the founder and president of Forecasting International, Ltd., 1001 North Highland Street, Arlington, Virginia 22210. He is the author of 10 books dealing with technology and the future, the most recent of which is *Encounters with the Future: A Forecast of Life in the 21st Century* (McGraw-Hill, New York, 1982, 320 pages, $12.95; available from the World Future Society Book Service; prepayment required, please include $1.50 for postage and handling). He will be a keynote speaker at the World Future Society's special conference "Working Now and in the Future" in August. He would like to acknowledge the help of Clyde Helms, president of Occupational Forecasting, in developing the projections of new occupations for the 1990s.

S. Norman Feingold

Emerging Careers

Occupations for Post-Industrial Society

Once upon a time Ben Franklin could take his son for a walk through the streets of Philadelphia and point out all the jobs that were available. Today there are more than 30,000 different job titles.

Careers have changed from time immemorial. First, food gathering was done by women, while men did the hunting. Then came a period when most people were subsistence farmers, growing plants and animals to meet their needs for food, clothing, and shelter.

In the Middle Ages, the emerging careers were those of craftsmen and artisans. These workers made a living in the villages by serving the needs of the upper classes. The serfs continued to grow food for themselves and the overlords and to provide military service.

During the Renaissance, a whole class of artists and craftsmen, assistants and guilds developed. Business, trade, and manufacturing expanded. People worked in jobs that never existed in the preceding agricultural age.

Next, the Industrial Revolution expanded the number and types of jobs and careers. Boosted by science and technology, the expansion of jobs has intensified.

We are now entering the post-industrial period. In 1980, just 28% of the work force was in manufacturing, and it will probably be only 11% in the year 2000 and 3% in the year 2030. More people now work at McDonald's than at U.S. Steel. Businesses are adapting by diversifying their operations. Today, for example, sewing machines make up only 1% of Singer's business; the rest is in electronics.

New occupations and careers emerge all the time while others become obsolete. In comparing a

The future holds in store a multitude of exciting new occupations, from treasure hunting to moon mining, says a careers expert.

past *Dictionary of Occupational Titles*, published by the U.S. Department of Labor, with the most recent one, many changes are readily observed.

Numerous job titles have been added, and many hundreds of others have been deleted.

One career, for example, of short duration in the nineteenth century was that of the pony express rider, though vestiges reappear in today's courier and messenger services. The elevator operator, the bowling pin setter, the milkman, and hundreds of other jobs and careers have virtually disappeared, and others will follow them into oblivion. The meter-reader will soon be extinct; instead of somebody reading the gas meter at your home, gas meters can be tied in to a com-

CYNTHIA FOWLER

puter and monitored more cost effectively. In 1977, the *Dictionary* added 2,100 titles while dropping 3,500.

All of us are in occupations and careers that are in transition. For some, the job titles will remain the same while the work tasks and concepts change. For some, there will be new titles and new tasks.

An emerging career has all of the following characteristics; it is one that:

- Has become increasingly visible as a separate career area in recent years.
- Has developed from pre-existing career areas, such as medical care and personal or business services.
- Has become possible because of advances in technology or actual physical changes in our environment. For example, home computers, solar industries, satellite television, and water pollution equipment are a few of the many areas that have engendered new, emerging careers.
- Shows growth in numbers of people employed or attending emerging education and training programs.
- Requires skills and training.
- Does not appear and then disappear in a very short period of time.

Careers in the Information Industry

One of the biggest areas of emerging careers is the information industry. Today, 55% of the workers in the United States are in information industries. More people are involved in information and communication than in mining, agriculture, manufacturing, and personal services combined. Some experts are calling the changes an "information revolution." By the year 2000, 80% of the work force will be information workers.

Here are some of the emerging career areas in the information industry:

Operation of information systems. Abstractor-indexers process the intellectual content of documents for convenient retrieval. Bibliographic searchers use modern computerized information systems and data bases to identify or

> ## "More people are involved in information and communication than in mining, agriculture, manufacturing, and personal services combined."

retrieve pertinent publications. Information brokers perform specialized information retrieval services for a fee.

Management of information systems. Information center managers supervise facilities that organize knowledge of a specific subject area.

Design of information systems. Application or systems programmers write large-scale computer programs or modify existing programs in order to solve information problems in business, science, education, and other fields.

Research and teaching. Computational linguists analyze word and language structure to determine how the computer can manipulate text for indexing, classification, abstracting, search, and retrieval. Information scientists conduct basic research on the phenomenon

of information. Teachers of information science educate others in the planning, design, management, evaluation, and use of the total information process.

Consulting (or the selling of information). There has been an explosive growth of consultants of all kinds. For example, image consultants work with clients on a variety of problems such as dress, speech, and color. One of the earliest types of image consultant was the public relations consultant, who handles information and communications problems for a variety of organizations.

Information is a limitless resource. Unlike finite industrial resources such as oil, ore, and iron, there is an inexhaustible supply of knowledge, concepts, and ideas as people gain further education.

Robotics Careers

Robots are to manufacturing and mining jobs as calculators are to white-collar jobs. Each takes the monotony of repetition out of the job. Additionally, robots can do the hazardous tasks—with bottom-line effectiveness, no retirement pay, no vacations, no coffee breaks, and no strikes.

Robotics means that people will have to be trained for new skills or remain unemployed—and this includes thousands of people who

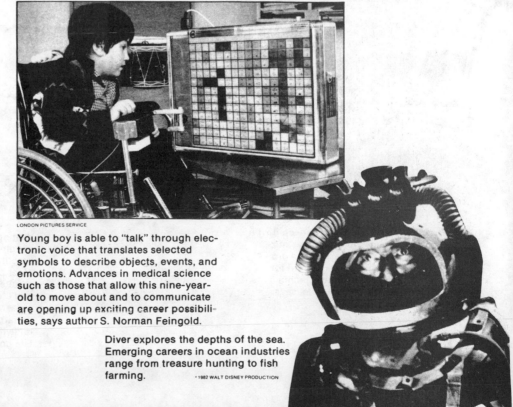

LONDON PICTURES SERVICE

Young boy is able to "talk" through electronic voice that translates selected symbols to describe objects, events, and emotions. Advances in medical science such as those that allow this nine-year-old to move about and to communicate are opening up exciting career possibilities, says author S. Norman Feingold.

Diver explores the depths of the sea. Emerging careers in ocean industries range from treasure hunting to fish farming.　　© 1982 WALT DISNEY PRODUCTION

formerly worked in the automobile and steel industries.

In addition to the new jobs for scientists, mechanics, and technicians that the development of robotics has created, there will be an increasing need for such workers as robots' supervisors in new, largely automated factories. But whether the development of robotics will create more jobs than robots displace is unknown at this point.

Robots are taking away thousands of blue-collar jobs. The jobs they are creating are not in these fields. The changes are of a magnitude comparable to those the Industrial Revolution created.

Overall employment in robotics is small but will grow with the increasing demand for robots. The three general types of jobs now available in the robot industry are:

> **"Unlike finite industrial resources such as oil, ore, and iron, there is an inexhaustible supply of knowledge, concepts, and ideas as people gain further education."**

Planning. Robotic engineers select jobs a robot could perform based on a thorough knowledge of the robot's capacities and of the tasks to be performed and the environment in which they are done.

Installation. Technicians install the robots and adjust them to the specific tasks involved. These people could be technical-school graduates with a special interest in robotics.

Monitoring. Supervisors check the operation of the robot on the line and keep it supplied with any needed raw materials, such as wire for a welding gun.

Ocean Industry Careers

The ocean industry is growing, with new careers ranging from catching new kinds of fish to finding ships that have sunk at sea carrying gold and other precious items. We are now cultivating the ocean the way we do the land. And researchers have discovered new kinds of sea-grown food that could

UNIMATION WESTINGHOUSE

Engineer controls robot connected with vision system designed by Westinghouse. As the robotics industry grows, there will be increasing demand for robot scientists, engineers, technicians, supervisors, and salespeople, says author Feingold.

Astronaut Edwin E. (Buzz) Aldrin, Jr., walks on the moon. Astronauts are not the only professionals who will be needed as we explore and develop space and its resources. Among the emerging extraterrestrial careers are: aerospace engineer, astrophysicist, lunar miner, planetary engineer, selenologist, and space colonist.   NASA

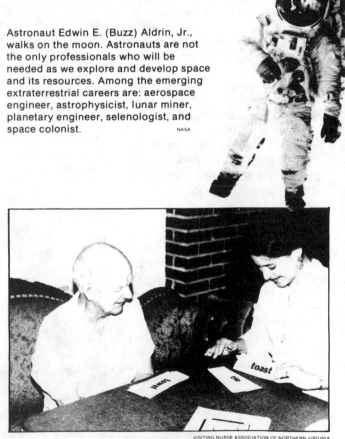

VISITING NURSE ASSOCIATION OF NORTHERN VIRGINIA

Visiting nurse works with home-bound patient needing speech therapy. The home health-care practitioner, especially those working with older patients, is an emerging career that has resulted from changes in society, population, and lifestyles. Other emerging health-care careers include stroke rehabilitation nurse, geriatric nurse, physician's assistant, nurse-midwife, child mental health specialist, alcoholism counselor, and music therapist.

have tremendous value to feeding the world's people.

Fishing and other occupations exploiting the sea are almost as old as the human race, but marine technology is making possible many exciting emerging careers, such as ocean mining, fish farming, oil prospecting, treasure hunting, and underwater archaeology.

Now let's take a closer look at some of these emerging career areas.

Ocean mining. Scientists and engineers work to solve the problem of how to retrieve and process the millions of tons of undersea minerals. Marine ecologists study how ocean mining operations could affect the ocean's environment. International sea-mining claims and law-of-the-sea treaties are new specialties for maritime lawyers.

Other areas such as off-shore drilling and deep-sea exploration require people with knowledge in more than one area, including oceanography, geology, seismology, marine engineering, and meteorology.

Underwater archaeology and treasure hunting. Until recently, no technology was available to recover artifacts from sunken ships. Now, treasure hunting using the most modern underwater techniques can be profitable, although the chances of making a fortune are small. Among the positions relating most directly to underwater exploration are project directors, professional divers, crew members, equipment handlers, sonar operators, and television camera operators.

Aquaculture. As fish supplies diminish and world population increases, scientific farming of fish and other seafoods will expand. One technique used with increasing effectiveness is polyculture, or the raising of several species together, which maximizes utilization of food and water.

Fish farming requires workers skilled in land and water management and in the care, feeding, managing, harvesting, and marketing of fish.

Exploring New Frontiers

Space, "the final frontier," has already opened up undreamed of

---

"Treasure hunting using the most modern underwater techniques can be profitable, although the chances of making a fortune are small."

---

occupations and will demand many new kinds of pioneers in the future.

Exploring space and developing its resources will require highly skilled technicians in addition to the astronauts and pilots now serving in U.S. and other space programs. Specialists in communications, computers and electronics, energy, and pharmaceuticals, for example, will work on the space shuttle or Skylab.

Eventually, as humans can remain in space for longer and longer periods of time, space programs will require miners, mechanics, ecologists, geologists, and other technicians to explore extraterrestrial materials and energy resources; to mine raw materials on lunar bases; to build and staff industrial facilities, factories, processing plants, and solar-power stations; to build space habitats and work in closed-ecology agricultural production; and to develop transportation systems connecting a growing number of space facilities.

Health Careers

Breakthroughs in genetics, bionics, cryology, laser surgery, and other medical sciences are creating exciting new career possibilities. The replacing of body organs with transplants or artificial parts represents a marriage of medical and engineering fields that has engendered such emerging careers as bionic-electronic technicians; orthotists or prosthetists, who develop surgical devices to activate or supplement weakened limbs or functions; spare-human-organs technicians; and many other previously unimagined occupations.

Electronic devices activated by voice, the blink of an eye, or a puff of breath have enabled mobility-impaired people to open doors and

---

windows, use the telephone, etc. Closed-captioned television and movies allow the deaf to "hear."

Other new health-related careers result from changes in society, population, and lifestyles. As the population ages, for example, there will be a greater need for geriatric nurses and social workers, home health aides, nursing home counselors, stroke rehabilitation nurses, and thanatologists.

Unemployment and other economic and social ills call for mental-health professionals in new specialties such as certified alcoholism counselors, family therapists, licensed psychiatric technicians, mental-health nurses, corrective therapists, and community psychologists.

Emerging Energy Careers

After the Arab oil embargo of 1974, people began to think about energy conservation, and new career opportunities appeared:

Nuclear energy. All kinds of new jobs are emerging in the area of nuclear fission and fusion. Construction of nuclear energy plants requires thousands of skilled workers ranging from boilermakers, pipefitters, welders, and sheet metal workers to office workers, laborers, and truck drivers.

Emerging careers for operating personnel include engineers specializing in ceramics, human factors, materials, reactor safety, systems, and standards development.

Technician jobs include power-plant inspectors, nuclear fuels specialists, quality assurance specialists, instrument servicepersons, and systems reliability analysts.

Scientists needed include those specializing in health physics and the environment as well as chemists, soil and air specialists, radio chemists, and geochemists.

Fossil fuels. Though few new careers are emerging in this field, which has been automating many traditional jobs, there is a big demand for people who combine skills and knowledge in more than one area. For example, engineering geologists are crucial to coal mining, as are mineral economists, who combine knowledge of mining, petroleum, and geology with

Fifty-Four Ways to Get a Job

All things being equal, the more job-seeking techniques used, the better your chances of locating a truly appropriate position. The following ways can be used. They are not listed in any order of priority.

1. Newspaper: Place or answer an ad in a newspaper.

2. Magazine: Place or answer an ad in a periodical.

3. Read the *Professional and Trade Association Job Finder* (available from the Garrett Park Press, Garrett Park, Maryland 20896).

4. Job banks: Use services that list candidates for jobs.

5. Job registries: This is another form of a job bank.

6. Clearinghouse of jobs: Use employment services that list candidates and vacancies.

7. Clearinghouse of jobs: Use employment services set up in conjunction with national or regional meetings of professional organizations.

8. Cold canvass in person: Call on employers in the hope of finding a vacancy appropriate for your skills, personality, and interests.

9. Cold canvass by telephone: Call employers to identify organizations with appropriate vacancies.

10. Union hiring hall: Use employment services set up by labor organizations.

11. Alumni office contacts: School or college alumni offices may suggest former students in a position to help you.

12. Public career and counseling services: Use state employment and other public career-oriented services.

13. Private career and counseling services: The fees charged by these organizations may be more than justified by the job search time saved.

14. Employment agencies: These may charge a fee or a percentage commission—but only if you take a job through them.

15. Executive search firms: These are "head hunter" organizations retained by employers to identify persons for specialized jobs.

16. Volunteer work: Millions have begun their careers by first gaining experience or a "foot in the door" through unpaid work.

17. Part-time work experience: A part-time job may be easier to obtain than full-time work and may lead to a permanent position.

18. Temporary or summer work: These provide experience and an introduction to the employer's organization.

19. Make your own job: Free-lance work may lead to self-employ-ment or a job with an employer.

20. Join a 40-plus group: Most cities have these job clubs that specialize in older workers.

21. Join a 65-plus group: These organizations provide jobs and other services for senior citizens.

22. Join a job search group: Sharing job hunting experiences can provide new ideas and psychological support.

23. Tell friends and acquaintances: Most studies show that friends and family are the best single source of job leads.

24. Federal job centers: These offices, located in major cities, are a good source of job leads. Look them up in the telephone book under "U.S. Government."

25. Computerized placement services: Many organizations inventory candidates and employers by computers to make job matches.

26. Social agency placement services: Along with social services, many of these groups now provide job counseling and placement assistance.

27. Membership services: Many professional and other organizations maintain employment assistance programs to aid their members.

28. Mail order job campaign: Send out dozens or hundreds of

---

skills in economics, management science, and business.

Alternative energy. Generation of power from water, the sun, organic wastes, the wind, and geothermal resources; from co-generation using two or more of these sources; and through energy conservation and recycling has expanded the need for workers with old-fashioned skills: electricians, pipefitters, plumbers, carpenters, and builders.

Small Business: Going Out on Your Own

From the end of World War II until the mid-1970s, small business was not looked upon favorably by the mass of young entrants into the labor force. Ten years ago, one study showed that while 27%

of the parents of high-school students owned their own small business, only 3% of the children were willing to enter the same business.

This has changed. In the past five to ten years, the number of self-employed rose significantly. Small business is the key to high employment today and in the year 2000.

Twelve hundred new businesses are formed each day in the United States. In an era of bigness, more and more people are now starting to see that small is beautiful and that they can turn their interests, potential, and abilities into salable products and services. The root of American economic success has been in entrepreneurship. Today, high schools and colleges all over the United States are offering courses in small business.

Women are more involved than ever before in starting their own small businesses. Many are entering small business for self-actualization, growth, and development. Though money is still important to them, more and more people want to be able to control their lives and to believe that they are making some sort of contribution to society.

Many new small businesses are at the cutting edge of new career developments, such as communications, aids for the handicapped, and the information industry. But there are all kinds of people needs. Creative people can translate them into a successful small business.

For example, one man who earned a high salary but just couldn't get along with his supervisors decided to start his own letters to potential employers, hoping to identify suitable openings.

29. School or college placement services: Both current students and alumni generally are eligible for help from these groups.

30. Association placement services: Many professional and other organizations include employment assistance as part of their service program.

31. Trade placement services: In many occupations, an organized placement program operates.

32. Professional placement services: Use professional career placement specialists, particularly if seeking a high-level job.

33. Hotlines: Use these answering services (many operate 24 hours a day) maintained by community organizations or libraries.

34. Federal civil service offices: Contact employment offices of federal agencies in your area of interest.

35. State merit service offices: Get in touch with appropriate state government agencies.

36. County or city personnel office: File for suitable openings with agencies of local government.

37. Internships: Use a paid or unpaid short-term internship to gain experience and make contact with potential employers.

38. Work-study program: Use a cooperative work-study program to gain experience and to make contacts in a field of prime interest.

39. Networking: Expand contacts that may help you by working with peers, supervisors, friends, and others.

40. Mentor: Cultivate an older, more experienced person to whom you turn for advice. Such a mentor may take a special interest in your proper placement.

41. Television job and career announcements: Don't overlook ads placed on television for employees.

42. Radio job and career announcements: Many employers, with numerous jobs, use radio to help solicit candidates for them.

43. Bulletin board posting: Check ads placed on career-related bulletin boards.

44. Check the *College Placement Annual,* published by the College Placement Council (P.O. Box 2263, Bethlehem, Pennsylvania 18001).

45. Check in-house job vacancies: Most progressive employers now post all vacancies for their current employees to examine and, if interested, apply for. This permits maximum use of upward mobility techniques.

46. DVR job placement services: All state divisions of rehabilitation services offer disabled persons extensive job counseling and placement services.

47. Former employers: Don't hesitate to ask former employers for help.

48. Fellow employees: Persons who work with you might know of suitable vacancies in other offices or organizations.

49. Personnel office counseling: Many times, the personnel office will counsel with you about career paths or alternative jobs in your organization.

50. Religious leaders: Often ministers, rabbis, and priests know of potential employers among their members.

51. Library resources: Check Moody's Industrials, the Fortune "500" list, and other library reference books for employment suggestions.

52. Overseas work: Major religious groups and other international agencies may hire for jobs in other countries.

53. Sponsored interviews: If possible, have persons you know set up employment contacts for you.

54. Military services: Enlistment in one of the armed forces may provide both an immediate salary and job training in fields of interest.

chauffeur business because he loved to drive a car; he now has a Rolls-Royce and drives it for anyone who wants to rent it for a special event. He is busy every day and is now on the way to buying another Rolls.

What kind of economic impact does small business have? Plenty. Of all nonfarm businesses in the United States, 97% are considered "small" according to the Small Business Administration's definition. Small business accounts for nearly $7 out of every $10 in sales made by retailers and wholesalers annually. Nearly 80% of all U.S. businesses (excluding farms) employ fewer than 10 people. The small business part of the economy creates more jobs than any other; it provides, directly or indirectly, the livelihood of more than 100 million Americans—that's almost half of the current U.S. population.

Small business has been growing at the rate of 2.4% annually for the past couple of years. With more sophisticated financial planning and action by entrepreneurs, the failure rate will undoubtedly drop during the next five years.

Computers and the Changing Workplace

Computers and the information revolution are changing the workplace in many ways, and these changes affect how people work, relax, travel, think, and feel.

Recently I visited a paperless office in Washington, D.C. Most of the staff worked at home with their computers and came together only once every three or four weeks. They got their instructions for the day or week via their computers.

Computers may markedly change human behavior by altering the ways people relate to each other. Over the phone, you hear the other person's tone of voice. Face to face, you see a person's smile or anger. You also see who takes the head seat at a meeting. When people use a computer to communicate, they lack nonverbal cues since they cannot see or hear the other person. There are no cues as there are when you meet someone in person or talk to someone on the phone.

Over the next 20 years, there will be more pressure to increase job satisfaction by changing the content of jobs; today, few people seem to deeply enjoy their work

Occupational Titles of the Future

Here is a list of job titles that might appear in a *Dictionary of Occupational Titles* of the future:

Aquaculturist
Armed courier
Artificial intelligence technician
Arts Manager
Asteroid/lunar miner
Astronaut
Battery technician
Benefits analyst
Biomedical technician
Bionic medical technician
Cable television auditor
Cable television salesperson
CAD/CAM technician
Career consultant
CAT scan technician
Certified alcoholism counselor
Certified financial planner
Child advocate
Color consultant
Communications engineer
Community ecologist
Community psychologist
Computer:
  analyst
  camp counselor/owner
  designer
  graphics specialist
  lawyer
  microprocessor technologist
  programmer (software writer)
  sales trainee
  security specialist
  service technician
Contract administrator
Cosmetic surgeon
Cryologist technician
Cultural historian
Cyborg technician
Dance therapist
Dialysis technologist
Divorce mediator
EDP auditor
Electronic mail technician
Energy auditor
Ethicist
Executive rehabilitative counselor
Exercise technician
Exotic welder
Family mediator/therapist
Fiber-optics technician
Financial analyst
Financial consultant
Forecaster
Forensic scientist
Fusion engineer
Genetic biochemist

Genetic counselor
Genetic engineer technician
Geriatric nurse
Graphoanalyst
Hazardous waste technician
Health physicist
Hearing physiologist
Hibernation specialist
Home health aide
Horticulture therapy assistant
Hotline counselor
House- and pet-sitter
Housing rehabilitation technician
Image consultant
Indoor air quality specialist
Information broker
Information research scientist
Issues manager
Job developer
Laser medicine practitioner
Laser technician
Leisure counselor
Licensed psychiatric technician
Market development specialist
Massage therapist
Materials utilization technician
Medical diagnostic imaging technician
Medical sonographer technician
Microbial geneticist
Microbiological mining technician
Mineral economist
Myotherapist
Naprapath
Neutrino astronomer
Nuclear fuel specialist
Nuclear fuel technician
Nuclear medicine technologist
Nuclear reactor technician
Nurse-midwife
Ocean hotel manager
Ombudsman
Oncology nutritionist
Orthotist
Paraprofessional
Peripheral equipment operator
PET scan technician
Physician's assistant
Planetary engineer
Plant therapist
Plastics engineer
Pollution botanist
Power plant inspector
Protein geometrician
Radiation ecologist
Recombinant DNA technologist
Relocation counselor

Energy consultant reviews thermograms and photographs in a heat-loss survey to show homeowners where they can save money. Energy industries offer a broad variety of job opportunities requiring a range of skills. In addition to workers with traditional skills—such as welders, pipefitters, carpenters, materials handlers, and truck drivers—emerging energy careers will require more and more people with knowledge in a number of areas.

Retirement counselor
Robot:
  engineer
  salesperson
  scientist
  technician (industrial)
  trainer
Security engineer
Selenologist (lunar astronomer)
Shrimp-trout fish farmer
Shyness consultant
Software club director
Software talent agent
Soil conservationist
Solar energy consultant
Solar energy research scientist
Solar engineer
Space botanist
Space mechanic
Sports law specialist
Sports psychologist
Strategic planner
Systems analyst
Tape librarian
Telecommunications systems
    designer
Thanatologist
Transplant coordinator
Treasure hunter
Underwater archaeologist
Underwater culture technician
Volcanologist
Waste manager
Water quality specialist
Wellness consultant

and to have real psychic satisfaction. At the same time, people are likely to spend less time at work, either through shortened workweeks or through absenteeism.

While there is likely to be greater employee participation in decision-making, loyalty to one's company will probably continue to decrease. More people will change jobs or even careers more often. Training policies will be reassessed to meet an increasing need to train and retrain people. The proportion of women in the work force is likely to increase, and more of them will be career-oriented.

More people will work at home. There will probably also be more work for people in neighborhood work centers. These centers will be similar to the firms that offer a business address, an answering service, and an office to rent on an hourly or daily basis. There also can be community communication centers for sharing particularly expensive facilities, including video telephone booths, rooms for electronic meetings, etc.

While sophisticated technical skills will be needed in the twenty-first century, I believe we need to add life- and love-enhancing skills or our technology will accelerate alienation.

The concept of Win-Lose must be replaced by a Win-Win ideal. Rather than "King of the Mountain," the game we must learn now is "People of the Mountain."

When people are made to feel that their self-image and worth depend on their being on top, complex problems are created. They experience high levels of anxiety, display destructive tendencies, and show increased insensitivity to the feelings of others. They lie, cheat, hurt, maim, and kill to make it to the top. In the process, some people destroy not only their colleagues but their families and themselves.

We need to develop a special kind of sensitive balance for cooperation and individualism that allows people to live and work in harmony. People can compete in a psychologically healthy way.

We can enhance individual initiative and creativity and, at the same time, stimulate the ability or potential to work well as a team.

Keeping Up with New and Emerging Careers

Newspapers, particularly ones like the *Wall Street Journal,* and magazines, especially trade and professional journals, carry news items that relate ongoing, current developments that affect companies and their products, earnings, and number and kinds of employees.

In addition to the World Future Society's three periodicals (THE FUTURIST, *World Future Society Bulletin,* and *Future Survey*), these newsletters and magazines might be helpful to anyone wishing to keep up with emerging careers:

CAM Report, Priam Publications, Inc., 1330 Beach Street, East Lansing, Michigan 48823-6862.

What's Next, Congressional Clearinghouse on the Future, 555 House Annex #2, U.S. Congress, Washington, D.C. 20515.

The Financial Post Magazine, Mclean-Hunter Business Publishing Co., 481 University Avenue, Toronto, Ontario, Canada M5W 1A7.

Occupational Outlook Quarterly, U.S. Department of Labor, Bureau of Labor Statistics, Washington, D.C. 20212.

Spinoff 1982 (National Aeronautics and Space Administration), Superintendent of Documents, U.S. Government Printing Office, Washington, D.C. 20402.

Washington Counseletter, Chronicle Guidance Publications, Moravia, New York 13118.

National Business Employment Weekly, the *Wall Street Journal,* 420 Lexington Avenue, New York, New York 10170.

For Further Reading

THE FUTURIST has recently featured many articles about new careers, including:

"Life/Work Planning: Change and Constancy in the World of Work" by Richard N. Bolles, December 1983.

"Getting Ready for the Jobs of the Future" by Marvin Cetron, June 1983.

"Managing the Issues of the 1980s" by William L. Renfro, August 1982.

"Careers with a Future: Where the Jobs Will Be in the 1990s" by Marvin Cetron and Thomas O'Toole, June 1982.

"Living and Working in a Sustainable Society" by Lester R. Brown, April 1982.

"Winning Through Mediation: Divorce Without Losers" by Patricia Vroom, Diane Fassett, and Rowan A. Wakefield, February 1982.

"Libraries in the Year 2010: The Information Brokers" by S.D. Neill, October 1981.

See also: *The World of Work: Careers and the Future,* edited by Howard F. Didsbury, Jr. (World Future Society, 1983), and *Careers Tomorrow: The Outlook for Work in a Changing World,* edited by Edward Cornish (World Future Society, 1983).

About the Author

S. Norman Feingold, a licensed psychologist, is president of the National Career and Counseling Services (1522 N Street, N.W., Suite 336, Washington, D.C. 20005). This article is based on his speech at the World Future Society's special conference, "Working Now and in the Future," held in August 1983, and on his latest book with co-author Norma R. Miller, *Emerging Careers: New Occupations for the Year 2000 and Beyond* (1983, Garrett Park Press, $10.95), which is available from the World Future Society Book Service (pre-payment required; please include $1.50 for postage and handling).

Work in a High-Tech Future

The proportion of American workers involved in agriculture and manufacturing declined from 83% to 30% between 1860 and 1980, while services expanded proportionately. Recent trends indicate that this historical transformation will continue, if not accelerate. In the medium-range future, this will not mean an *absolute* decline of jobs in agriculture and manufacturing sectors, but a *relative* decline as the size of the work force increases. However, as advanced technology is applied to heavy industry during the last decades of the twentieth century, some analysts speculate that the proportion of the work force employed in manufacturing will gradually decline to about 3% over the next 50 years.

The relative decline of employment in manufacturing and agriculture does not indicate that they will become less important to our economy; rather, these sectors will produce more with fewer workers. Just as the number of persons fed by the average American farmer increased from 9 to 25 between 1940 and 1962, advances in technology and management will allow workers in manufacturing and other sectors to produce far more per hour of labor.

California, a recognized center of technological innovation, exhibited shifts in the distribution of its work force that parallel national trends. Many forecasters speculate that the large and growing proportion of businesses involved in the development and production of high-technology products within California will foster a rate of change that is faster than that seen nationally. To provide an overview, the number of jobs within the United States is projected to increase 15.9%, from 103 million to 119 million, between 1981 and 1990; the number of jobs in California will increase some 24.9%, from 11 million to 14 million.

Projections to 1985 from the California Employment Development Department indicate considerable variation of job growth among different occupations. These forecasts, which roughly parallel those for the nation, indicate a greater than average growth rate for most technical occupations, as well as skilled craft and operative positions. However, many observers feel that these forecasts are conservative due to the growth of California's high-tech industries and the demand for highly skilled labor.

As in the past, shifts in the skills required for employment will be due primarily to technological change. The high-technology sectors will increasingly account for new jobs created in the coming decades and will change the skills required throughout the entire economy.

These high-technology industries include computers, communication equipment, instruments, electronic components, and computer services. The aerospace industry is occasionally included in the high-tech category, as are a variety of fledgling enterprises such as energy innovations, biotechnology, robotics, chemicals, new materials, selected medical products, and home entertainment equipment.

Although high technology now employs a relatively small proportion of the total work force, job growth within these sectors has been phenomenal. Between 1970 and 1980, job growth for the five core high-tech industries within California was 80.3%, compared with 38.8% for the state work force as a whole. During the 1980s, job growth for these same industries is projected to be 47.6%, compared with 24.9% for the entire state economy. Moderate projections indicate that the number of California jobs in these core high-tech industries will increase from 591,795 to 726,700 between 1980 and 1990.

The aerospace industry is expected to add at least 24,400 new jobs (possibly more due to defense contracts) to the California economy during the 1980s, and fledgling high-tech enterprises are likely to add another 10,000 jobs during the same period. Consolidation of all high-tech related industrial growth suggests that these sectors will account for approximately 268,900 new jobs during the next decade. To put these figures into historical perspective, these high-tech industries and enterprises directly created 6.9% of overall California job growth during the 1970s and are expected to account for 9.7% during the 1980s. Some studies have forecast even greater growth.

These high-tech sectors will require workers with more extensive and diverse training than the work force in general. Engineers, scientists, technicians, and computer specialists, representing 5.7% of the total California work force, will make up about 28.7% of the employees in the state's five core high-tech industries by 1990.

The growth of California's high-technology industries will foster an increasing demand for technical, scientific, and skilled workers. Demand for computer specialists will increase 106% among the five core high-tech industries between 1980 and 1990. The demand for technicians will increase by about 46% and for qualified assemblers and operatives by about 30% over the same period.

As a result, high-technology industries will probably need 19,000 additional technicians, 21,000 additional skilled craft persons, and 44,000 more qualified assemblers and operatives by 1990. Correspondingly, there will be increased demand for managers, clerical workers, and other support personnel who are familiar with basic technical issues.

—Fred Best

David C. Borchard

MARY KAYE O'NEILL/PRINCE GEORGE'S COMMUNITY COLLEGE, LARGO, MARYLAND

NEW CHOICES

Career Planning in a Changing World

Not so long ago, career/life planning would have served little purpose. People had few career choices available: most men were farmers or factory workers, and most women were homemakers or teachers. Those circumstances were perceived to be as stable as the dollar, and the future promised little change other than growing older. Those were the days when America's work and lifestyles were associated with agriculture and manufacturing.

There is little doubt that we have left the old world behind and are now in the post-industrial revolution—the transition to a new age. The realities that once restricted occupational and lifestyle choices are no longer the governing realities of today. The magnitude of today's possibilities is staggering. Now life seems as *unstable* as the dollar.

Career/life planning is the process of identifying your choices and then choosing goals suited to both your individual uniqueness and to the realities of the world of work. This is a time-consuming and on-

As society enters the post-industrial age, career choosers and changers have more options than ever before. Yet traditional methods used by career counselors fail to take into account the rapid changes affecting the world of work.

going process. For people to have invested much effort in this process in the agrarian and industrial eras would have been essentially futile. Today, however, we live in an age of almost unlimited choice. This makes career/life planning an essential undertaking for anyone desiring a satisfying career and life.

A Career/Life Planning Model

John L. Holland, a vocational psychologist at Johns Hopkins Uni-

versity, created an occupational-choice model that has become a very popular career-planning tool over the past decade. Holland's model establishes a general classification system for personality styles and another for occupational environments. In this theoretical framework, personality styles are classified into six general categories based on patterns of interests (see Figure 1). The six styles are linked to a classification structure that organizes occupations according to similar traits (see Figure 2).

Therefore, the task in Holland's model for career planning is to identify your strongest interests and to see where these fit in the personality style hexagon. You then select your occupation from among those choices that are included within the corresponding category of the occupational environment hexagon.

For example, let's assume that you complete an interest-assessment evaluation, using assessment tools such as Holland's *The Self Directed Search* or Edward K. Strong,

Figure 1

The Six Personality Types

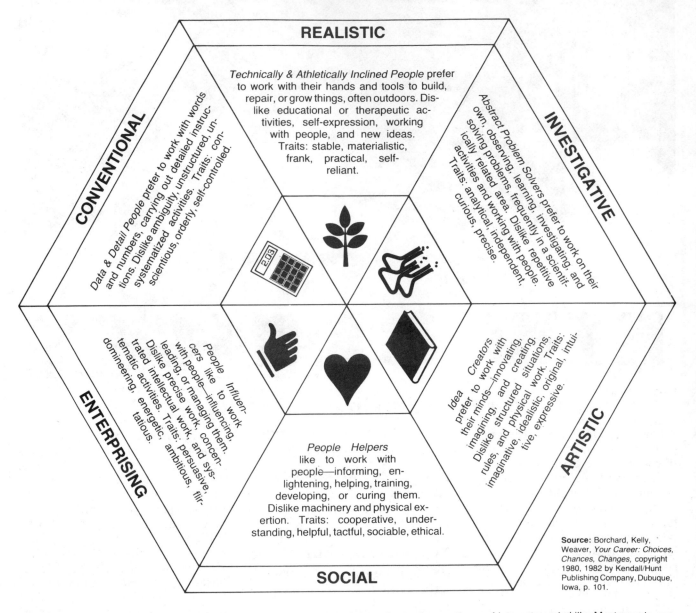

REALISTIC

Technically & Athletically Inclined People prefer to work with their hands and tools to build, repair, or grow things, often outdoors. Dislike educational or therapeutic activities, self-expression, working with people, and new ideas. Traits: stable, materialistic, frank, practical, self-reliant.

CONVENTIONAL

Data & Detail People prefer to work with words and numbers, carrying out detailed instructions. Dislike ambiguity, unstructured, unsystematized activities. Traits: conscientious, orderly, self-controlled.

INVESTIGATIVE

Abstract Problem Solvers prefer to work on their own, observing, learning, investigating, and solving problems, frequently in a scientifically related area. Dislike repetitive activities and working with people. Traits: analytical, independent, curious, precise.

ENTERPRISING

People Influencers like to work with people—influencing, leading, or managing them. Dislike precise work, concentrated intellectual work, and systematic activities. Traits: persuasive, domineering, energetic, ambitious, flirtatious.

ARTISTIC

Idea Creators prefer to work with their minds—innovating, imagining, and creating. Dislike structured situations, rules, and physical work. Traits: imaginative, idealistic, original, intuitive, expressive.

SOCIAL

People Helpers like to work with people—informing, enlightening, helping, training, developing, or curing them. Dislike machinery and physical exertion. Traits: cooperative, understanding, helpful, tactful, sociable, ethical.

Source: Borchard, Kelly, Weaver, *Your Career: Choices, Chances, Changes,* copyright 1980, 1982 by Kendall/Hunt Publishing Company, Dubuque, Iowa, p. 101.

Psychologist John L. Holland's identification of six personality types is based on unique patterns of interests and skills. Most people can be placed in one to three of these categories, which can then be used to help them to discover the occupations for which they are best suited (see Figures 2 and 3).

Jr., and David P. Campbell's *Strong-Campbell Interest Inventory.* You learn that your primary interest patterns fall within the Artistic (A), Investigative (I), and Social (S) categories. A career counselor might then assist you in identifying a list of occupations to consider from the A, I, and S groups, such as psychologist, psychiatrist, biology instructor, writer, architect, graphics designer, etc. While this is an overly simplified description of the process, it does serve to illustrate the general nature of Holland-oriented career planning.

Career Planning and Change

One of the major problems confronting the neophyte career/life-planning professional is the pace at which the occupational world is now changing. Many of the specific career-related programs that college freshmen and technical-school students enter into today may no longer offer good employment prospects or long-range career potential by the time they obtain their degrees.

Rapid change does not alter the effectiveness of the Holland model for assessment purposes, but it certainly could affect its utility as a vocational-selection methodology. The Holland model works well in a stable world where the occupational future remains consistent with the past. Vocational choice in stable conditions is a simple matter of selecting the occupation that

Figure 2

Occupational Environments

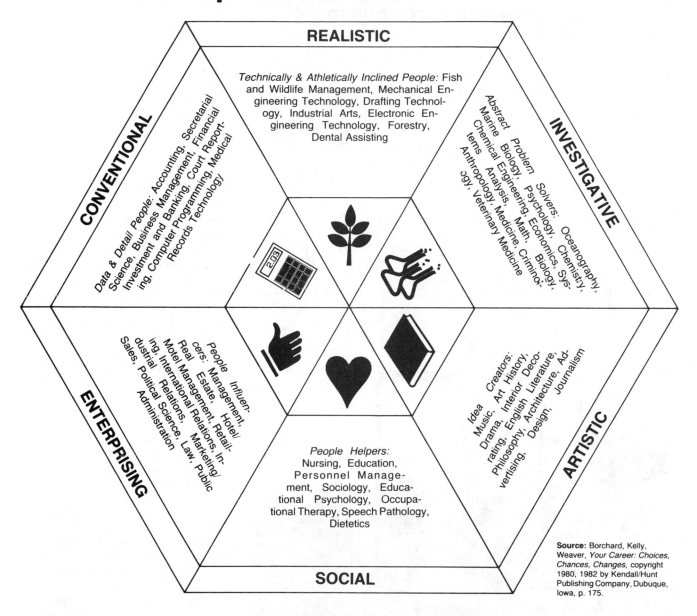

REALISTIC

Technically & Athletically Inclined People: Fish and Wildlife Management, Mechanical Engineering Technology, Drafting Technology, Industrial Arts, Electronic Engineering Technology, Forestry, Dental Assisting

CONVENTIONAL

Data & Detail People: Accounting, Secretarial Science, Business Management, Financial Investment and Banking, Court Reporting, Computer Programming, Medical Records Technology

INVESTIGATIVE

Abstract Problem Solvers: Oceanography, Marine Biology, Psychology, Chemistry, Chemical Engineering, Economics, Systems Analysis, Math, Biology, Anthropology, Medicine, Criminology, Veterinary Medicine

ENTERPRISING

People Influencers: Management, Real Estate, Hotel/Motel Management, Retailing, International Relations, Industrial Relations, Marketing/Sales, Political Science, Law, Public Administration

ARTISTIC

Idea Creators: Music, Art History, Drama, Interior Decorating, English Literature, Advertising, Architecture, Journalism, Philosophy, Design

SOCIAL

People Helpers: Nursing, Education, Personnel Management, Sociology, Educational Psychology, Occupational Therapy, Speech Pathology, Dietetics

Source: Borchard, Kelly, Weaver, *Your Career: Choices, Chances, Changes,* copyright 1980, 1982 by Kendall/Hunt Publishing Company, Dubuque, Iowa, p. 175.

This chart shows traditional occupations associated with the personality types identified by Holland (see Figure 1).

best fits your interests and skills. But how do you know what occupation your interests suggest when the future is so uncertain? In a time of rapid change, you can't even be sure what choices will be in existence in the future, let alone which has the best match for your particular attributes.

However, two features of the Holland model make it an excellent tool for futures prediction in the occupational arena. The first has to do with the assumption that an in-

dividual's dominant personality-based interest patterns have pretty much crystallized by the end of adolescence. These patterned interests then remain fairly stable throughout life. What this means is that when your personality style has been accurately classified in Holland's terms, your primary interest patterns have been revealed for life. Thus, if an assessment test found you to be an Artistic or an Investigative type at age 20, a similar test retaken at ages 40 and 60

would again detect the same prevailing interests.

The second feature of the Holland model that gives it credence as a tool for futures prediction lies in the relationship between human interest patterns and the structure of the occupational world. In essence, Holland found that occupational activities in the workplace are reflections of human interest patterns. It seems unlikely that the evolved structure of our occupational world is due to chance or ac-

"While we can't be sure what specific names the occupations of the future will have, we can be rather sure that these unknown occupations will possess characteristics that conform to the Holland structure."

cident. The fact that Holland was able to classify the inner world of personality so neatly into six general styles seems to attest to a natural ordering. But why does this same pattern exist in the occupational world? The answer, no doubt, is that people gravitate to, or create, work that enables them to express their primary interests. In this regard, the Holland structure appears to be an occupational model for all time.

No matter what historical period we might select as a reference, we could fit all of the known occupations in existence at that time into Holland's six categories. We know,

for example, that the alchemists were Investigative types, blacksmiths Realistics, court jesters Artistics, cattle barons Enterprisings, and midwives Socials.

There is every reason to believe that the Holland model will continue to serve as a convenient scheme for organizing the occupations of the future. We can also assume that people in the future will be happiest when they enter occupations best suited to their natural interests. Thus, while we can't be sure what specific names the occupations of the future will have, we can be rather sure that these unknown occupations will

possess characteristics that conform to the Holland structure. The Holland model helps us to know a lot about what people's interests will be in the future, and a little about the nature of work in the future.

Designing Occupational Scenarios

Figure 3 illustrates how the Holland model can be used as a reference for facilitating occupational-scenario designing. Three scenarios have been developed around six factors that shape the nature of jobs and career patterns over the next 20 years. These six factors are: technology, economics, international politics, brain/mind capabilities, health and longevity, and values. Figure 4 depicts a continuum representing extremes for these variables. From this continuum it is possible to weigh the overall effect of possible trends and then to envision likely occupational scenarios using Holland's six categories as a base for prediction.

The three scenarios are:

1. Little change in the environment or in human qualities.

2. Rapid change in human creations, such as technology, economics, and politics, with little change in humans themselves.

3. Rapid change in humans, such as brain/mind capabilities, health, and values.

Scenario 1 lists a few sample occupations that we might expect in each of Holland's six code categories if there is little change over the next 20 years. In this scenario, the occupations would not be very different from those of today. However, there are some current trends that would probably continue modifying the occupational environment. For example, there will almost certainly be fewer physical-labor jobs of the kind associated with a heavy-manufacturing-based industry and more of the highly skilled jobs associated with high technology.

JOE DI DIO/NATIONAL EDUCATION ASSOCIATION

People who like to work with other people—teaching, healing, developing, informing, or training them—are attracted to occupations in such fields as education, sociology, and therapy. This teacher has the rapt attention of his young pupils.

Figure 3

Three Scenarios for Occupations in the Year 2000

PERSONALITY TYPE	1·LITTLE CHANGE	2·EXTERNAL TRANSFORMATION	3·INTERNAL TRANSFORMATION
Realistic *Technically & Athletically Inclined People* 	Electronic Technician, Robot Technician, Pre-Fab Construction Worker, Cable-TV Technician, Medical Technician	Laser Technician, Solar Technician, Space Station Technician, Satellite Communication, Bionic Limb Technician	Brain/Mind Lab Technician, Bioenergetic Technician, Actualization Abode Carpenter, Thought Transmission and Recording Technician, Health Food Farmer
Investigative *Abstract Problem Solvers* 	Pollution Control Scientist, Systems Analyst, Nuclear Engineer, Computer Scientist, Intelligence Analyst	Space Medicine Scientist, Computer Scientist/Medical Analyst, Space Habitation Analyst, Extra-terrestrial Geologist, Weapons Disposal Engineer	Genetic Engineer, Well-Being Medical Doctor, Mind Expansion Researcher, Human Communications Specialist, Peace Scientist
Artistic *Idea Creators* 	Graphics Design/Commercial Artist, Cable-TV Writer, Conservation Architect, Military Musician, Curriculum Developer	Computer-Assisted Design and Computer Graphics Artist, International Satellite Communications Script Writer, Solar Energy Architect, Computer Musician, Right Brain Curriculum Developer	Thought Transmission Artist, Human Expansion Writer, Human Milieu Architect, Mind Expansion Musician, Whole Brain Curriculum Developer
Social *People Helpers* 	Nurse, Stress Psychologist, Marriage/Divorce Counselor, Public Education Teacher, Geriatrics Nurse	Computerized Medicine Nurse, Space Psychologist, New Modes of Living Counselor, Private Computer Learning Facilitator, Retirement/Longevity Counselor	Psychic Healer, Actualization Psychologist, Mind/Body/Spirit Counselor, Personal Enlightenment Tutor, Age 70 + Career Counselor
Enterprising *People Influencers* 	Industrial Robot Salesperson, Hospital Administrator, Military Officer, Electronics Office Manager, Criminal Lawyer	Solar Car Salesperson, Electronics Medical Diagnosis Center Manager, International Peace Project Officer, International Data Bank Manager, Euthanasia Lawyer	Rapid Learning Machine Salesperson, Actualization Center Manager, Quality of Life Projects Manager, Brain/Mind Data Bank Manager, Genetic Manipulation Lawyer
Conventional *Data & Detail People* 	Data Entry Clerk, Word Processing Specialist, Medical Records Technician, Computer Programmer, Accountant	International Data Base Clerk, Paperless Office Administrative Aide, Electronics Medical Diagnostic Records Technician, Computer Security Inspector, Computer Accountant	Brain/Mind Data Bank Clerk, Thought Transmission Recorder, Actualization Center Administrative Assistant, Psychic Research Aide, Personal Efficiency Advisor

This chart shows what job titles might be found in Holland's Occupational Environment hexagon (see Figure 2) in three different scenarios of the year 2000.

Figure 4

Factors Shaping Careers of the Future

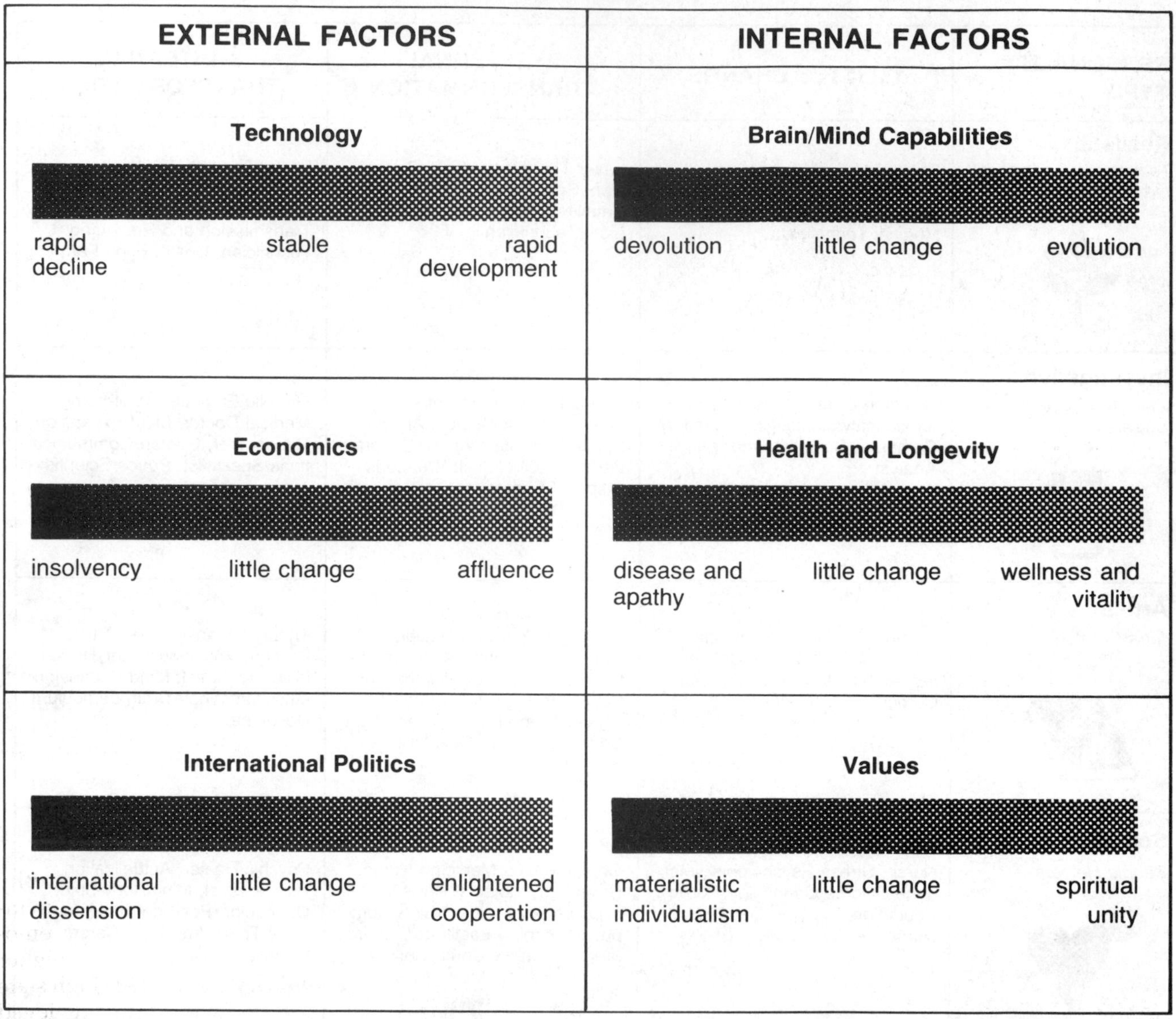

EXTERNAL FACTORS	INTERNAL FACTORS
Technology	**Brain/Mind Capabilities**
rapid decline · · · stable · · · rapid development	devolution · · · little change · · · evolution
Economics	**Health and Longevity**
insolvency · · · little change · · · affluence	disease and apathy · · · little change · · · wellness and vitality
International Politics	**Values**
international dissension · · · little change · · · enlightened cooperation	materialistic individualism · · · little change · · · spiritual unity

This chart summarizes a continuum of possible changes—from negative to positive—in six factors affecting the future of work. Author Borchard's occupational Scenario 1 assumes "little change" in either external or internal factors. Scenario 2 assumes rapid positive change in external factors, but little change in internal factors. Scenario 3 assumes little change in external factors, but rapid positive change in internal factors. Other scenarios can also be developed assuming rapid negative changes in either external or internal factors or both.

The current upheaval in the school and college system generated from the baby-boom years will have stabilized. The result should be a much rosier employment situation than is currently the case, and the education field may once again offer promising, prestigious, and stable careers.

In a population that is growing older, increased numbers of workers serving the over-60 age group are sure to be needed. With most of the U.S. population possessing home computers and cable television service, the early twenty-first century should be a boom time for the deliverers of life-long learning services, including educational-system designers and software developers.

Scenario 2 illustrates the kinds of occupations we can expect if rapid, positive transformation should occur in government, technology, and economic conditions over the next 20 years. Major breakthroughs in the technological areas that produce better living conditions (abundant and cheap energy, clean environment, food sufficiency, clean and efficient mass transportation, space capabilities, etc.), combined with rapidly developing world affluence and international cooperation, would create profound changes in the array of occupations available. This would be especially true in the defense, health, and education industries.

Under these circumstances we could expect to see a great reduction in military expenditures with significantly more capital resources available for health, education, and

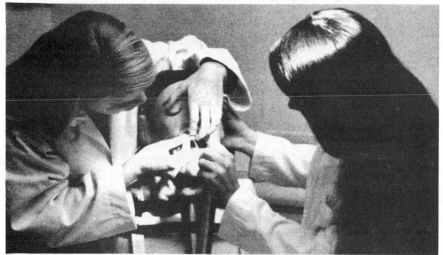

MONTGOMERY COLLEGE, ROCKVILLE, MARYLAND

Dental-assistant students prepare for a career suited to "Realistic" type individuals—those who are technically or athletically skilled and like to work with their hands. Other Realistic careers of today include mechanical and electronic engineering, drafting, and forestry.

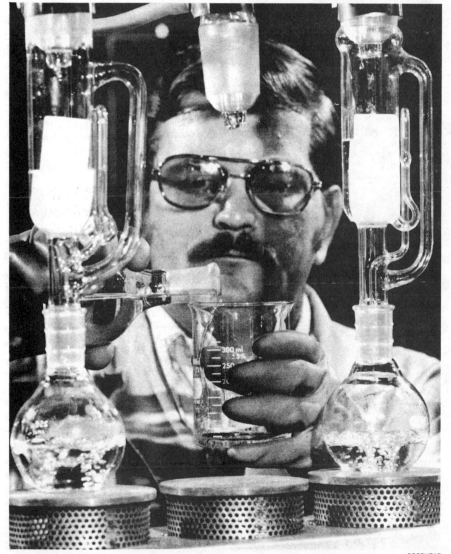

GOODYEAR

People who are analytical and precise and who prefer to work on their own frequently gravitate toward scientific and technical careers such as chemistry, biology, medicine, and mathematics, says author Borchard. Here, a technician measures chemicals during research at Goodyear lab.

nonmilitary research and development. The emphasis might shift from protecting national interest and security to global problem solving through science, technology, and education.

In this scenario, the year 2000 ushers in an age of international peace and cooperation. The world's military expenditures might be re-employed for international construction projects, peace-keeping missions, environmental restoration tasks, and space and ocean exploration. Multinational corporations would become aware of the business benefits created in an affluent, cooperative, and peaceful world, while industries with vested interests in promoting the arms race would transform their product lines into goods and services with market value in a peaceful world.

Scenario 3 envisions a revolutionary transformation in people, with a growing awareness of the amazing potential of the mind. Here we would see a value-system transformation from individual materialism to spiritual wholeness. People would live long, healthy lives through their ability to manage personal, mental, and emotional health and to move to higher levels of well-being. This high state of wellness would be achieved through inner transformation rather than through advances in medical technology. In this scenario, the major focus for career activity might center on "inner technology" and our ability to expand our creativity and intellect, promote mind/body/spiritual well-being, and conduct fully expressive and loving relationships.

Career Planning Example

Mark, a 30-year-old automobile-assembly-line worker, was laid off from his job in 1982. After several months of lying around the house waiting for the union to get his job back, he realized that the automobile industry wasn't rehiring

Artists and musicians, along with art historians, writers, journalists, and philosophers, are "idea creators," individuals whose skills and interests place them in the Artistic category of vocational psychologist John L. Holland's model of personality styles.

PHOTOS: GRINNELL COLLEGE

very many laid-off workers. Mark also knew that the plant was using robots to do the tasks that he used to perform.

At first he felt bitter and angry; later, helpless and depressed. His job was gone, his self-concept was devastated, and he felt he had no skills to do anything else.

After much encouragement from a friend, Mark visited the career-development center at a nearby community college for assistance. There, a career counselor introduced him to the career-planning process, and he began to explore new possibilities. After completing several interest- and skills-assess-

ment exercises, Mark learned that his top interests could be classified as R-I-C (Realistic-Investigative-Conventional) on the Holland model. He was pleased to learn that he had valuable skills that were transferable to other jobs and careers.

The counselor then showed Mark how to develop a list of occupational alternatives suited to an R-I-C personality style by using the traditional sources of occupational information, such as the *Dictionary of Occupational Titles* and the *Occupational Outlook Handbook*, as well as computerized searches and group brainstorming. From these sources, Mark was able to compile a lengthy list of options that offered both good employment prospects and future development potential.

With the assistance of his career counselor, he narrowed down his choices to these occupations: electronics technician, radiology technician, computer operator, solar technician, cable-TV technician, and laser technician. After researching these options in the college's career library and conducting information interviews with people working in these fields, Mark chose to pursue a new career as an electronics technician. This occupation both suited his interests and seemed to be viable in almost any future scenario that he and his counselor could envision.

Now, one year later, Mark is beginning his second year at the community college and soon expects to complete the electronics-technology program. He obtained financial aid to assist with family finances while pursuing his degree. After successfully completing a semester of work experience through the college's cooperative-education program, he obtained a part-time job at a nearby electronics firm. He has already had several job leads and is excited about beginning his career in either the robotics industry or computer production.

ROBERT A. ISAACS

The average secretary's skills and interests place her in Holland's "Conventional" category—people who are orderly and efficient and prefer to work with words and numbers. Other Conventional types include accountants, medical records technicians, and computer programmers.

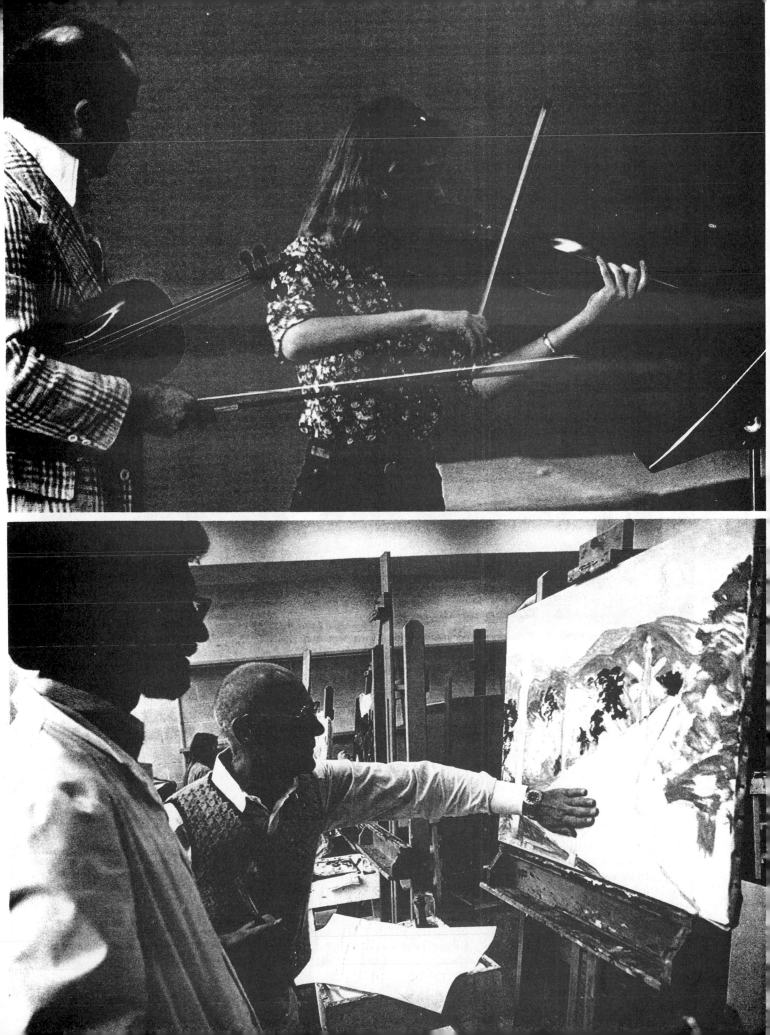

"Career-planning practitioners need to become occupational-scenario designers as well as personal-assessment experts."

MARY KAYE O'NEILL/PRINCE GEORGE'S COMMUNITY COLLEGE, LARGO, MARYLAND

Students seek the advice of career counselor at a community college. To help career choosers make wise choices, the counselor must also be a futurist capable of constructing alternative occupational scenarios.

Life/Career Planner As Futurist

Career planners need to tune in to the future if they are to remain equipped to assist today's career choosers and changers. Many of the methods, tools, and resources currently in use are outdated. Even our current computerized career-search systems are not fully adequate sources of occupation information for people who wish to have careers that span into the future.

Career-planning practitioners need to become occupational-scenario designers as well as personal-assessment experts. By educating themselves about the future, counselors can develop new resources and rejuvenate existing tools. Most counseling tools are showing their age when it comes to assisting people with career planning toward the year 2000.

For example, the Holland model has features that make it particularly adaptable for occupational-scenario development and future-oriented career planning. With a bit of creativity, the counselor can use the model to predict the kinds of occupations likely to develop in the future, even when the times are changing as dramatically as they are now.

About the Author

David C. Borchard, president of the Middle Atlantic Career Counseling Association, is director of career development at Prince George's Community College, 301 Largo Road, Largo, Maryland 20772. He is co-author of *Your Career: Choices, Chances, Changes* (1980) and *Winning Your Career Game* (1983), both published by Kendall/Hunt Publishing Company, for whom he is career planning consultant.

The Changing Unive.sity

Survival in the Information Society

by Samuel L. Dunn

The universities of tomorrow—the ones that survive—will combine a medieval style of professorial tutoring with a futuristic brand of instructional delivery.

The university of tomorrow will differ considerably from today's university, borrowing from the past and adapting to the future as it evolves new links between students, faculty, and community.

Surprisingly, the role of the professor and the organization of the curriculum will be more similar to that of a medieval university than the university of the last 100 years, with students attending fewer lectures and working more independently. On the other hand, new information and communications technologies will transform the classroom and campus as the university moves toward the twenty-first century. And the student body will include a much higher percentage of older adults.

Universities will form linkages with businesses and industries to provide new kinds of educational programs. More human resource development leaders in business will be recognized as educators as they provide full-scale educational programs in competition with the universities. Many students will obtain degrees without even setting foot on a university campus.

Both exciting opportunities and perplexing uncertainties will accompany the shift to the new university. Many institutions will close over the next 20 years, falling victim to demographic changes, new technologies, funding problems, external degree programs, and competition. But exciting days are ahead for those institutions that can make the transition and realize the unlimited potential of the information society.

End of a Monopoly

While universities and colleges will continue into the foreseeable future as teaching institutions, the traditional university will not have a monopoly on higher education. High-quality educational programs will be available in many other institutions.

At present, it is customary to divide U.S. post-secondary institutions into three groups: (1) the private nonprofit college; (2) the public college; and (3) the private entrepreneurial institution. However, this breakdown ignores the significant educational programs that are carried on in business and industry.

The total budgets for training and development in business and industry now run at about $80-$100 billion per year. American Telephone and Telegraph alone spends approximately $1.3 billion per year on training. There are approximately 700,000 full- and part-time educators in business and industry.

The educational and training programs run by business and industry offer a good deal of diversity in terms of quality, intent, and philosophy. Some courses of study are clearly training programs at a basic level, while others equal or surpass typical college courses in terms of theoretical content, quality of instruction, and demands on the student.

Many organizations offer integrated programs leading to certificates that are recognized by other

Graduate students attend a lecture at the Arthur D. Little Management Education Institute. A growing number of companies, such as this international consulting firm, offer master's degree programs in management and other fields related to their business.

ARTHUR D. LITTLE, INC.

"A growing number of corporations are granting bachelor's and master's degrees in fields related to management and disciplines of interest to that corporation."

employers, and a growing number of corporations are granting bachelor's and master's degrees in fields related to management and disciplines of interest to that corporation. Mona Milbrath's book *Credentials: A Guide to Business Designations* (Blue River Publishing Co., P.O. Box 882, Sheboygan, Wisconsin 53081) lists over 100 recognized credentials, many of which are available through corporate training and development programs. Other organizations that provide high-level instruction include the armed services and other governmental organizations, professional societies, unions, and community service groups.

In addition to their formal educational programs, business and industry invest heavily in informal educational programs through on-the-job training of higher-level employees. New managers generally need start-up time before they can become full, producing members of the corporate team.

Job experience will have a greater effect on a worker's formal education, since universities and colleges will increasingly recognize and certify experiential learning. Over 1,000 colleges and universities now have programs that award credit to students for learning obtained through experience. Thus, older adults can get a head start when they return to formal educational programs. These programs, of course, blur the lines between the traditional university and training programs in business and industry.

Universities will be increasingly willing to consider a variety of arrangements as they move to improve services to adults. Many more consortium arrangements will link universities and colleges with businesses and industries. Even now, some universities give credit for courses sponsored and taught by corporations. Universities will contract to provide training and devel-

opment programs for specific companies and even offer on-site degree and certificate programs to complement the corporations' own human resource development programs.

Universities will make increasing use of businesses for internship and cooperative education programs. Many disciplines—not just teacher education and nursing—now use internship programs to provide significant percentages of the programs for majors. These programs provide experience, learning, access to employers, linkages between professors and potential consulting clients, and a source of inexpensive labor.

The educational preparation of the human resource development personnel in American corporations is steadily improving. There are now over 100 formal academic programs for human resource development personnel in the United States, with at least 40 at the master's and doctoral levels. As human resource development leaders become credentialed as educators, the lines will be further blurred and it will be easier for universities to create linkages.

Electronic Consortia

In another kind of consortium, traditional colleges will band together to pool resources for nontraditional educational delivery systems. These arrangements will be important from an economic perspective, particularly when entire degree programs are offered via television, computer, videocassette, videodisc, or combinations of these technologies. Typically, a large student base will be needed to cover the investment costs in terms of the hardware and software needed to deliver the programs, especially since the software will be short-lived due to rapid increases in knowledge.

Public television, public radio, and newspapers will also deliver course programming. This will lead, of course, to situations in which stu-

dents can exercise an option to earn credits from one of many different colleges. Consequently, universities will more readily accept transfer credits from a student not enrolled at the college from which the transcript comes. External degree programs will be common, with most universities of tomorrow providing access to degrees with no residence requirements at all.

The university of the future will no longer be a stand-alone institution, providing in and of itself all aspects of a student's educational program. Linkages will be all-important to its survival and significance in the future.

Educating for the Information Society

Tomorrow's university will provide both education and training. The distinction between the two may be somewhat artificial, but it may also be helpful. To paraphrase Robert Theobald's description, the study of a problem whose solutions are known is training; the study of a problem whose solutions are unknown is education. At present, over half of all instruction at the undergraduate level in U.S. colleges simply presents facts and solutions—and hence may rightly be called training. In some disciplines, over 90% of the instruction is at this lower cognitive level. Training *must* occur for education to occur, but on the other hand, it will be a constant challenge to the university to instruct at higher cognitive levels.

The university of tomorrow will provide three categories of educational experiences:

First, it will provide general educational programs that will prepare students to be knowledgeable and useful citizens, family members, and workers. Courses in communication, problem solving, decision-making, societal issues, the arts, and human nature should be taken by younger adults to make their lives

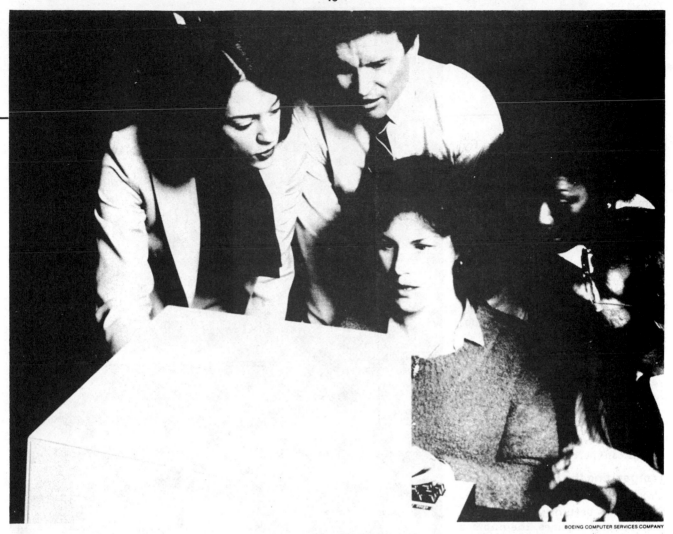

BOEING COMPUTER SERVICES COMPANY

At the Boeing Company's computer services training center, students get "hands-on" experience plus credits from Seattle Pacific University. In the future, many more consortium arrangements will link universities with corporations.

more satisfying and productive. This category of educational programming is especially important in a dynamic society such as ours, since students can no longer prepare in advance for a specific lifetime career. The liberal arts or general education approach is the most practical for individuals in the information society.

Second, the university of tomorrow will provide educational programs—both for young adults and mid-life career switchers—that can be used to gain entry to career opportunities. Universities will find it very important to provide these programs for older, working adults in a manner that does not disrupt their income.

Third, the university will provide educational programs for adults at all levels of instruction. Courses in basic skills, taking into account adult needs and learning theory, will be common. The university of tomorrow will be a place where adults go to learn, regardless of level.

The university will also continue its other tasks of discovering, originating, critiquing, and disseminating information and knowledge, as well as its research and consulting services.

Toward More Flexible Programs

Today, more than one-third of all full-time and part-time college students are over 25. In the future, most students will be over 25 years of age. Most will be working adults and will not be able or willing to forgo income for long periods of time. These students will want programs that enhance knowledge and skills useful in their present careers or ones that will help them gain entry to new careers. Some will want programs that enrich the quality of their personal, family, and social lives, but most adults will go to school for pragmatic purposes.

These older learners will, on the average, be more highly motivated than the 18- to 22-year olds. They will want to have easy access to courses or programs, to move through the educational experience as rapidly as possible with maximum learning, and to receive certification of their new knowledge and skills.

These students will desire a broader range of offerings in the evenings, early mornings, and weekends, through courses by audiocassette, videocassette, and independent study. They will prefer programs that do not have extended prerequisite structures, and in many cases they will want courses that are shorter and more focused than typical college courses. Total immersion, high-impact courses that meet for about 12 hours per day for a period of two to five days will be popular, as will modules—one or one-half credit segments of a three- to five-credit course.

Many younger students, unable or unwilling to spend four years obtaining the baccalaureate degree, will also desire more flexibility. They will be willing to attend school full time only if they can complete their programs more quickly, in time-compressed programs of two or three years.

Of course, many students will still want a more leisurely approach to their programs while in residence on campus. Thus, while the residential component will be relatively less important, it will continue to include a significant percentage of students.

Reorganizing the Curriculum

Over the past 300 years, the curriculum has been organized largely in terms of disciplines, the number of which has grown greatly. This division promotes the tendency to view the world, nature, life, and work as segmented, differentiated into separate parts. Particularly at the secondary level and above, information and learning now come in fairly rigidly defined categories, an approach that will be detrimental to the citizen of the information society, who will need to know much more about the interactions of various bodies of knowledge.

The modern world is complex and interconnected. Problem solving must be considered from a systems perspective, taking into account the total knowledge base. A narrow view of life, discipline, or career is inappropriate in these circumstances.

The need to prepare citizens for the telematic society will lead to new organizations of the curriculum in the future. However, despite some experimentation, the present approaches are still firmly entrenched

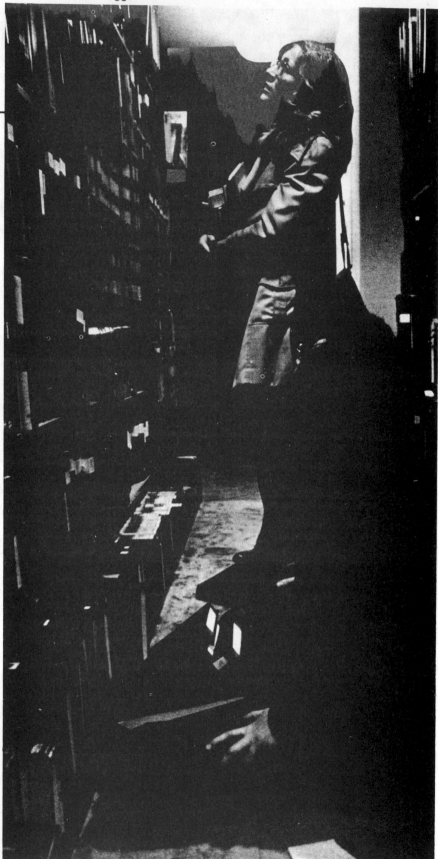

CARL J. DAHLMAN/PRINCETON UNIVERSITY

Students look for books in campus library: a scene that may become less common in the future. Personal computers will give students access to data banks from their homes or dorm rooms, and they will get much of their information through such nontraditional methods as computer discs, audiocassettes, and videocassettes.

"The model of the professor as the manager of a mini-educational system involving staff support, hardware, and courseware appears to be a promising one for meeting changing academic and economic goals."

and it may take 10 to 20 years before other methodologies become widely accepted.

One approach that looks promising is to organize the curriculum around the concept of problem solving. In this system, the student works through a series of problems, researching information as needed. Teams of professors work with certain classes of problems.

For example, a student might tackle the problem of planning a new suburb. In the process of working with this problem, the student would have to work with a great deal of information in the disciplines of sociology, urban planning, statistics, business, the biological or environmental sciences, and law, and would consult with a team of professors from these various fields. Preparing written and oral reports would sharpen communication skills, and accessing information from data banks and interviewing experts would add retrieval skills.

Whether this particular approach will be widespread in the future cannot be predicted, but it does appear clear that different approaches to curricular presentation will be utilized. The telematic society will significantly affect the curriculum.

Emphasis on Results

The quality of today's university is generally measured in terms of inputs to the learning process. That is, the quality of the program is judged by the number of faculty members, the percentage of faculty holding doctorates, the student/faculty ratio, the admissions requirements, the number of books in the library, etc. In the future, this system of quality assessment will be complemented and then replaced by an emphasis on measurements of outputs. As consumers, students will demand full value for the investment they make. They will be inter-

ested in the ability of the university to provide programs that fulfill the claims it makes about its graduates, and many schools will strengthen their general education programs accordingly. The university of the future will certainly require all students to be competent in using information technologies.

Because of the emphasis on outputs rather than inputs, universities will introduce exit competency programs. Before this century, most universities and colleges had significant exit requirements, such as the undergraduate thesis or the undergraduate major examination that students had to successfully complete before receiving a bachelor's degree.

Changing Faculty Roles

The heart of the university is the faculty. Faculty members teach, advise, motivate, model, publish, consult, testify, and do research. The reputation and future of the university rest with the faculty—and this dependence will continue in tomorrow's university.

The faculty of tomorrow's university will perform the same tasks as in the past, but in a different way.

Faculty members will need to spend more time keeping up with their disciplines. Direct study of new material being generated, with extended periods of refreshing and retooling, will be mandatory. The professors of tomorrow will also have to spend more time keeping abreast of changing teaching technologies. Considerable amounts of time will be devoted to collecting, formatting, and presenting information via the new technologies.

Another task that will require more time will be that of diagnosing student needs and prescribing individual courses of study. Diagnostic tests must be located or constructed and updated regularly. This system will permit students to learn in a more individualized manner as they

master the materials in a given course.

The model of the professor as the manager of a mini-educational system involving staff support, hardware, and courseware appears to be a promising one for meeting changing academic and economic goals. In a typical situation, the undergraduate professor would have one full-time professional-level support person with a bachelor's degree in the discipline being taught. The helper would be able to program a computer and do word processing. This assistant would also be able to run the typical educational machinery (minicomputers, videotape players, videodisc players, film projectors, etc.) as well as manage a records system and administer and correct objective diagnostic and course tests.

Courseware would be available to be checked out by the support helper for the student to use on site. Some courseware—largely audiocassettes and discs—might be available for purchase in the university bookstore.

Most students in tomorrow's university will have their own personal computers and will be able to access information banks with ease and skill. The personal computers will be linked to university-wide networks that will allow students to call up most library materials and view them from their dormitory rooms or homes.

The course support system supplemented by the student-supplied equipment would be used in the following way: The student would enroll for a course or module, then go to an assigned classroom for initial instructions and diagnostic tests covering the course material. On the basis of the diagnostic results, a personalized course of study would be prescribed that would involve interaction with a collection of courseware materials, submission of papers, attendance at occasional

Princeton University students take time out to play catch. The residential experience will remain an important part of college for many students, even though many will be able to obtain degrees without even setting foot on a campus.

lectures given by the professor, individual consultation with the professor, and examinations to demonstrate mastery.

The Medieval Model

In this approach, the professor spends less time preparing and presenting formal lectures to large groups of students and more time keeping abreast of the information in the subject being taught and formatting that information in ways that students can access readily. The professor is then available for more interaction with students who need counsel or assistance. The net result is that the professor spends less time lecturing and more time responding to the individual needs of the students.

In this model, the professor assumes duties that are similar, at least conceptually, to those of professors in the European universities of 500 years ago. In the medieval universities, the typical student came to a professor who, through discussion, analyzed the student's needs, then prescribed a course of readings and study. The student started working through the materials on his own, checking back with the professor if he encountered difficulty or wanted to discuss some aspects of the readings. The student discussed the material with other students on his own initiative. When he thought that he had mastered the material, he returned to the professor for an examination (formal or informal), turned in any required papers or theses, and received approval for or failed the course. The professor might give a small number of lectures, usually announced in advance, to the entire university community.

One can see the similarities between the telematic university of the future and the medieval university. The significant difference is that the professor in tomorrow's university will be able to use more

sophisticated procedures to diagnose and track the student's experience more readily, working with more students at a time.

Survival Strategies

To help professors make the transition to this kind of teaching, the university will need to provide learning experiences, staff, and equipment. The transition in any given situation must be well planned, with the faculty development staff providing the leadership. There will certainly be resistance, and only if the rewards are adequately described and the experiences of the first professors making the transition are pleasant will the new approach be easily accepted.

The university of tomorrow will be considerably more complex than today's university. Varied approaches to the curriculum, linkages with other organizations, blurred lines between public and private funding, increased quality expectation, severe competition, and teaching/learning from a distance will make the university more difficult to manage. Universities will need

professional academic administrators with special skills not directly related to those of the teaching and research faculty to manage the transition. Only those institutions with the ability to adjust to the challenge of the future will survive into the twenty-first century.

About the Author

Samuel L. Dunn is dean of professional, graduate, and continuing studies at Seattle Pacific University, Seattle, Washington 98119. This article is adapted from a speech given at the World Future Society Education Section Conference, Dallas, Texas, in February 1983.

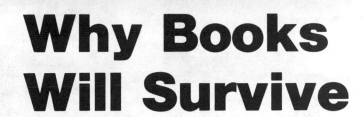

Why Books Will Survive

by Lane Jennings

High prices, paper that self-destructs, and competition from computers and video forms may mean hard times ahead for books. But the unique experience they provide will ensure their survival.

CYNTHIA FOWLER

For me, as a booklover, the future arrived a few days before Christmas, 1982. That was when my favorite secondhand-book shop put a new sign in its window: "Special! Save 30% to 60% on Used Videotapes."

Five good bookstores had closed nearby in as many years. Two new video stores had opened in the past five months. Now here was secondhand video moving in on the used-book market. Could this mean that the Age of the Book is about to end? We may soon find out.

Until the invention of writing, some 5,000 years ago, all literature was oral. Yet complex civilizations rose and flourished. Some cultures, like the Incas of South America, never developed writing. Others functioned for centuries with only a tiny minority able to read and write. The invention of printing made more books available and encouraged more people to learn to read, but volumes remained rare and expensive. Making paper from wood pulp instead of rags and using cloth rather than leather for book covers brought down the price of books substantially in the mid-nineteenth century. But only since World War II, with the explosive growth of paperback books, has it been possible for the average citizen—at least in Western Europe or America—to afford a private library containing many volumes.

Books on the Ropes

But now this brief era of books for all is about to end. Book prices have risen sharply in response to higher costs for paper, printing, and postage. The standard price for a new paperback novel now stands at $3.95—up from less than a dollar in the late 1960s—and new hard-cover fiction seldom costs less than $10.00 and can often be $15.00 or more. Prices for nonfiction books are generally even higher.

In the 1960s, large corporations began taking over independent pub-

Cozy "old-fashioned" bookstores like Quill and Brush, in Bethesda, Maryland, may see a resurgence in the future. In recent years, chain stores modeled after supermarkets have increasingly dominated bookselling. But as publishing costs continue to climb and electronic alternatives to print become common, connoisseurs and collectors may be the main buyers of printed books, with booksellers serving clients on a more individual basis.

lishing houses, and many smaller firms were swallowed up by large ones. In all, more than 300 mergers took place in the U.S. publishing industry between 1960 and 1980. The results, chronicled by Thomas Whiteside in his book *The Blockbuster Complex* (Wesleyan University Press, 1982), have included enormous pressure on editors and writers to produce works that can be easily repackaged and sold to a mass market in different forms, including television and movie adaptations, paperback, foreign-language translations, and tie-ins to toys, records, novelty items, etc.

Yet, while sales volume has grown (up nearly 75% for hard-cover books between 1976 and 1980), profit margins for publishers have remained stubbornly at around 8%—unchanged from the days before the big corporations poured in their cash and streamlined management to bring the industry up to date. This has prompted some conglomerates to begin selling off their insufficiently profitable publishing opera-

tions, while others intensify the pursuit of "big" books that will pay back quick profits on a large investment.

Books As Consumables

At the selling end, book clubs and chain bookstores that buy in large quantities now dominate the market. Because they make their buying decisions well before publication, nationwide chains like B. Dalton and Waldenbooks can practically decide a book's fate in advance. And because chain bookstores pattern their atmosphere after supermarkets, which encourage customers to "shop," not "browse," and to buy on impulse, new books and new displays always get top priority. Books that do not sell quickly are returned to the publisher, who in turn will most likely "remainder" the books (sell them in quantity at a loss to get a tax write-off).

The remainder piles can be a source of real bargains to book-lovers who know what to look for, but the wastefulness of this form of

distribution is high. The shelf life of an average new book today in a shopping mall bookstore has been estimated as somewhere between that of whole milk and yogurt in a supermarket—in other words, less than six weeks.

Smaller booksellers, who can't match the pace of new purchasing or the volume discounts of the national chains, are being forced out of business. And even at bigger bookstores, profits were down 3% in 1981, according to the American Booksellers Association. Worse yet, what profits there are seem to come not from quality fiction and serious nonfiction titles that can be expected to remain in print for years to come. Instead, the big sellers are fad books—cat cartoons, how to solve cube puzzles, diet and exercise books, etc.—that are easy to "presell" through advertising and public relations efforts.

But if publishers and booksellers seem hard pressed, consider the plight of readers! With 40,000 new titles appearing each year (up from

"Smaller booksellers, who can't match the pace of new purchasing or the volume discounts of national chains, are being forced out of business."

2,000 a year in the 1880s), and most of these only remaining on bookstore shelves for a few weeks, readers can't possibly hear about (let alone read) all the new works that might amuse or interest them.

More and more new books are being published as "trade paperbacks," oversized volumes with heavier, more durable covers than the familiar pocket-sized mass-market paperbacks. Yet despite their growing popularity (44 million trade paperbacks were sold in 1980, up from less than 1 million in 1971), these books are rarely reviewed by critics. As a result, publishers continue to issue new works of literary merit in hardback first for the prestige, even though their higher prices put them out of reach for many buyers, who must either wait until the paperback version appears months later, or hope that the work will flop and be remaindered soon so they can buy it at a sizable discount.

What's Wrong with Reading?

The U.S. Census Bureau reports that 99% of the population is able to read, a mark that has risen from 83% in 1880. Yet, the American Booksellers Association estimates that only 25% of the U.S. population buys books. Since more than 95% of U.S. households have one or more TV sets, the small size of the book-buying public is a matter of concern to everyone connected with literature in any way.

There seems to be a curious double standard of values with regard to books today. On the one hand, we tend to admire those people who buy and display books. So much so that several firms offer collectors' editions of famous books in expensive leather bindings intended for display, and never explain in their advertising how the books were chosen, what paper was used, how large the type is, or even whether the texts are complete or abridged. As one such ad proclaims: "The books will symbolize your respect

for culture and tradition. And, of course, they will immeasurably enhance the decor of your home."

Although people in today's society may admire books as decorative objects, the act of reading is rarely taken seriously. The same people who would gladly invite the neighbors in to see their collection of elegant books would be offended if those neighbors were to decline the invitation by saying, "Oh, we can't tonight. We have to stay home and catch up on our reading." Once we leave school, we tend to regard reading as a leisure activity—the least important job, and usually the last one we get around to doing—ranking below even the most trivial chores at home and at work.

The problem with reading is partly that it appears antisocial (you do it alone), partly that it looks so easy to do (unless you take notes,

there is no sign to show anyone watching what you have accomplished in the time spent with a book), and partly that reading, even for pleasure, takes considerable effort. Unlike television and radio, which can run on unattended and still leave impressions on the memory, reading demands concentrated attention. The faster you read, the more completely you need to focus on the page. This is one reason why speed reading often makes remembering facts and details easier—the reader's eyes and thoughts have no time to stray.

The effort of reading and its low status as an activity in much of Western society today encourage the tendency to put books aside to read later. But for many books, time may be running out. The quality of materials and workmanship in books has declined steadily since the mid-

Conservation lab of the Folger Shakespeare Library (Washington, D.C.), where rare books are treated and restored. Although people often think of books as lasting forever, many books today are printed on acidic paper that actually self-destructs. Books can be made to last by using better paper or by treating the paper to neutralize the acids.

JULIE AINSWORTH/FOLGER SHAKESPEARE LIBRARY

"The factor most likely to assure the survival of books into the future is [that there is] simply no experience in life that matches silent reading."

nineteenth century. Today, in spite of their attractive appearance, many books are literally self-destructing. Acids in the wood-pulp paper commonly used today turn book pages brown and brittle in a few decades. Already several million volumes in the Library of Congress have deteriorated so badly that they are no longer available for general use. And few of the books being printed today —even expensive hardbacks and limited editions—are very likely to survive much beyond the first decades of the twenty-first century.

Books on the Bounce

Are there no signs of hope, then, for a future of books and book readers? Yes, a few. In recent years, schools have put more emphasis on reading and writing skills; in 1982, there were indications that this effort may be paying off. The average scores in verbal skills of high-school seniors taking the pre-college Scholastic Aptitude Test (S.A.T.) rose slightly for the first time in 19 years. And grade-school children in major cities across the United States achieved better results on reading tests in 1982 than were common a few years earlier.

Books written specifically for teenagers (known as "young adults" in the publishing trade) encourage reading, and sales of such books have tripled since 1980. While authors like Judy Blume and S.E. Hinton offer believable stories of characters dealing with problems from everyday life, other books engage young readers by making them part of the action. Titles in the "Choose Your Own Adventure" series of paperbacks published by Bantam Books, for example, introduce a character in some exciting situation and let the reader choose between several possible actions that character might take. Depending on which choice is made, the reader turns to a different page in the book and con-

tinues reading to the next decision point. In this way, hundreds of variations on a single plot are possible, and the same story can turn out differently every time it is read.

New technologies are helping make sure that more of today's books will be available for the readers of tomorrow. Paper manufacturers have known since the 1950s how to make chemically stable papers that would last for centuries, but these low-acid papers have been more expensive to produce. In the long run, however, they may actually prove to be economical. Low-acid paper pulps cause less corrosion of machine parts, and the manufacturing process uses less energy than conventional high-acid paper-making. Even the waste water produced can be more cheaply disposed of because it requires less treatment to meet environmental-quality regulations. In Europe, 60% of book paper is alkaline based today, but the U.S. lags behind. Only 20% of the books

currently published in the U.S. use low-acid paper.

Advanced technologies are also helping to protect books against another danger: thieves. One technique that has proven especially effective for libraries is to place a strip of metal tape inside a book's spine. Electronic sensors near each exit trigger an alarm if anyone tries to carry a book out without presenting it at the checkout desk first. The Chicago Public Library installed a new computerized circulation control system in 1981 after losing $2 million worth of books to thieves in two years. The University of Pennsylvania reports that book thefts from its library have dropped 40% in just over three years, thanks to its electronic protection system. A computer service firm in New York now registers rare books and manuscripts reported missing from libraries and book dealers, thus making it harder for thieves to sell their choicest items.

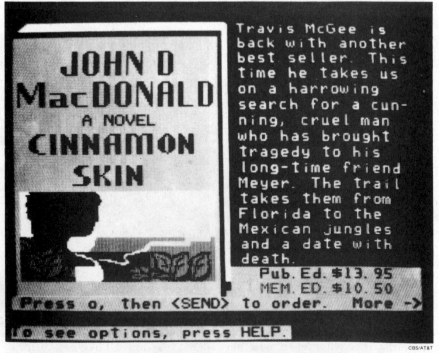

CBS/AT&T

Advertising a book electronically, via a television videotex system. Electronic advertising and publishing will undoubtedly become more common, but many kinds of books will remain more effective in their traditional printed form, author Jennings says.

THE SOURCE

Author Burke Campbell writes his novel *Blind Pharaoh* using his personal computer. The novel was made available to readers immediately over an electronic information network.

Investing in Books

One reason book thieves have become more active is that the value of books as collectible objects has soared. In the last 20 years, prices for rare books at auction have gone up as much as 3000%, making rare books a better investment than stocks, diamonds, gold, or oriental rugs. First editions in perfect condition are especially prized. While not every book rises in value (the demand for most titles by Robert Frost, Ernest Hemingway, William Faulkner, and George Bernard Shaw is reported to be sluggish or actually falling at the moment), first editions of twentieth-century poetry and fiction offer good prospects for a high return on a small investment. A book that fails to move quickly and ends up remaindered, selling at half price or less, can gain value over-night if another work by the same author suddenly becomes popular.

Astute book dealers point out that under current tax laws a book collection built up over many years can be donated to a library or university for an income tax write-off based on what the books would cost today. The firm of Francis Edwards, in London, England, will assemble a portfolio of valuable editions as a service to investors too busy or too wary to shop for rare books on their own.

But the factor most likely to assure the survival of books into the future is perhaps so obvious that it is easily overlooked. There is simply no experience in life that matches silent reading. Unlike spectators, who watch a show, or even participants, who must deal with reality as they find it, readers make every-thing happen just the way they want it to. The actions, scenes, and voices in a book come to life entirely inside the reader's mind.

With a minimum of outside influence—enough light to see the page and somewhere to sit or stand in comfort—a book can transport its reader into a reality more vivid and believable than life itself because it is largely self-made. Authors supply the outlines of character, setting, and plot, but the true skill of writing lies in *not* telling everything and suggesting much more than is explicitly stated. The reader's imagination supplies the missing details. This collaboration between author and reader makes the reading experience intense and absorbing.

Books and Beyond

Not every book holds readers spellbound, and many don't even try. Almanacs, encyclopedias, textbooks, and how-to-do-it manuals merely seek to pass on information. That this information happens to appear in book form is only incidental. As the cost of manufacturing and distributing material in the form of print on paper continues to climb, it may well be that publishers and readers alike will no longer rely on books unless total absorption rather than mere information transfer is the object.

Woody Horton, a Washington-based information management consultant and former staff director for the U.S. Commission on Federal Paperwork, has proposed a test that publishers and readers can apply to determine how satisfactorily material now normally supplied in book form might be displayed on a video monitor or computer screen. Horton's test includes rating both intellectual and emotional factors, and considering the objectives of both producers and users of the material in question. For example, an electronic encyclopedia might prove better than today's printed version by offering more timely information and making it easier to locate specific information in a short time. An electronic novel, on the other hand, might prove to be less convenient, attractive, and comfortable on the eyes than its paper counterpart.

Both these experiments have already been tried, and readers with access to the Source and CompuServe computer networks can evaluate the results for themselves. The entire 10-million-word text of the *World Book Encyclopedia* is available on-line through CompuServe. Every one of the more than 32,000 subject entries in the printed version is included in Online World Book. There are no graphics or illustrations in Online World Book (photos and artwork could not be reproduced on most home computer terminals presently in use), but simplified search procedures make Online World Book enjoyable for beginners of grade-school age, yet still factual enough for adult users. Also, unlike the printed version, Online World Book articles can be revised as often as four times a year, keeping their information constantly up-to-date.

Last November, a Canadian author named Burke Campbell spent 62 hours composing a novel on his Apple III computer. He then transferred the text electronically on the Source computer network to the headquarters of Source Telecomputing Corporation in McLean, Virginia, and the entire 20,000-word novel, entitled *Blind Pharoah*, was made available to Source network subscribers.

Campbell received no royalties for his writing, and Source subscribers who read or print out the text on their own computer terminals pay nothing beyond the normal hourly rate for connect time to the network. But the same process has been used on a for-profit basis to produce electronic magazines of articles, news stories, editorials, and fiction.

A "fireman" burns books in the movie version of Ray Bradbury's *Fahrenheit 451*. In Bradbury's society, books are outlawed as dangerous; they can only be preserved by people willing to memorize them and pass them on to others.

"An electronic novel might prove less convenient, attractive, and comfortable on the eyes than its paper counterpart."

Fewer But Better Books?

For those who have a special affection for books, the years ahead will not be easy ones. Many old books will disintegrate before they can be copied or preserved. New books seem certain to continue to go up in price, and volumes of special interest and importance (such as first editions of famous authors) may become too expensive for any but the wealthiest collectors or university libraries to own. Bookstores designed like supermarkets are fast replacing the low-key establishments of the past; and even rare and secondhand book shops will decline as the stock of older books decreases due to age, and as other forms of information and entertainment materials (audio recordings, videotapes, videodiscs, computer software, etc.) become common.

But we must remember that the market for books—indeed for writing of any kind—was small until quite recently. The prospect that it may shrink again need not mean that books will disappear. Fewer books may mean better books.

The first volumes in a series designed to make available the major works of the best American authors, durably bound and printed on acid-free paper, appeared last year. More than 100 volumes are planned for this series, and 21 of these will be in print by 1985. Projects like this in the U.S. and other countries promise to pass on to future generations the thrill of reading at its very best.

It is the less-famous works, including whole genres routinely dismissed by scholars and critics as trivial, that may be lost to the future. Few books of topical humor or verse, or works of fiction in the so-called "pulp" genres—western, gothic horror, mystery, pornography, fantasy, or "space opera" sci-fi—were written with any conscious thought of speaking to the future. But they do speak: the trashiest, the corniest, the least skillful writing can still convey a powerful sense of what it meant to be alive—thinking and feeling—when that work appeared.

Books are not only things we *own*, they are surrogate memories that reveal the values and concerns of those who wrote and read them. The best-seller lists of the past 90 years include many works that are forgotten today, but which meant a great deal to the public that first read them. Having these old books available for reading is one of the few ways that people of the future will be able to share an experience and compare outlooks and expectations with those who lived before them. When only the best survives from the past, it is easy to believe in the myth of a golden age that can never again be equaled. Chance may preserve a few lesser works, as it has in the case of ancient Greek and Latin authors. But why should we depend on chance?

Save a Book for the Future

Computer enthusiasts predict that whole libraries will soon have all their contents safely stored in electronic form for instant access by anyone from a personal computer terminal. But however quickly the technology spreads, and however inexpensive it eventually becomes to transfer words from a printed page into a computer file, someone must do the actual work of transfer and decide which books get top priority for transfer and which will have to wait. For some books, inevitably, the wait will be too long.

So if some printed work—a book, a magazine story, even a single poem—has special importance to you, consider sharing that work with the future by taking an active role in helping to preserve it. Take a favorite old paperback that is falling apart and have it permanently bound—or better still, pay to have it chemically treated to preserve the paper. If you have access to a small computer, you might build up your speed at the keyboard by typing your favorite obscure or forgotten work onto a disc or tape.

You might even try flexing your memory. Learn by heart some text you really love and find someone younger than you who would also like to learn it, and who will pass it on in turn. This is what the "book people" do in Ray Bradbury's novel *Fahrenheit 451*. Bradbury depicts a society in which books are outlawed: only outlaws own books, and only memorization can keep a book's contents both hidden and available for use.

The future of the book may not be as bleak as suggested in Bradbury's novel. But which books survive into the twenty-first century and beyond will depend on the role we ask books to play in our lives, and on how much we value the reading experience.

More than a quarter century ago, the American poet and critic Randall Jarrell neatly summed up the case for a future of books in these words:

Sometimes when I can't go to sleep at night, I see the family of the future. Dressed in three-tone shorts-and-shirts sets of disposable papersilk, they sit before the television wall of their apartment; only their eyes are moving. After I've looked a while I always see—otherwise I'd die—a pigheaded soul over in the corner with a book; only his eyes are moving, but in them there is a different look.

—from "The Year in Poetry," *Harper's,* October 1955

About the Author

Lane Jennings is the World Future Society's research director and editor of the *WFS Bulletin.* He denies that he would sell his firstborn child to support his book-buying habit, but admits that the thought has crossed his mind.

The Future of Sex Education

Computerizing the Facts of Life

by Parker Rossman

New information technologies such as computers and videodiscs can help defuse the controversy around how children should be taught about sex.

We may joke about a loving, comforting computer robot as teacher and counselor in sex education, but in fact the electronic tutor or electronic textbook—videodisc plus computer—may help solve many of the problems and controversies that often now plague schools or churches attempting sex-education programs.

Most young people today have a variety of sources for sex education, including:

• Personal experimentation.

• People they see and know, especially those just a few years older than they are (often family members).

• Films, television, popular books and magazines (not textbooks), and easily available pornography.

The result? U.S. government-funded research on materials and programs of sex education found that:

• There is a disturbing lack of communication between parents and children about sexual matters.

• Teenagers receive conflicting messages from peers, from the media, and from various adults.

• Consensus about public sex education is almost impossible to achieve in many communities because, in a complex, pluralistic society, people have fundamentally different convictions and value systems. Some citizens, for example, believe that sex education (at least outside the family) destroys morality, increases juvenile sexual activity, and therefore increases out-of-wedlock pregnancies. Controversies have shattered schools and neighborhoods, resulting in teachers being fired.

But educators believe that society can hardly leave sex education up to families alone since many parents do little to inform their children. The situation has become catastrophic:

• Each year 1.3 million teenage girls—some as young as 11 or 12—become pregnant, often as a result of ignorance.

• Ten million persons were infected with venereal disease in one recent year, 65% of them youngsters.

• Films and television are becoming increasingly explicit in their presentations of all kinds of sex.

The question now is not whether or not there will be sex education outside the home, but who will help interpret these experiences properly for young people.

Who is to teach sex education and who is to answer the hard questions

CONTROL DATA CORPORATION

"Youngsters could talk frankly . . . about a wide range of sexual problems, fantasies, fears, and so forth, if they recorded what they wanted to say on tape and then received replies and comments on a tape that they could listen to privately."

(not the biological facts) that worry most young people at one time or another? For example, there is the central issue of pleasure: What is allowable, when, and with whom? The question is posed daily in the media, over and over, and parents disagree violently over answers. Another fundamental need is the preservation of privacy and confidentiality for the young person.

Electronic Solutions

Ideal education, it has often been suggested, would be the nineteenth-century educator Mark Hopkins at one end of a log and the pupil at the other. But until now it has not been possible to provide such individualized tutoring for all pupils. Costs have been prohibitive. And in sex education, Mark Hopkins-type quality (combining moral and intellectual training within a close student-faculty relationship) can hardly be provided by less than a team of interdisciplinary experts in each classroom if all needs and interests are to be satisfied.

Now, however, the computer plus the interactive videodisc—with its 54,000 frames or pages of information and films—may soon be able to provide excellence in a far more efficient way than has ever before been possible by textbooks or teachers.

In 1977, a Yale University physician reported that students preferred to learn about sex through tapes they could listen to in private. And the pastor of a Congregational Church in Connecticut found that junior-high-school youngsters could talk frankly with him about a wide range of sexual problems, fantasies, fears, and so forth, if they recorded what they wanted to say on tape and then received replies and comments on a tape that they could listen to privately.

Even more interesting was the willingness of these young people to give consent for parents or counselors to listen to some of the tapes

C.G. WAGNER

A Unitarian-Universalist church's sex-education class begins with a back-rubbing exercise to loosen up before their discussion begins. Methods of teaching about human sexuality vary widely, and the values included in one sex-education curriculum may not coincide with the beliefs and values of some members of a community, making a consensus about public sex education difficult to achieve, says Rossman.

privately—an easier way for youngsters to speak to adults about things they usually found it impossible to talk about face-to-face.

Add a computer and this process can be dialogical. The computer might answer questions, or it might ask questions the way a counselor would to lead the pupil in learning. It also can make comments appropriate to the age, experience, and needs of the learner.

I say "experience" because adequate sex education must be rooted in the real experience of the learner and must help young people communicate their real worries, fears, emotions, and needs with those persons they most care about and who most care about them. "Experience" means much more than genital activity, although one would not minimize the importance of helping a young person properly interpret whatever his or her experience might be. Experience, however, includes fantasies, jokes, the media, and much more than overt sexual activity. A learner, of course, must have the assurance of privacy—a key to be pushed to erase or prevent the recording of anything the learner wishes to keep private.

Since as much of the instruction as desired by family or community could be personal and private with the electronic tutor, a first step is taken to meet potentially serious criticism and controversy. The electronic tutor can further mollify critics by making it possible for a family to choose from alternative value-systems. Parents and pupils could review facts and presentations, providing for value comments from one of a variety of possible programs, such as Orthodox Jewish, Catholic, Protestant, secular humanist, and many others.

Learners could be given "annual checkups," which would involve goal-setting and an examination of values in sex education. The computer could answer a learner's questions in ways that are difficult for human counselors to deal with; these answers would include continual reminders of the value concerns of the young person's family, church, or whatever the program selected might include.

Learners would thus be reminded of what their own actual or recommended values would require of them in specific situations. A range of alternative decisions and actions could be discussed and explored for consequences. The program would be designed to help the learner to interpret the meaning and implications of his or her own real experiences.

Interdisciplinary Cooperation

A formidable barrier to the creation of Intelligent Computer Assisted Instruction and sophisticated videodisc programs for education is the tremendous cost of research and production. However, since large sums are usually more easily available for medical research and education, schools might be able to piggyback on the shoulders of the health-care establishment, which has a large stake also in sex education. For instance, the technology now being developed in medical education (such as interactive videodiscs for teaching surgery) can easily be adapted to other educational uses.

More cooperation may come as physicians realize that up to 70% of their patients have "illnesses" such as drug and alcohol abuse, VD, ulcers, and stress, for which treatment requires a holistic approach and more involvement from schools, the community, and the patient's entire family.

Computerized Sex Education in Practice

One experiment in computer-assisted sex education, conducted in Dallas by Ron Lien of Control Data Corporation, used a course prepared

in cooperation with C. Wayne Banks of Southern Methodist University. A significant thing about this course is that the young people were not "taught" by a computer; rather, the computers were simply "resources" and "textbooks" for homework by learners and their parents.

Instruction took place in a formal class, with group discussions and other normal classroom procedures; but the learners—having done their homework by Computer-Assisted Instruction (CAI)—came to class better prepared.

The junior-high-school students used terminals in Dallas connected to a large computer in Minneapolis. Of the 22 ninth graders evaluated, 82% of them said CAI had helped them understand that sex is a normal part of their lives; 77% said it helped them to be more comfortable with their own sexuality; indeed, they rated the computer higher on personal matters than on facts or instruction in terminology, and so forth. Sixty-three percent of the participating pupils said that as a

result of the CAI sex education they could make more intelligent decisions about sexual activities.

But a more important dimension of this computer program was the involvement of parents—a major objective of any effective sex-education program. And the cooperation of parents in the computer instruction suggests another way in which community controversy can be reduced through the use of electronic instruction.

On the videodisc, the films used to illustrate and educate would also vary in accordance with the design of the alternative packages. They might be as frank as those used in some Unitarian-Universalist Church sex education, or they might be very conservative, in accordance with the choice of parents and educators. Long-term evaluation would compare the results in the lives of learners who used alternative programs.

The goal, the final test, would be in the healthy adult lives of the learners. How were their personal

C.G. WAGNER

Students meet for a weekly sex-education class offered by a Unitarian-Universalist church near Washington, D.C. Despite their attempts to provide a relaxing atmosphere, teachers find that adolescents in group situations are uncomfortable discussing sex. Using computers for answering difficult questions could help avoid such uncomfortable situations, says author Rossman.

"It is going to be possible now to do almost any electronic thing that educators want to do. The issue is: What should be done in sex education and how?"

---

and social needs met? To what extent are they loving adults with creative, fulfilling personalities, a caring sense of responsibility, and so forth?

Now Where Do We Go?

Since talking to scientists at the World Computer Center in Paris and elsewhere who are working on the marriage of videodisc and computer, I am convinced that it is going to be possible now to do almost any electronic thing that educators want to do. The issue is: What should be done in sex education and how?

Educators are now confronting the enormous potential of Intelligent Computer Assisted Instruction with limited vision and outmoded educational theory. It is as if the automobile had just been invented and we could go anywhere we wanted to go, but few of us know where to go! We need roads and maps. It is time for educators to end their concentration on what is under the hood of the car and to start deciding where to build the roads.

In any case, the videodisc is probably just interim technology. Arthur C. Clarke has described a small device he calls an "electronic tutor," which by the end of the century will be as common, he says, as the pocket calculator is today. He says: "It is hard to imagine a single subject which could not be programmed into it at all levels of complexity, from elementary to advanced."

At the heart of electronic sex education will lie the resources of the "Coming Great Comprehensive Electronic Encyclopedia" (see THE FUTURIST, August 1982), which can put all information at the fingertips of the learner. This potential, plus the impact of television, films, and other media, requires that the emphasis in sex education be largely on helping the learner interpret what he knows and experiences, with the selection of "facts" to be presented as secondary.

Clarke suggests that with the electronic textbook you could change subjects, or update courses, merely by plugging in different modules or cassettes. Clarke laughs at the notion that electronic technology can ever replace teachers: "Any teacher that *can* be replaced by a computer *should be*." But the potential of the new technology calls for new styles of teaching that are more individualized and more personal.

In his recent book *The End of Sex*, George Leonard discusses the need now in sex education to emphasize love and affection, words hardly found, he says, in many sexuality courses. In his 1968 book *Education and Ecstasy*, Leonard described a future school in a vision that continues to challenge those educators who are ready to quit looking under the "electronic" hood and begin talking about where teaching should go with the computer technology.

He began with the assumption that educators must use the computer to encourage uniqueness rather than sameness in learners. He would tie the ongoing educational program to "referents from a memory bank consisting of all of the learner's past responses, the learner's distinctiveness" from all other persons.

Educators would then discover that existing programs were too narrow, since they tend to concentrate on one subject at a time. Sex education, for example, involves nearly everything: life-style, values, and religious faith as well as biology and psychology.

Leonard's future school illustrates another direction that electronic technology might take us: Sensors might in time be used to identify students' brain wave patterns and states of consciousness; the data would then be fed directly into the computer for ongoing analysis. If Leonard is right in suggesting that sex education must say more about affection and love, then it would be appropriate for testing in sex education to in-

volve an examination of emotions and feelings and of the pupil's psychology.

This type of electronic monitoring of learning raises the issue of the nature of the learning environment for sex education. Through the computer videodisc a learner may be taken into almost any kind of experience. Deviance discovered in a young child might tempt officials to abuse freedom and privacy by demanding psychiatric treatment or whatever. On the other hand, different kinds of "deviance" discovered in everyone might help pupils and teachers discover that every human being is, indeed, "unique." In any case, all kinds of information about the pupil are going to be gathered, correlated, evaluated, and used.

Content: What Is To Be Taught?

Most communities are likely to see more controversy, not less, if ways are not found to individualize the content of sex-education programs and make them more private. The conflict between home and school can make a helpful contribution to the pupil's education if teachers and parents engage in dialogue; as the Dallas sex-education program showed, parental views and values can be presented fairly. Young people realize that people differ and disagree and that there are very different alternatives in sexual behavior and politics. They need help to understand how to evaluate different possible actions or life-styles.

In Leonard's future school the pupils play games, such as a history game on the Peloponnesian War, in order to help them understand human nature and issues in moral decision-making. It is already possible to keep a record of the steps leading to a decision—and of the decisions youngsters make while playing computer games. It is possible now to have the computer ask the player why he has made a particu-

Students work together at a computer terminal in their classroom. An individualized computer curriculum would not necessarily isolate students from one another, says Rossman. While students can have their privacy when needed, they may still enjoy helping each other in the electronic environment.

lar decision and to point out consequences of alternative decisions.

Although educators would prefer to stick to "objective facts," there really is no way to separate sex education from ethics, morals, and religion in most American communities. In time, perhaps, an educational program can be evaluated in terms of how it helps a learner progress to higher and higher stages in becoming a more responsible, loving human being.

The whole notion of a "course" begins to disappear as learning programs are especially designed for each individual learner. The context for sex education in the not-too-distant future may be something like this:

First, each pupil will have access to what Leonard calls "a full bank of the basic, commonly agreed-upon cultural knowledge." The content of this easily accessible electronic "text-book" on the 54,000 pages or frames of a videodisc, much more sophisticated and comprehensive than present materials, will include films, slides, case studies, graphics, and a complete encyclopedia of scientifically established facts related to sexuality.

Second, a specific learning program, tailored for the individual, would consist of a computer dialogue that not only poses specific questions but also provides learners with the opportunity to ask any question they wish. Youngsters in the Dallas experiment were highly pleased with this confidential computer tutor. So were their teachers. I can imagine fewer snickers in class and a much more satisfactory answer than "go ask your father" for what one writer calls the unwritten curriculum.

Third, even though each particular pupil is working on a specially designed program at the computer terminal, the learning process is far from being solitary work. Learners still work as a group in a classroom, but they can have privacy and solitude when needed. One has only to visit a school where young people are using computers on individual programs to see how much they work together, help each other, and enjoy each other's company. The teacher, too, is much more relaxed and able to give personal attention to each pupil. The electronic environment, surprisingly enough, can be more personal and human. Sex education, therefore, will take place in a mixed-media learning environment involving teacher, computer, counselor, videodisc, other members of the class, and books, too.

Bringing it All Together

Values and science can be brought together in the context of an emerging cultural paradigm that is more complex, holistic, and valuing. We must remember that failures of technology are most often failures of policy; nowhere is this so true as in sex education.

As educators struggle with how to use electronic technology, one of the hardest questions they must face is how to attain and share wisdom.

**About
the
Author**

Parker Rossman (Box 382, Niantic, Connecticut 06357) is an interdisciplinary scholar in sociology, communications, theology, sexuality research, and education. This article is based on his addresses to the Educational Testing Service in Princeton, New Jersey, and the World Future Society's Fourth General Assembly in the summer of 1982.

Roy Mason with
Lane Jennings and Robert Evans

A Day at Xanadu
Family Life in Tomorrow's Computerized Home

Imagine yourself in a house that has a brain—a house you can talk to, a house where every room adjusts to your changing moods, a house that is also a servant, counselor, and friend to every member of your family. A science-fiction tale of the far future? Not at all. The idea of the "intelligent house" has been around for years, and today's "architronics"—the application of computer technology to architecture—is transforming that idea into reality.

Prototype "homes of the future" are open to the public at several locations. In them you will find many applications of electronics to

Tomorrow's computerized home will be more than a residence; it will be servant, counselor, and friend to each member of the family. Here, we see what a typical day would be like at "Xanadu"—a "house of the future" that already exists.

family living that may become commonplace within a few years. You will also see gadgets and gimmicks that are likely to remain costly luxuries for decades, and others that will probably be outdated in a few months. No model home can accurately depict the "best" or even the "most probable" lifestyle of the future. There are too many uncertainties—too many unrecognized problems and undiscovered opportunities ahead for anyone to build the definitive House of Tomorrow today.

But you can explore alternative lifestyles—compare different house designs and computer applications to find out which combinations of old and new, traditional and modern, flexible and solid, inner-focused and community-minded, high tech and handmade, automatic and labor-intensive best match your tastes, ambitions, and interests.

The Xanadu House, located just outside Orlando, Florida, is designed to showcase some of the options that architronics will add to family and home life in the 1990s. Although conceived as the luxury home of a wealthy family in the mid-1990s, Xanadu's various computer-enhanced security, telecommunications, energy monitoring, entertainment, and climate control systems are all adaptable for use in far smaller and less expensive houses.

"Using sensors built into each bed, the House Brain can measure body temperature, brain activity, and pulse rate."

The electronic equipment described here is more elaborate than can be easily found today. But talking computers, a self-selecting telecommunications center—an "electronic hearth"—and the various computer-activated sensors and control systems that regulate energy, lighting, etc., are all plausible extensions of existing tech-

nologies, and in many cases can be bought or custom-built today.

Now, let's spend a typical early spring day in the mid-1990s with an imaginary family living at Xanadu.

6:30 a.m.

As the sun begins to rise, the analytical left side of Xanadu's House Brain computer system comes to life. A quick scan through its memory banks shows that the automatic systems operated during the night by its more reflexive right side (without human command or reprogramming) are all functioning properly. Every six minutes around the clock, the computer monitors its sensors to confirm that water pressure is at correct levels in the plumbing system, the solar sinks hold adequate heat reserves, the hydroponic garden greenhouse has the correct levels of moisture and nutrients, all electrical circuits are functioning, all windows and doors are secure, no structural faults or leaks have developed, and no high-priority messages have been received since the previous status check. If anything had gone wrong, the appropriate sensors would have alerted the House Brain's analytical circuits and fed them the information available to decide whether the problem could be handled by computer or if it warranted waking someone for instructions.

Now comes the most important task of all—checking each of the

GRADY ALLRED

The "Great Room" in the home of the future corresponds to today's living room. Heating and cooling equipment is concealed within tree-like structures. Elevated areas contain stereo and video equipment, along with the "sensorium"— a space specifically designed for meditation and relaxation.

house's still-sleeping human residents to make sure that they too are all "functioning correctly." Using sensors built into each bed, the House Brain can measure body temperature, brain activity, and pulse rate.

Next, the House Brain tunes in to the outside world. Using the outside sensors, the temperature, humidity, and barometric pressure are checked and compared with its memory banks to detect the possibility of upcoming storms or other radical weather changes. Since it is relatively cool and dry, the Brain opens extra ventilation ducts and windows to circulate outside air throughout the house while activating humidifiers to add a comfortable amount of moisture.

The House Brain now searches the videotex system for items that the master and mistress of the house have preprogrammed under key words such as "real estate," "stock market," and specific company names. Once found, these items are separately stored for retrieval on request.

Then, the House Brain puts itself into a standby mode and waits for its next chore: waking the individual family members at the time and in the manner that each has requested.

7:15 a.m.

Slowly, the temperature on the mistress's side of the bed begins to

> **"Talking computers, a self-selecting tele-communications center—an 'electronic hearth'—and the various computer-activated sensors and control systems that regulate energy, lighting, etc., are all plausible extensions of existing technologies, and in many cases can be bought or custom-built today."**

rise and a gentle massage like thousands of tiny fingers becomes more obvious. Since the master does not have to wake up for another 45 minutes, the Brain has decided it should communicate today's messages for the mistress using only text instead of voice synthesis. As her eyes open, the mistress hears the click of the large-screen monitor as it turns on to relay her first message of the day:

Good morning. It is now 7:16 a.m. Your appointment in Tampa is at 9:30, but since traffic is light today you will not have to leave until 8:15 if you take Route I-4.

The temperature is now 67 degrees and is expected to reach 79 by 2:00 p.m. There is zero chance of precipitation today. No important priority messages for you have been received since you last checked.

I have retrieved four articles on real estate for you to view when you are ready. Your shower will be at your requested temperature in three minutes. You will not be exercising this morning, but do not forget to do so tonight. Your coffee will be ready at 7:40. Now please get up!

She gets out of the bed quietly in order not to wake her still-sleeping husband and hurries to the master bath, where her perfect-temperature shower awaits.

Once it's time to dress, she gives the vocal command to allow the Brain to speak and goes to the Clothes Retrieval Closet.

"I need help in deciding what to wear. What would you suggest for my business appointment?"

"How about your blue dress, the one you wore to the Stevenses' anniversary party? You'd better hurry—your coffee is ready in the kitchen and you have to leave in 25 minutes."

"I'm hurrying—you just keep the coffee warm."

7:45 a.m.

After dialing for and receiving her freshly cleaned blue dress from the Clothes Retrieval Closet, she hurries to the kitchen, where she

The home of the future will contain many architectural features not commonly found in today's homes. Besides raised or sunken dining areas (pictured above), there will likely be indoor hydroponic gardens, "spas" replacing today's master bathroom, and geodesic solariums.

COURTESY XANADU

grabs her coffee and proceeds to her computer work station. Here she retrieves the special videotex items that the Brain has stored, and after finishing her coffee she again gives the command for computer voice activation.

"Before I go, I want to give you a message for my husband when he wakes up. Remind him that we have the Carlsons coming over tonight for dinner and Johnny has Bob coming over to spend the night, so we'll have to have our family meeting at 6:30 instead of 7:30."

"You'd better leave or you'll be late for your meeting. What time will you be returning if anyone wants to know?"

"2:00 p.m."

Mary runs out the door to her waiting, fully charged electric runabout.

8:00 a.m.

As the bed warms up and begins to vibrate vigorously, the House Brain's voice wakes the master of the house:

"Time to wake up, John. It's 8:01. You still have to do your morning exercises and make sure Johnny has his breakfast before he starts his school work. It's a beautiful day and you must be at your best for your teleconference.

"You have two messages, but none with a high priority. I have stored three articles for you to read; one of them is about your company. As soon as you are ready, I will retrieve them for you. Now you really must get up!"

Reluctantly, John pulls himself out of bed and steps into the master spa, where he is awakened further by the voice of the House Brain:

"Time to wake up that tired body. Not only do you have your board meeting, you also have the Carlsons coming for dinner tonight, and your son is having Bob over to spend the night. By the way, the regular family meeting will have to be at 6:30 instead of 7:30 tonight. You have 20 bench presses and one mile on the exercycle to do before you have your shower and coffee."

8:15 a.m.

Johnny's warm bed rocks like a boat as the voice of his "tutor"—the House Brain—calls out:

"Wake up, Johnny. Your father is planning to have breakfast with you in 45

"Advances in tele-communications and computerization have made it possible [for John] to run his business from home, over 3,000 miles from Canadian headquarters."

---

minutes. Your mother has left on her morning trip but she wants to remind you that the Carlsons are coming for dinner, and Bob will be here tonight also. Now get up—your shower is ready and waiting, and Paul and George will be coming over at 9:30 to study with you this morning. Better get moving."

9:00 a.m.

Johnny dashes into the kitchen just as his father is finishing his first cup of coffee. After hearty "good mornings," both go to the computer dietitian and punch in their break-

---

fast orders for the autochef. Johnny's order of hot cakes, orange juice, and milk goes through with no trouble, but John, Sr.'s scrambled eggs, bacon, and toast are quickly nixed for their high cholesterol count. He is forced to settle for an English muffin, orange juice, and another cup of coffee.

With instructions not to disturb him until lunch at 1:00, John, Sr., is off to his home office; his son heads for the family room to wait for his friends to arrive for their morning studies. It's Johnny's turn to have them at his house today.

9:30 a.m.

Looking around his home office/study, John thinks back to the time when he had that tiresome daily commute to his office. Thankful that advances in telecommunications and computerization have made it possible to run his business from home, over 3,000 miles from Canadian headquarters, he is also reminded of how the office has

GRADY ALLRED

The "intelligent" bedroom of Xanadu features a voice-activated house monitoring and command center. When you are ready to sleep, the bed converts itself into an environmentally-controlled "sleep module," and the house's computer system turns off lights and heat in unoccupied rooms to save energy.

changed over the last 20 years. In place of the typewriter there's now a computer and video monitor doubling as a word processor and file storage unit. A single unit combines telephone/data receiver/transmitter-monitor-answering machine and video camera. Instead of bulky filing cabinets, only a few small cabinets and computer disk files remain. And no secretary anymore—the House Brain, with its voice synthesizer, fills this role.

"Good morning, boss. What would you like to tackle?"

"I'll just review my notes and files for the board of directors' teleconference at noon. In the meantime, unless something urgent shows up on your sensors or in your message box, I won't be needing anything."

9:45 a.m.

Now that Paul and George have arrived, John, Jr., leads the way to the family learning center, where the tutor part of the House Brain has prepared their morning study regimen. Each boy goes to his own computer terminal. The "tutor" has prescribed work in the specific areas where they have demonstrated deficiencies. This required earlier consultation with the visiting boys' own House Brains.

Periodically, the "tutor" gives the boys a short break. They relax, compare notes and lessons, and complain about their strict "teacher."

Noon

Paul and George head home to lunch. John, Sr., is ready for his board meeting after first calling upon the House Brain for any messages, articles, or other data stored since he last checked. He adjusts his shirt collar, combs his hair, and then turns on the video camera and dials up company headquarters. This connects him with all the board members scattered throughout North America and even with one vacationing in Europe.

1:00 p.m.

After the meeting, John, Sr., calls his son to lunch and decides that they both deserve special treats. Putting the family dietitian on "override," they each make a

"The tutor part of the House Brain has prepared [the children's] morning study regimen. Each boy goes to his own computer terminal."

selection: pizza and a chocolate shake for the boy; lasagna, a cola, and a hot fudge sundae for dad. Obediently, the autochef prepares each selection. But father knows that the House Brain, while presently silenced, never forgets and will be sure to prescribe an exhausting workout.

Suddenly a buzzer goes off and John, Sr., reluctantly gives the vocal command to release the House Brain from silence.

"Out of the kitchen, both of you. It's time for John, Jr., to get back to his afternoon studies, and you, sir, have an appointment."

2:00 p.m.

As Johnny returns to his afternoon solo studies, his father returns to his office and activates his "secretary":

"Good afternoon, boss. You have an appointment with a client."

"I know. I'm not looking forward to talking to the treasurer of the university. Our company has been managing their investment portfolio for five years and given them a very decent return on their money. But somehow he always manages to make me feel like a freshman again."

"The best way to overcome that is to have all the information available that he may want. Study it ahead of time. I have prepared a report on your last conference with him. You can retrieve it on your monitor. Assume his questions will be very much the same. You can start by calling up the Dow Jones Information Service to get an update on all the university's holdings."

He turns to his computer terminal, reviews the questions asked at their last conference, and then calls up the Dow Jones service and transfers the preprogrammed stock-and-bond quotations to the special disk

for the university. As an afterthought, he also calls up the news information service for an update on the international situation, with special attention to the countries in which the university's investments are located. "Don't want to look uninformed," thinks John.

2:30 p.m.

Mary returns home in a good mood. Noticing the activated light showing that the kitchen is still in voice operation mode, she requests the status on the other members of the family.

"John, Jr., is in the family learning center working on his afternoon lessons. Your husband is in his office in a meeting with a major client."

"As soon as my husband is free, let him know I have returned and that I will be at my work station if he wants me for anything. Don't bother Johnny, but let him know I'm home when he's finished his lessons. Any messages for me?"

"The Carlsons called to confirm their arrival tonight for dinner at 8:00. I told them everything was fine unless they heard from you otherwise."

Going to her telephone/computer terminal at the work station, Mary prepares herself for more work.

3:30 p.m.

After making some required business calls, Mary settles down to catch up on her household affairs. Using her terminal, she checks with the "dietitian" on any special dietary needs the Carlsons might have on file and then checks on what the autochef has in storage that would be appropriate. Noting that the files list the Carlsons' favorite meal as Chicken Cordon Bleu, Mary instructs the autochef to prepare the dinner around that as a main course. Next, using her computer, Mary balances her bank account, authorizes the bank to pay certain regular bills, and transfers some of their funds to the savings account. She then heads off to the exercising she missed this morning.

4:30 p.m.

With his last call of the day out of the way and his wife in the spa, John decides to retire to the Sensorium to relax. As he enters the Sensorium, its lights come up to the minimal level for vision and the familiar voice is activated:

"Good afternoon. What will be your pleasure today? Some music, a hypno-light show, a regular video broadcast, a reading from the library?"

"Actually I just want to relax. How about some soothing music and a relaxing light show?"

As John takes a seat in one of the specially contoured chairs, the light-wall erupts in an apparently random pattern of swirling lights. The built-in sensors and massagers in the chair go to work with the first strains of the music growing in volume from the hidden speakers. The biofeedback sensors in the chair make note of his muscle tone and pulse and begin to adjust the show, room temperature, lighting, and other stimulants to correspond to his need for a relaxing environment—for a deeper state of meditation.

"What time would you like to have me end your session?"

"Unless someone needs me for something earlier, let me know when it is 6:30 so I can go to the family meeting."

6:15 p.m.

As time for the daily family meeting approaches, Mary stops by the

"Once they are seated by the 'electronic hearth'—various television monitors and video cameras connected to the House Brain—the parents ask for a report on Johnny's studies."

hydroponic greenhouse/breakfast room to check on her herb garden. Although the garden is regularly looked after by the House Brain, she likes to give the herbs the "personal" attention they need. She prunes several plants and takes cuttings from the ones she wants to use with the dinner tonight. Summoning up the voice of the House Brain, she inquires which ones are ready for cutting.

"The parsley and the basil should be ready. The others won't be ready for at least another week. Take my advice and leave the basil cutting until then, too. The

The "electronic hearth". Television monitors and video equipment connected to a central computer may serve as the family gathering place in the home of the future. The electronic hearth will be used not only for entertainment but also for education and family business.

An electronic home office. Forecasters believe that by 1995 one out of every five workers will be working at home. Computers and videotex equipment will replace the typewriters—and in many cases the secretaries—of today.

'cook' tells me you won't be needing it for this dinner anyway."

Priding herself on her abilities as a garden enthusiast, Mary snips the parsley and deposits it in the autochef's storage bin before the family meeting.

6:30 p.m.

John, Sr., Mary, and Johnny gather in the family room for their daily family meeting. Once they are seated by the "electronic hearth"—various television monitors and video cameras connected to the House Brain—the parents ask for a report on Johnny's studies.

"Even though we have added the extra social interaction recommended by the psychoanalyst program by having Johnny's friends over for morning studies, he still doesn't seem to be studying hard enough. His grades have continued to slip. Perhaps he is not being challenged sufficiently. But if he wants to be a bio-genetic engineer as he says he does, certainly he needs to study harder."

When Johnny can offer no reasons for his falling grades, the father calls on the House Brain to provide some possible insight to the problem.

"The Carlsons arrive and let themselves in with the special password that Mary had given them last week when she invited them to dinner."

"It seems, from an analysis of Johnny's study habits, that he's still not being challenged enough. Not that the family 'tutor' isn't doing its job. It's just that Johnny needs more of a challenge from his studymates who come over three times a week. After consulting with the neighboring House Brains, we have decided that Phil Johnson would make an ideal studymate for Johnny on the other two mornings a week. Phil is an excellent student and Johnny would be stimulated to work harder if he had someone to compete with. Otherwise, all of Johnny's social behavior is quite normal for a developing teenager."

John and Mary decide to call the Johnsons and see if they will agree to let their son Phil come over twice a week to take lessons with John, Jr. But his parents also warn Johnny that if his grades don't improve soon they will not take him on their annual vacation next month.

With their minds finally on the vacation, the family asks for a report on the research they have asked the House Brain to perform.

"After analyzing all of your vacation needs and desires, as well as your set budget, I have carefully gone over the geography section of the city library and monitored the video, cable, and satellite channels for travelogues and geographic documentaries. I've contacted travel agency computers and from this data I have determined that a two-week safari in Kenya is the best selection you can make."

The monitors come alive with scenes of Africa, while the House Brain interjects pertinent information between commentary.

"I believe you're right," says John, Sr. "Go ahead and make reservations."

"Now you must all get ready. Your guests arrive in 45 minutes and you, John, still have to exercise before getting dressed. And Mary, you haven't selected the type of fantasy dining experience you want for the evening."

The family members set off to prepare for their guests.

7:30 p.m.

Johnny's friend Bob is the first to arrive. After letting himself in by using the special password his host had given him, he heads straight for the family room, where he knows he will find Johnny.

At the kitchen work station again, Mary is torn between having the House Brain create an intimate Parisian environment for the dining room or a festive Beaux Arts ball atmosphere. After deciding that the Carlsons are perhaps more conservative, she settles on the intimate evening, and the Brain searches its memory banks for the correct music and videoimages to play on the dining room viewing wall. The Brain also preadjusts the lighting effects for the room.

8:05 p.m.

The Carlsons arrive and let themselves in with the special password that Mary had given them last week when she invited them to dinner.

From the foyer they spot John and Mary coming from the "Great

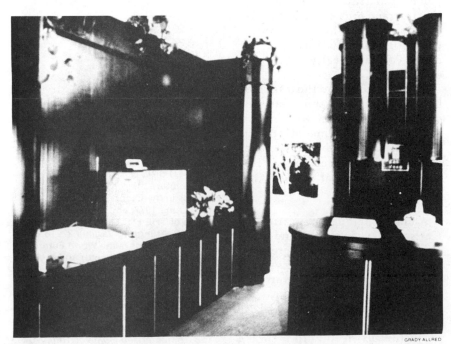

GRADY ALLRED

The kitchen of tomorrow will be equipped to both cook and serve food. Computers will be used for menu planning and teleshopping and will also aid in the preparation of meals.

Room"—Xanadu's central living and entertaining space—to greet them. But first, the House Brain has its say.

"Welcome to Xanadu. I am the House Brain and it will be my pleasure to serve you this evening. My master and mistress will be with you shortly."

Realizing that the Carlsons may not yet have adapted to the computerized artificial intelligence and voice synthesis that they enjoy, John quiets the House Brain with a quick vocal command. It will remain still for the remainder of the Carlsons' visit unless expressly asked to speak.

This is their first visit to Xanadu, and the Carlsons are immediately surprised by the size and "organic" feeling of the Great Room. After inspecting the "tree" that serves to support and heat and cool the large open space, they quickly walk up the steps to the dining room area, where they can hear the outdoor cafe sounds of Paris. This prepares them for the sight of a candlelit table that appears to be on the Champs Elysees.

This certainly will be an evening the Carlsons will enjoy and remember.

8:30 p.m.

While Johnny's parents and the Carlsons dine in Gallic splendor in the dining room, the two boys are busy in the breakfast room devouring their dinner while discussing what it must be like to try to play softball in reduced gravity on the Moon's new colony.

9:15 p.m.

Retiring with their guests to the Great Room conversation pit, John and Mary tell anecdotes about the years they spent building and upgrading Xanadu and its systems. The Carlsons, while still not totally converted to computerization, ask for a chance to meet and talk with the House Brain.

9:30 p.m.

While the adults are rediscovering the lost art of conversation, the two boys are exploring the new additions to the "audioasis" that Johnny's father had installed the week before. Within the glass bub-

"The left side of the House Brain comes to attention. Its remote sensors have sent it an alarm. Something is wrong."

ble balcony overlooking the Great Room, they are able to experiment with the new music synthesizer without disturbing the party below. At the end of an hour, however, the two boys decide they have had enough, retire to Johnny's room, and go to bed.

10:00 p.m.

The Carlsons have asked for a demonstration of the Sensorium. As they approach, they are greeted by the House Brain:

"Welcome to the Sensorium. It is my pleasure to provide you with an environment suitable for relaxation, meditation, or entertainment. How can I serve you tonight?"

John quickly makes a request:

"First, I'd like the Carlsons to see you demonstrate your capabilities for abstract musical and lighting entertainment. Then you can retrieve for us the stored copy of that movie you taped earlier this week off satellite."

The lights dim and the laser wall lights up with abstract patterns pulsating in rhythm with music. As soon as the demonstration is over, the same large wall switches into a viewing screen for the featured entertainment of the night.

12:15 a.m.

Alone in their bedroom after the Carlsons have left, John and Mary are in bed watching a pretaped segment of late-night news that they had missed while watching the movie in the Sensorium.

"What time would you like to wake up tomorrow?" asks the Brain's voice.

"Just let us sleep until we wake up naturally. We have nothing planned for the morning," replies John.

"Any special instructions for tonight or tomorrow?"

"No, nothing. Just leave us now so we can go to sleep."

The lights dim even further as the computer complies with its master's request.

Epilogue

2:47 a.m.

The left side of the House Brain comes to attention. What is it? Its remote sensors have sent it an alarm. Something is wrong. After going through its standard inspection program that includes checking on all occupants, the Brain determines that the problem is a minor plumbing leak in the hydroponic garden.

By contacting neighboring House Brains, it is able to find one with a similar problem in the past. Since the company that had done the repairs had proven reliable, the Brain takes the initiative and calls the plumbing company's computer, making an appointment for repairs the next afternoon.

With everything under control, the Brain once more returns to a standby mode, awaiting its first orders of a new day.

About the Author

Roy Mason, a futurist architect, writer, and designer, is architecture editor of THE FUTURIST. He has written widely on the future of architecture, including articles in the October 1975, February 1976, June 1977, and February 1982 issues of THE FUTURIST. His address is Box 558, Arlington, Virginia 22216.

Lane Jennings is the World Future Society's research director and is editor of the *World Future Society Bulletin*.

Robert Evans is curator of educational technology and education administrator at the Capital Children's Museum, 800 3rd Street, N.E., Washington, D.C. 20002.

This article is excerpted from *Xanadu: The Computerized Home of Tomorrow and How It Can Be Yours Today!* and is reprinted with permission. Copyright © 1983 by Acropolis Books Ltd., 2400 17th Street, N.W., Washington, D.C. 20009. *Xanadu* (260 pages, $18.95) is available from the World Future Society Book Service (pre-payment required; please include $1.50 for postage and handling).

Computer Chess: Can the Machine Beat Man at His Own Game?

by Lane Jennings

Chess-playing computers are winning new respect for "machine intelligence" and are raising important questions about the powers and limits of the human mind.

"Now the man who invented
*   that steam drill,*
He thought he was
*   mighty fine,*
But John Henry drilled down
*   sixteen feet*
And the steam drill
*   only made nine,*
*   Lord, Lord,*
Steam drill
*   only made nine."*
*   —The Ballad of John Henry*

John Henry's famous contest with the steam drill was a legendary "last stand" of human muscle against the power of the machine. As automation took over more and more tasks that once required enormous outlays of strength and stamina, the prestige of hard physical labor went into a decline. The engineer replaced the village blacksmith as the man to be admired, and human beings took comfort in the thought that however well a machine might do at lifting heavy weights or bending steel, it could never match the human brain. But the rapid development of electronic computers in the last few decades is raising some serious doubts about man's supposed intellectual superiority.

In July 1976, a computer program competed in a chess tournament for humans and won every game. This had never happened before. A few years earlier, most chess players and even many computer experts would probably have said that it never *could* happen. The computer's stunning tournament victory has since been followed by others, clearly establishing that its triumph was no fluke.

The possible long-term implications of a powerful chess-playing computer reach far beyond the world of chess. For if a machine can already "outsmart" its creators over the chessboard, tomorrow's machines may have powers that will force mankind to re-examine the whole question of what it means to be human.

Why Build a Chess Machine?

For centuries the game of chess has enjoyed a special place in Western culture. More than any other pastime, chess has been respected as an intellectual challenge, a battle of minds. Viewed as a test of intelligence that provides scope for strategy and planning, chess is often taught in schools and is a required subject at many military academies throughout the world. The element of chance plays no role in chess, and deciding which move to make requires the utmost patience, concentration and thought.

The decision-making aspect of the game intrigued Claude Shannon, one of the early pioneers in computer research, and led him in the late 1940s to begin looking for a way to program a computer to play chess. Shannon proposed several methods by which the various objectives of chess strategy could be assigned different mathematical values and reduced to a series of simple yes/no decisions. This procedure of breaking complicated choices into many small steps is how a computer approaches any problem. The job of the computer programmer lies in determining just how many "yes/no" questions have to be answered, and in what order. In the case of chess, there are so many such questions involved in each move that thousands or even millions of possibilities could be considered without exhausting every reasonable choice.

Shannon's objective was to develop techniques for programming a computer to solve complex design problems involving the ability to recognize and modify patterns. The knowledge that scientists have gained through experiments with computer chess has helped produce computer programs that are used today to design electronic circuits, handle complex telephone switching operations, plan and coordinate military operations, and solve other problems involving logical deduction.

Early attempts at teaching computers to play chess were not immediately suc-cessful. For a long time, any human player—even a complete beginner—could beat the computer fairly easily. But the computer programmers did not give up and rapidly learned more and more about how to identify and isolate the elements involved in solving chess problems.

Most of this work was performed in the United States, but the Soviet Union, where chess is regarded as the national game, has also been active in chess programming since the mid 1950s and has contributed to the rapid progress in computer chess. Milestones in this progress include:

1949—U.S. computer pioneer Claude Shannon presents the first paper describing how a computer might be programmed to play chess.

1956—U.S. scientists at Los Alamos Laboratory develop a program that plays a simplified version of chess using fewer pieces and a smaller board. In a demonstration game, their MANIAC computer beats its human opponent in 23 moves.

1961—The USSR releases the first reports of its research into computer chess.

1966—A four-game match is played between a computer at Stanford University in the United States and one programmed by scientists at the Institute of Theoretical and Experimental Physics in Moscow. The Russian computer wins two games; the other two are draws.

1967—MacHack VI, a chess program written by Richard Greenblatt (then a student at MIT) is entered in a local chess tournament and becomes the first computer program to score a victory over a human opponent in tournament play.

1970—CHESS 3.0, a program developed by three Northwestern University students (Larry Atkin, Keith Gorlen and David Slate), tops a field of six entries to win the First United States Computer Chess Championship with a perfect score: three wins, no losses, no draws.

1973-74—CHESS 4.0, an improved version of CHESS 3.0, finishes third in a tournament for humans with a score of 4½ out of a possible 6. Based on its performance here, officials of the U.S. Chess Federation estimate that CHESS

4.0 has a level of skill considerably higher than that of the average tournament player in the United States.

August 1974—Thirteen entries from eight countries compete in Stockholm for the First World Computer Chess Championship. The USSR's chess program KAISSA wins with a perfect score of four victories, no losses and no draws.

August 1975—KAISSA is called in to "advise" Russian chessmaster David Bronstein on a plan for winning a game already in progress. Bronstein follows the program's advice and wins the game.

December 1975—KAISSA demonstrates a forced win in an endgame position that top-ranked human chess players have argued about inconclusively for decades.

July 1976—CHESS 4.5, programmed by David Slate and Larry Atkin, becomes the first computer to win a chess tournament for humans, beating all five of its human opponents at the Paul

Chess can be an outdoor sport, as here at the Paul Masson Tournament in Saratoga, California. It was in this tournament, held July 24th and 25th 1976, that the computer program CHESS 4.5 made history by defeating all five of its human opponents, thus becoming the first "machine" to win a rated chess tournament.
Photo: Control Data Corporation

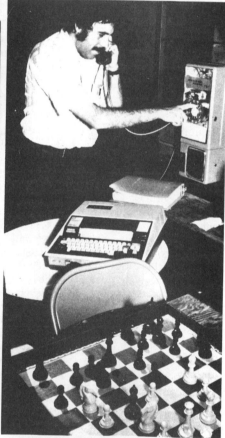

Control Data Corporation's CYBER 176 computer system, one of the largest and most powerful ever built for commercial use, is designed to handle the massive calculations required in such fields as weather mapping and nuclear energy research. Using this computer, the chess-playing programs written by David Slate and Larry Atkin have scored impressive tournament victories against human players. How serious chess players around the world react to this unexpected competition in their "Royal Game" may reveal what attitude society as a whole is likely to adopt toward other manifestations of machine intelligence in the future.
Photo: Control Data Corporation

Though playing in California, CHESS 4.5's "brain" was a computer at the University of Minnesota. After each move by its human opponent, programmer David Slate dialed the computer's number in Minnesota to report the move and to receive the computer's reply over the teletypewriter on the white table. Although this shot is posed, and the position on the board did not occur in actual play, the computer won all five of its tournament games to become undisputed tournament champion in its class.
Photo: Control Data Corporation

Masson Tournament in Saratoga, California.

February 1977—CHESS 4.5 again takes first place against human opponents, this time at a chess tournament in Minnesota.

March 1977—Humans strike back! Entered in another Minnesota tournament against stronger human competition, CHESS 4.5 finishes in last place with a score of one win, one draw, and three losses.

August 1977—With further improvements added, the Slate/Atkin program (now called CHESS 4.6) outscores KAISSA and 15 other entries from eight countries to win the Second World Computer Chess Championship.

October 1977—CHESS 4.6 wins the 8th U.S. Computer Chess Championship, marking the seventh U.S. Championship in eight years for the steadily improved Slate/Atkin program.

* * *

Computer chess has moved from the realm of science fiction to become an established fact in less than 30 years, and the end is nowhere in sight. There is no longer any doubt that computers can be programmed to play chess well enough to beat most human players. But if the day actually comes when a computer can "outthink" even the top grandmasters of the game, how are people likely to react?

Writing in the June 1977 issue of the U.S. magazine *Chess Life & Review*, Walter Goldwater, president of the Marshall Chess Club in New York City, described his thoughts after losing a game to the computer program CHESS 4.5:

I was very upset, and remained so for two days. . . . We are not, obviously, disturbed to learn that a machine can go on land, water, or in the air faster than a mammal, fish or bird. But if we were to feel that a machine could write a better play than Shakespeare, or a better quartet than Beethoven, . . . we would become disturbed; and the reason seems to be that we make a distinction between ability in a physical or even a mental sense and *imagination.*

Historically, chess has been ranked as an art in which imagination as well as calculation plays an important role. But are we willing to credit a machine with "imagination" if it can play better chess than its human opponents? How we answer this question may reveal much about the future relationships between man and machine.

Does Chess Have a Future?

Here are some of the suggestions that have been made for dealing with the "threat" of an "unbeatable" chess-playing computer:

• **Change the rules.** Adding new complications to the established rules of chess might reduce the computer's advantage over man in speed of calculation. *Chess Life & Review* editor Burt Hochberg has suggested a new rule that would allow each player to place pieces on the board in a different pattern at the start of every game. This would take away the computer's chance of gaining an early advantage by having stored in its memory the recorded best opening moves from the traditional starting position.

• **Downgrade our image of the game.** Mathematicians have long known that there is a finite limit to the number of possible legal moves that can be made in a game of chess. In theory, this means that chess, while more complicated, is just as solvable as tic-tac-toe or Chinese checkers. Thus we could take the view that the chess computer is only "calculating" and not engaged in "creative thought" when it outplays a human opponent. This would certainly be true if the computer were able to consider every possible move before it made its choice. But in fact, that "finite number of legal chess moves" is actually greater than the number of atoms in the uni-

verse, and millions of years would be needed to calculate all of the possible alternative consequences from the opening move of a game. In order to play chess, then, a computer has to examine certain moves in depth while ignoring other possibilities, just as a human being does. If we now choose to say that the thought process involved in chess is not creative because a "mere" machine can do it, then we will have to revise our opinion of human chess players too. David Levy, an international master of chess and one of the world's leading authorities on computer chess, argues that "a computer plays even more creatively than a man" because it "does not have stereotypes and it more often finds unexpected and therefore beautiful solutions."

• **Give up chess completely.** With computers able to beat the best human players, chess might suffer a sizable drop in popularity. It seems unlikely though that people would no longer find any enjoyment in the game. David Levy puts it this way: "Boats have been sailing the seas for centuries but I still like to swim." Monroe Newborn, professor of electrical engineering at Columbia Universtiy and co-author of a computer chess program named OSTRICH, suggests that if and when computers are able to play chess at the world championship level it will open "a new era in the history of chess . . . in which the game is not playing chess but programming computers to play." Newborn also predicts that these programs will have "their own individual 'personalities,' and will reflect the chess style of their authors."

• **Work out a partnership.** The idea that a skilled human chess player and a computer might someday work together as a team was suggested as long ago as 1962 by writer Fritz Leiber in a science-fiction story entitled "The 64-Square Madhouse." The story describes how some of the world's leading chessmasters might react if a computer were to be

Lane Jennings opens a game against *Boris* (a chess-playing micro-computer) by keying his first move into the computer's memory.

Boris signals its counter-moves on the lighted panel above its nameplate, and Jennings moves the corresponding piece on the chessboard.

Boris's light panel flashes out the words "Ahhhh ruthless!" as Jennings grins with satisfaction over a tricky move.

Photos: Sally Cornish

Artist Bob Walker's cover illustration for the June 1977 issue of the American chess magazine *Chess Life and Review* sums up the fears of many chess buffs that computers may soon dominate the game. Though computers cannot consider every possible variation on each move, their perfect memories and enormously fast calculating speeds have already proven more than a match for top human players in informal "rapid transit" games and have scored impressive victories against better than average human players even under tournament conditions.

Drawing by Bob Walker
courtesy of *Chess Life & Review*

Chess Challenger

Chess Challenger, introduced early in 1977, was the first computer chess game designed for the home market. Though users complained that the first model (since improved) was too easy to beat, the machine succeeded in providing a tireless, non-threatening companion for lonely chess players. Unlike a human opponent, *Chess Challenger* can admit defeat but cannot claim victory. In the future, "friendly computers" may become increasingly popular, offering companionship as well as entertainment on demand.

Photo: Fidelity Electronics

CONTROL CENTER

CHECK
Lights when the computer has you in check

FROM Window
Displays the position of the piece you want to move (your starting position)

REset
Starts the game —will cancel memory

Double Move
To be used for Casting and for En Passant

Keys
Designates Rank and File board moves

I LOSE
Lights when computer admits defeat and is in checkmate

TO Window
Displays the new position to which you have chosen to move your piece

ENter
To enter your move into the computer

CLear
To clear an unwanted move before pressing enter

entered in a tournament against them. Leiber has a human player winning the tournament by spotting and exploiting subtle weaknesses in the machine's program, but looking to the future the chess masters agree that all the best players will soon have computers to work out tactical complexities, with the human partner "taking over" at certain times to make strategic decisions.

• **Tame the machine.** Not every attempt to program a computer for chess has been aimed at producing the strongest possible game. In 1977, several electronics firms in the United States began manufacturing chess-playing microcomputers for the home market. The first of these, *Chess Challenger*, although advertised as being "programmed for aggressive play"—"like a skilled human opponent"—turns out in practice to play a very defensive game. *Chess Challenger* can only flash two messages: "check" (a warning to an opponent that his king is being attacked) and "I lose." The victory-cry "checkmate!" is not in its vocabulary.

More recently, a second-generation chess computer has appeared under the name *Boris*. Produced by a firm called Applied Concepts Inc., of Garland, Texas, *Boris* plays much more aggressively and even wages "psychological warfare" by occasionally preceding its moves by flashing out nerve-rattling messages at its opponent, such as a sarcastic "Have you played before?," an ironic "Really?," or a smug "I expected that." *Boris* may also flash out (not always at appropriate moments): "Good move!," "Interesting!," "I missed that," "Ah, ruthless!," and "May I cheat?"

Boris, Chess Challenger, and similar machines now becoming available really offer a chess *companion*. Now, at

The Battered Human Ego

The rise of the machine to its present position as man's physical superior and mental rival is only one of many developments that have compelled human beings to change their beliefs about themselves and their place in the universe.

Some of the more notable dates in the long history of blows to mankind's collective ego include:

1543—Copernicus demonstrates by mathematics that the earth is not the center of the universe but instead moves around the sun. Later confirmed by the telescopic observations of Galileo and others, Copernicus's discovery forces men to recognize that their senses are not always to be trusted.

1675—Anton van Leeuwenhoek, using his newly invented microscope, discovers thousands of tiny creatures, invisible to the naked eye, in a drop of rain water. Leeuwenhoek's microscope discoveries reveal a whole new world of living things over which human beings have little control.

1781—James Watt's steam engine becomes a practical device for powering machines to do work formerly done by muscle power. In the following decades, machines displace human workers in many industries.

1811—Luddite rioters at Nottingham and other towns in England storm factories and smash the machines that are taking their jobs.

1859—Darwin's *Origin of Species* undermines a major source of human pride by presenting evidence that mankind shares a common ancestry with other animals. Four years later, naturalist Thomas Huxley compounds the injury by suggesting that *Homo sapiens* is not even the end product of the evolutionary process, but merely a transitional stage on the way toward some more advanced being.

1895—Freud begins developing his theories of psychoanalysis. In the

1543   **1781**   **1859**

the flick of a switch, you can have a respectable (but beatable) opponent who will be ready at any hour of the day or night to play "just one more game," but who will never complain if *you* want to stop, or brag to someone about how easily "he" beat you.

This example of a "friendly" machine could become increasingly common in a world of limited resources. With travel growing more expensive, and long-distance friendships becoming harder and harder to maintain, computer games may increasingly be designed to provide companionship as well as amusement.

Man and Machine: Companions of the Future?

Computer chess is only one of many electronic games that use computer circuits to simulate the actions and responses of a human opponent. Electronic backgammon, checkers, poker, and football simulations are already on the market, along with a growing number of TV games. If the cost of small computers for the home continues to drop as expected over the next few years, and the number of easy-to-use programs for home computers continues to grow, we may very soon find

ourselves adopting a whole new attitude toward "thinking machines" and perhaps toward machines in general.

When a machine can do something that would earn our respect if done by a fellow human being, we can react in one of several ways. We can immediately downgrade our estimation of the achievement ("If a mere machine can do this, then it can't be so remarkable after all.") or we can become alarmed and resentful ("If a machine can do *this* already, how much longer will it be before machines take over *every* job?"). These have been common reactions to

years that follow, researchers in psychology produce a flood of books and papers arguing that human beings are the prey of primitive drives and instincts operating below the level of consciousness, and seldom act from purely rational or idealistic motives.

1914—World War I establishes the machine's power and versatility at producing mass destruction. The war destroys public faith in many traditional social institutions and systems of belief, but establishes weapons research as a high government priority. This adds new impetus to the development of advanced machinery of all kinds.

1945—ENIAC (Electronic Numerical Integrator and Calculator), the first electronic computer for general purpose use, is completed. Built for ballistics research, ENIAC can compute in 30 seconds a missile trajectory that would take a skilled human mathematician 20 hours or more to complete.

1960s—Computer teaching machines, which enable students to pursue a topic at their own pace, begin to be recognized as "more human" (more patient, less prone to anger or scorn) than human teachers in some situations.

1976—CHESS 4.5, a computer program run on Control Data Corporation's powerful CYBER 176 computer, defeats five human opponents to become the first computer program to win a rated chess tournament.

Still other blows to man's pride can be expected in the years ahead. Among those most often predicted are:

• Contact with extra-terrestrial intelligence greater than our own.
• Perfection of an electronic or chemical process for implanting memory patterns in the brain, making obsolete the traditional learning process of acquiring knowledge

through reading, listening, viewing, and practical experience.

• "Customizing" humans through genetic engineering, cloning, or selective breeding, with the probable result that individuality would be sacrificed to achieve greater standardization, reliability and ease of maintenance.

• A complete breakdown of civilization, leaving humans to compete for food and shelter as best they can without the advanced technology and social systems that now sustain them.

In the space of a few short centuries, man has moved from a world in which life was a simple, straightforward matter of earning one's bread, raising children, and obeying the commands of God and king, to a world where everything is complex, nothing is permanent, and man himself is often seen as a vicious animal that can be—and perhaps deserves to be—supplanted by machines.

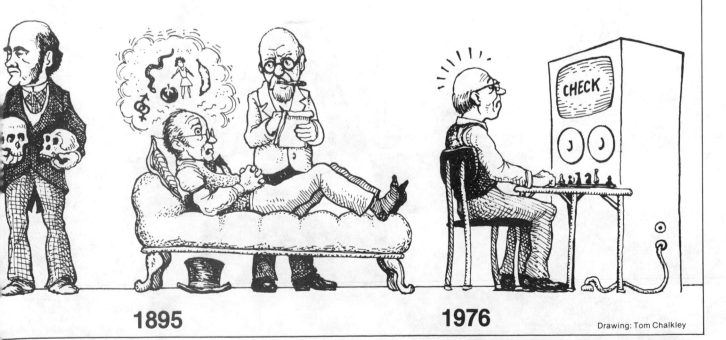

1895

1976

Drawing: Tom Chalkley

the automation of many manufacturing and raw materials processing activities since the Industrial Revolution. Physical labor, even when it demands special skill, has come to be regarded as somehow demeaning to human beings, as well as economically insecure, because a machine could be built to do the same job faster, longer, and more cheaply. We have therefore transferred our respect to those occupations requiring "brain work," secure in the knowledge that no mechanical contraption could ever replace the thinking human being.

But suddenly we find that there *are* machines—computers—that can do such intellectual tasks as planning, weighing alternative choices, issuing orders, and even imagining. Already we depend on these machines to carry out jobs we could never hope to do ourselves. If we now follow the same path we did before and deny there is any dignity in human brain work because machines—by whatever roundabout means —can produce the end-products of

thought in less time and at less cost, all we will accomplish is to deny ourselves the pride of intellectual achievement. If we decide that playing a good game of chess or planning a national budget or composing a piece of music are trivial accomplishments because a computer can do them all, then we are only downgrading our own image of human worth. We can do this, but there *is* another choice. Perhaps, instead of losing respect for ourselves, we would do better to increase our respect for the machine!

In practice, showing "respect" for machines means learning not to look on them simply as slaves. When a slave owner sees that his slaves are stronger, faster, and more efficient than himself, he is likely to fear that someday these slaves will realize their power and revolt. In the same way, so long as human beings see machines as slaves, they will continue to regard any machine that is stronger, faster, or "smarter" than themselves as a potential threat. It is

only when the stereotypes are broken and an individual human being makes the effort to become thoroughly familiar with a particular machine—however complex or powerful it may be—that this fear is overcome and the machine becomes a partner rather than a slave. Just as truckers get to know their "rigs," sailors their ships, and musicians their instruments, so ordinary people in the near future may get to know their computers.

There may never be a John Henry of the electronic age. Instead of fiercer and fiercer rivalry, man and machine may develop closer and closer cooperation. Once machines are able to perform thinking and planning tasks as well as physical labor, human beings could be freer than ever before to choose the particular jobs they themselves wish to work at. The status distinctions between those who work with their hands and those who work with their heads will no longer apply, and the "do-it-yourself" spirit that today leads people to tend a

About the Author

Lane Jennings is Research Director for the World Future Society and editor of the *World Future Society Bulletin.* He is also a confirmed chess addict.

Boris

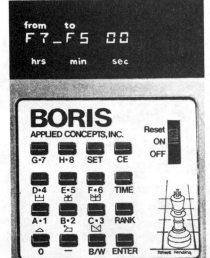

Boris, a micro-computer programmed exclusively for playing chess, signals its moves in code form (left) or can show the position of pieces on each rank using the symbols reproduced below. Opponent's moves are entered into the computer's memory using the keyboard (above). The computer can also flash out messages at random intervals to unnerve or entertain its human opponent, as shown at lower left photo.

Photo: Applied Concepts, Inc.

garden or remodel a house for the joy of it may become the prime motivation for *all* human work.

Far from "replacing" human beings, machines that can think as well as act could restore human pride of accomplishment in every field. For once the *compulsion* to work is removed, the *opportunity* to work at a chosen task becomes a source of potential pleasure no matter what the particular task may

be. Even jobs that are now despised as dangerous, dirty, dull or just unglamorous may never become fully automated. Instead, these jobs may be performed by machine-assisted human volunteers who will find they can *enjoy* such work once it no longer carries a social stigma.

This idyllic picture of man/machine partnership can only become a reality if humans are able to overcome their fear and envy of machine intelligence. This

is far from certain, however, for human egos are notoriously sensitive, and at first glance computers can be overpowering.

How the world's chess players react to the growing impact of computers—both large and small—on the theory and traditions of their "Royal Game" may provide a glimpse into the future of mankind's relationship with the machine.

Paul Hurly

The Promises and Perils of Videotex

The role of videotex as a communications tool is growing rapidly throughout North America and Europe. Videotex systems and services are gradually introducing significant changes to our social, political, and economic milieu. Some of these changes are the inevitable result of technology. A few may be the harbingers of emerging perils.

Videotex is in widespread use throughout the world—in Venezuela, Japan, Finland, Australia, the Soviet Union, Belgium, and Switzerland, just to name a few countries. Videotex applications can be classified in five general categories: retrieval (news, sports, weather, travel schedules, stock market reports), computing (computer-assisted instruction, management information services, income-tax aids), transactional

> Videotex has the potential to significantly change and improve communications. Now is the time to determine whether we let videotex development take its own course or direct it ourselves.

(teleshopping, telebanking), messaging, and downline loading (transmitting telesoftware programs to intelligent terminals).

Society has reached an important decision point. Should we allow a technology like videotex to transform society seemingly at will, or should we direct the change process triggered in part by videotex toward goals consistent with our present values?

Videotex is a generic term for systems that provide easy-to-use, low-cost, computer-based services via communication facilities. There are several basic types:

Viewdata is fully-interactive videotex. The user's requests for services or information are actually

AT&T

"Some, believing that the planning of systems like videotex should no longer be monopolized by so-called experts, call for participatory strategies."

sent to, received by, and acted upon by the system computer. In North America, the terms "videotex" and "videotext" have become synonymous with viewdata.

Teletext is pseudo-interactive or broadcast videotex. While the user can select the information or service to be received, only a one-way communication link is involved.

A final variation of videotex is *open-channel teletext*. One version of open-channel teletext, called closed captioning, has become an important communication aid for the deaf. Other applications include cable television information channels, open captioning, and airline arrival/departure displays.

Videotex services may be transmitted to the receiver's terminal by coaxial cable, fiber-optic cable, telephone line, radio, conventional satellite or Direct Broadcast Satellite TV, or microwave. Both viewdata and teletext may be transmitted by narrow- or broadband video frequencies. Narrowband employs part of the unused portion of a video signal, while broadband makes use of the entire video channel and thus can transmit more data.

Videotex data can be displayed on a wide range of devices, including TV sets, microcomputers or other terminals with a cathode ray tube, and thermal or impact printers.

Issues, Promises, and Perils

As the importance of videotex as a communications technology grows, a number of issues arise concerning its use and regulation. Among the issues to be faced are:

Regulation. Critics argue that government administration of telecommunications is essential to ensure equitable access. Some, believing that the planning of systems like videotex should no longer be monopolized by so-called experts, call for participatory strategies. These advocates point to the

EXTERNAL AFFAIRS, CANADA

Videotex display of stock-market information. Private videotex systems provide financial data, forecasts, analyses, and other information to selected clients.

EXTERNAL AFFAIRS, CANADA

Advice for shoppers from an electronic shopping guide. Videotex services make shopping more convenient but could reduce the consumer's range of choice and services, says author Paul Hurly.

deteriorating state of commercial television in the United States and the lead that European public telecommunications authorities have in videotex and fiber optics to demonstrate the weaknesses of present U.S. regulatory methods.

Rate setting. High videotex costs established by market demand may exclude access to videotex by lower socio-economic groups. Government-approved tariffs could help lower access charges and thus promote greater dissemination, but could also increase the financial risk of investing in videotex, possibly reducing the present level of participation by private enterprise.

Billing. Techniques sensitive to individual user practices require more expensive viewdata systems. Centralized billing systems can provide savings to users and service providers, but the amount of detail collected can expose users to a possible breach of privacy.

System ownership. The involvement of major broadcasters such as CBS in teletext tests and of newspaper and book publishers such as Knight-Ridder and Reader's Digest in viewdata systems raises serious concerns regarding the increasing concentration of the private ownership of information distribution systems in North America. Is this growing monopoly, and the power it confers, in the best interest of the general public?

System compatibility. If the ultimate promise of videotex is a global communications village, a single international videotex specification will be required. Network interconnection can be promoted most effectively through system compatibility.

The peril is that, with so much money already invested by industry and users in videotex equipment that complies with other standards, there will be little incentive to move beyond the current situation. If a user's equipment has access to only one system, the result would be like needing two telephones, one for local calls and the other for long distance.

Transborder data flow. TBDF is the movement of data or information by electronic means across national boundaries. There are four basic benefits. First, TBDF will pro-

EXTERNAL AFFAIRS, CANADA

Information for customers at a shopping mall. Public-access systems are already in widespread use as mall or store directories in the United States and Canada.

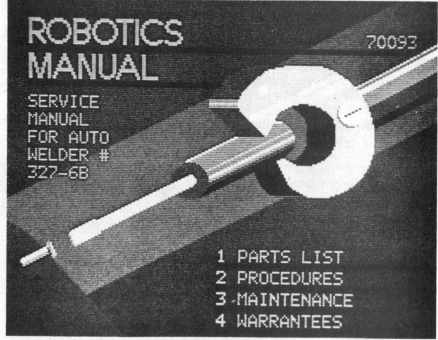

EXTERNAL AFFAIRS, CANADA

Videotex robotics manual can be easily updated as new data become available.

mote the global village concept. Second, it will give the largest number of people access to information. Third, it will allow information to be processed where the costs are lowest. And fourth, it will reduce the cost of retrieving and storing information.

Major concerns regarding TBDF have been raised by various nations and groups. One peril is that the free movement of information could undermine national sovereignty and cultural identity. An

economic peril is that the outflow of funds to purchase information from foreign data bases could result in job loss and weakened economies in some countries. A third peril is the potential for invasion of privacy due to jurisdictional ambiguities, the vulnerability of communication transmissions, and the lack of strong national legislation regarding data theft.

Employment. While new jobs are being created and old jobs made more interesting by the

Videotex Systems in Europe and the United States

Public videotex systems have been available in most Western European nations since 1981. The United Kingdom also has a large number of private videotex systems. These generally fall in one of two categories: intra-company communication systems, or services provided by a company to selected clients, such as stock brokerage firms providing online videotex market forecasts and analysis, and stock ticker and stock marketing services.

British Telecom's Prestel videotex format, along with the Antiope-DIDON and Antiope-Teletel formats coordinated by Intelematique of France, provided the world's first public videotex systems featuring both visual displays as well as words and numbers. Prestel has introduced such capabilities as the digital reproduction of photographic images, to be used by such services as real estate companies to picture their listings.

West Germany used the Prestel videotex protocol to create a domestic system called Bildschirmtext. This system allows users to gain access to a wide variety of data bases, from airline schedules to mail order company catalogs.

France has promoted the public acceptance and use of Teletel by distributing more than 250,000 Minitel viewdata terminals free of charge. The videotex system is testing the use of a "smart card" for teleshopping and other transactional services.

A common European videotex format called CEPT was adopted in 1983. This will open the way for a fully integrated viewdata network that will permit system users to gain access to data bases anywhere on the continent, in much the same manner as a telephone user can place a long-distance phone call to any nation in the world.

The United States and Canada approved a common viewdata standard in 1984 called the North American Presentation Level Protocol Syntax (NAPLPS). While direct viewdata network interconnection between Europe and North America is still some way off, NAPLPS will gradually help the growth of the North American viewdata market. This is likely to occur for two reasons:

First, the common NAPLPS standard will increase the market for one type of equipment, thus slowly decreasing the cost of terminals and system hardware. Second, a common standard will help to promote greater access between systems and data bases.

While national boundaries in Western Europe have served as an impediment to a continental viewdata network, competition between corporate-owned systems in the United States has been a far greater barrier to the development of a national viewdata network.

A number of major equipment manufacturers, including IBM, Commodore, Wang, and DEC, now manufacture NAPLPS software decoders for microcomputers. This, coupled with the declining cost of modems, will open up an enormous potential pool of terminals in offices and homes to viewdata systems in the United States.

—Paul Hurly

INTELEMATIQUE

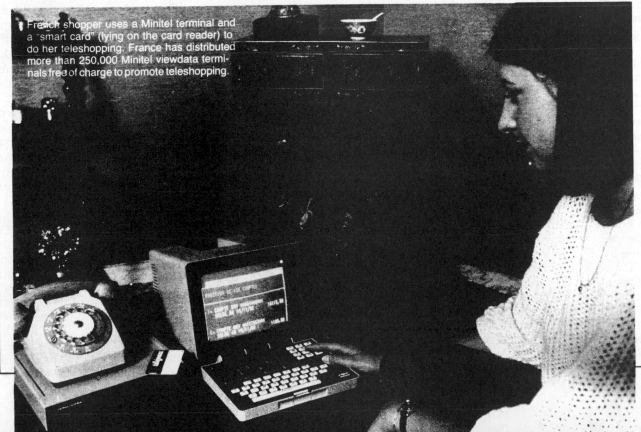

French shopper uses a Minitel terminal and a "smart card" (lying on the card reader) to do her teleshopping. France has distributed more than 250,000 Minitel viewdata terminals free of charge to promote teleshopping.

"Videotex will not transform boring tasks into stimulating jobs, and it has introduced some of its own dull tasks."

adoption of videotex, the gradual introduction of videotex into the integrated office will facilitate the elimination of many white-collar, middle-management jobs. Furthermore, videotex will not transform boring tasks into stimulating jobs, and it has introduced some of its own dull tasks.

For example, copying line drawings or photographs with an optical digitizer or copying typing (word processing) for a videotex program are not more fulfilling activities because they are done electronically rather than electrically. Or suggesting that cab drivers follow routes prescribed by a map projected electronically by videotex in the taxicab may be more efficient but takes all sense of individual decision-making out of the task.

Privacy and security. While important judicial and technical strides regarding privacy have been made in Europe, neither the United States nor Canada has effective measures in place to ensure personal data privacy and to prosecute violators. The U.S. military has begun to harden data communication facilities, but successful attacks on data bases by radical groups in Europe have graphically demonstrated their vulnerability. The massive compilation and correlation of personal information now possible using modern computers make it extremely difficult to enforce any reasonable form of privacy and confidentiality controls on videotex systems.

Participatory democracy. Although videotex polling mechanisms have been hailed by political scientists as a vehicle for implementing participatory democracy, the peril is that society will adopt rule by electronic plebiscite. There must be requirements that the participants be well informed, be able to comprehend issues, be able to distinguish parochial from national interests, and empathize with opposing viewpoints for participatory democracy via videotex—or any other medium—to be successful.

For example, commentator and columnist Andy Rooney criticized television ads prior to this year's U.S. elections that encouraged all Americans to get out and vote. "I don't want some ignorant person canceling out my vote," Rooney proclaimed. He pleaded for voters who couldn't name their local candidates or tell a Republican from a Democrat to stay home.

The need for proper controls was illustrated by an experiment in Columbus, Ohio, on video polling, using the Warner-Amex Communications system called QUBE. One couple reported coming home to discover that their pre-school son had turned on the television and had participated in a QUBE poll intended for adult viewers.

Cultural dissemination and diversity. Videotex promises to become an electronic library, publishing vehicle, archive, and gallery. Open access will put the best of what is known at everyone's fingertips. The peril is that, with the rapid rise of "information overload," it will be difficult to locate the best.

Communications critic Gary Gumpert has referred to the advent of mini-communication or "mini-com." Unlike mass communication, mini-com, utilizing such technologies as videotex, can deliver nonstandard information or entertainment to specific, selected audiences.

Some critics of mini-com fear that the lack of the single unifying symbols that the mass media have in the past projected will cause national identity to be fragmented and unfocused. Others argue that the existence of large, centralized videotex data bases further removes from small communities, subgroups, and individuals the power to shape what is communicated and concentrates power in the hands of an elite.

Social-class divisions. While videotex has the capability of making information universally available

CABLESHARE

Robot sales clerk: This "shopping machine" utilizes images stored on videodisc and displayed on the top screen and on a videotex screen below. The machine accepts orders and credit-card payments, allowing for a totally electronic sales transaction.

to all, some predict that the gap between socio-economic classes will be heightened by the availability or lack of availability of information technologies. If this occurs, the haves and have-nots will be divided by access to videotex and computers as well as by economic wealth.

Information handling. Viewdata services, due to their interactive dimension, make it easier to locate specific information. Videotex services are providing customized information presentation and synthesis for users.

Yet research by Nobel laureate Herbert Simon has shown the fallacy in the argument that making more information available improves decision-making. Limitations in human memory and reasoning limit the number of facts that can be weighed when solving a problem.

The utility of information is judged by its accuracy, timeliness, and applicability. When data bases

"As the implementation of videotex evolves and the technology is refined, its impact on society is likely to broaden."

are not updated consistently or strict editorial controls enforced, these measures of videotex's effectiveness can be compromised.

There are other perils. The intermingling of sponsored pages with content pages and the lack of clearly defined editorial standards may blur the distinction between fact and opinion on videotex. People may forget that videotex data can be just as subjective as other sources.

For example, a Canadian citizen was recently charged with knowingly publishing false information that harmed or was likely to harm social or racial tolerance. In addition to allegedly publishing this information in pamphlet form, he had created an electronic "bulletin board" in the United States that Canadians could gain access to via computer.

The control of information is a growing public concern, but censorship by omission is hard to detect. Detection of censorship will become increasingly arduous with the information explosion.

Interpersonal communication. Videotex communication may be effective for such tasks as problem-solving, discussion of ideas, and policy decision-making. However, the lack of verbal communication is a major problem. People form less accurate perceptions of others via media.

Electronic bulletin boards, telegaming that involves networks of simultaneous players, and computer conferencing have created new subgroups and communities across North America. Videotex has fostered new forms of socialization and expanded some people's sense of community. But the absence of immediacy and other interpersonal communication factors, along with the lack of tactile experience, is identified by critics of videotex as a serious weakness. Some fear a consequence of the electronic cottage will be electronic seclusion.

Teleservices. Videotex will change the television set from a passive to an interactive device. Teleservices like travel reservations and ticket ordering, teleshopping, and telebanking will improve the convenience of services for consumers; will help manufacturers, wholesalers, and retailers to pare costs; and will allow businesses to receive immediate payment through electronic funds transfer.

On the other hand, the proliferation of TV-based services may reduce public participation in live events and travel for business or pleasure. The definition of a "vidiot" might be the person who prefers videotex to human or social interaction.

As computer-communication improvements reduce travel, the travel and hospitality industries could be adversely affected. Teleshopping could seriously reduce the consumer's range or choice of services, limiting, for example, the method of payment. And some businesses could become unviable due to competition from videotex marketing and retailing activities.

Strategy Choices

As the implementation of videotex evolves and the technology is refined, its impact on society is likely to broaden. Gradually, videotex is finding niches or roles it can play as business and institutions identify the unique attributes of the technology and methods by which videotex may complement existing media. Society is faced with two fundamental choices in determining the course videotex will take.

One strategy is basically hands off—laissez faire. Market and social forces would render judgment and shape the direction of videotex. This is the strategy in place today, and some of its effects are already visible. For example, critics of current videotex operations point to the blue-ribbon price tag—and the

fact that no one really asked for it in the first place—as reasons that consumers are wary. And telecommunications officials have admitted that they are marketing videotex chiefly for additional revenues needed to offset slow growth in telephone service.

Alternatively, governments could recognize the concerns being expressed by various groups and begin to regulate the videotex industry more closely, accepting that videotex is becoming an essential service required for the benefit of all, not just for those who can now afford it or visualize an application.

The advent of each new communication or travel technology has required a certain measure of regulation. The establishment of uniform railway line widths, an efficient interstate freeway system, highway and air travel safety rules, and reasonably equitable rural-urban telephone rates have ultimately assisted each innovation. Acceptance of each system increased as public confidence and access were facilitated.

Even in the present deregulatory climate in North America, a strong case can be argued for the regulation of videotex services. Some measure of government assurance that videotex will benefit the majority of society and that personal privacy will not be infringed upon would benefit both the videotex industry and the citizen.

About the Author

Paul Hurly is an information and training officer with Online Services, Canadian Centre for Occupational Health and Safety, Hamilton, Ont., Canada L8N 1H6. This article is adapted from his book *The Videotex and Teletex Handbook* (Harper and Row, New York, forthcoming, 1985, 380 pages).

Ruth E. Smith

Computer Bulletin Boards
New Wave in Teen Communications

How vividly I recall lying on the floor in the middle of the hallway with my feet propped on the door jamb, talking for hours to my friends on the telephone and listening to the latest Elvis Presley hit! We didn't realize it at the time, but my friends and I were learning a skill that we would use in the business world: expressing ourselves through the most common tool a manager uses—the telephone.

Today, many teenagers are communicating with one another using what will be one of their main management tools—the microcomputer. Teens all over the United States

Computer "bulletin boards" are preparing teenagers for their future business lives—and giving them a forum for sharing their views.

and in many countries around the world are using electronic message systems to "conference" on a daily basis.

Many teenagers are creating their own computer "bulletin boards," which are relatively sim-

ple for an experienced computer buff to set up. Bulletin Board System (BBS) software such as ABBS (Apple Bulletin Board System) or PMS (Public Message System) is readily available. Also on the market are "smart modems," devices that allow the user to transmit data over telephone lines and that will automatically dial a number or answer the ring of an incoming call and connect it to the computer. With this in place, computers can be the focal point for the exchange of electronic memos or bulletins.

Some teens who are skilled at programming write entire message system software programs themselves and build in a "chat" mode, enabling two users to converse simultaneously. Normally, only one user can be "logged on" to the system at a time.

Once a user logs on to the message system, he can post a bulletin, much like a traditional bulletin board, or send a private electronic message to one individual. The message would then be waiting

when the recipient logged on. Most teen computer users now are communicating through local bulletin boards that do not require the cost of a long-distance telephone call, although some with bigger allowances call bulletin boards all over the country.

One of the most active computer bulletin boards is Teen Line in San Diego, California. The system's operator (or "sysop"—the person responsible for running and maintaining the computerized bulletin board) is a 13-year-old girl named Meredith in Del Mar, California. Her father, a pathologist, originally bought the computer to search medical data bases. When Meredith became interested in computer bulletin boards, they decided to set one up for local teens.

T.D. CROWE

Peyton, a 16-year-old from Del Mar, says that he likes electronic messaging because "I enjoy being able to 'reach out and touch someone' in the privacy of my own room." Craig, a 17-year-old who is one of Teen Line's more active users, says that most of the area's 17 or so local bulletin boards are busy all the time.

More Than Just "Hi"

The teenagers use their electronic messaging to say more than just "Hi, how are you?" Their group discussions include such topics as programming tips, global politics, and philosophy.

There are also light-hearted dialogues, with participants using pseudonyms and calling for group camaraderie. And Meredith, Teen Line's sysop, writes short stories on the computer for other bulletin board users to browse.

Participants on a Milwaukee-based bulletin board called SUE (Serious Users Exchange) use electronic messaging for such diverse purposes as expressing their school spirit for upcoming football games, offering "thoughts for the day," or alerting others to magazine and newspaper articles that would affect all home-computer buffs. One of the longest-running public discussions on SUE, for example, was that of the recent adverse publicity on the "414s," a group of local teenage computer buffs named after Milwaukee's telephone area code. They were caught breaking into more than 60 business and government computer systems.

Gary, a 16-year-old user of an El Paso, Texas, bulletin board named Forum 80, reports that he first became interested in computers because of "peer group pressure" and that electronic messaging can be just as addicting as drugs or alcohol for teenagers.

WCCC is a bulletin board in Wise County, Virginia, a community of

"One of the longest-running public discussions . . . was that of the recent adverse publicity on the '414s,' a group of local teenage computer buffs . . . [who] were caught breaking into more than 60 business and government computer systems."

about 4,000 people. The board is residing on the computer at the Wise County Vocational Technical Center, where a 16-year-old named Bryan is the system operator. Bryan says that many of his friends had bought small computers and saw the advertisements on how to use them to communicate. After finding out that the closest place to communicate was a long-distance telephone call away, Bryan encouraged the school to provide a bulletin board system. "It's a great way to make new friends," he says.

There are currently at least 500 bulletin boards open to the public. Many more are private or just not known about yet. After getting a computer, using it to send or receive messages is a natural extension. The teens of today are less threatened by technology and expect to use electronic conferencing tools in their future careers. Teenagers—by using their microcomputers to "talk" for hours—are becoming acclimated to the technology they will be using in their working future.

About the Author

Ruth E. Smith is a consultant in management communication systems training and marketing. Her address is R.E. Smith & Associates, William Heath Davis Building, 440 Davis Court, Suite 1322, San Francisco, California 94111.

Telecommuters:
The Stay-at-Home Work Force of the Future
by Peter F. Eder

We live and work in a world in which the telephone, the television, and the computer are being linked together. With that linkage will come whole new ways of learning, relaxing, playing, and working. Indeed, we may be beginning to reach that impossible ideal of Johann Gutenberg in the fifteenth century: all information in all places at all times.

In this evolving environment, many people will become "teleworkers." These workers—whether they are owners, managers, specialists, generalists, secretaries, or clerks—will be able to work out of the home and use telecommunications as their link to the workplace.

Beyond a doubt, the day will come when telecommunications will serve as an effective and efficient replacement for a substantial amount of "in-office" work. It's the timing and intensity of the change that's uncertain, and achieving the transformation may not be easy.

Trade journals, consumer magazines, and the business press are full of forecasts and estimates of the impending impact of teleworking. If one were to listen to the "hype," one could draw the following conclusions to why teleworking will pay tremendous dividends in a short period of time:

- It saves fuel and reduces auto usage.
- It saves time.
- It can provide tax advantages to the at-home worker (at least under current tax regulations).
- It fosters the spread of population.
- It has been proven to increase productivity (where it has been measured among certain levels of clerical workers).
- It expands the labor pool by giving the opportunity for fruitful

Much of the work in the coming information society will be done by teleworkers—people who stay home and "commute" to work via telecommunications. But a host of complex issues will determine exactly how fast and how far teleworking will spread.

labor to people who want to or have to stay at home, such as certain handicapped people.
- It reduces personnel operating costs for companies.

But what about the disadvantages of teleworking, the factors we often don't hear about? Let me enumerate some of these:

- It can create feelings of isolation in workers.
- It can foster workaholism. (You've always got it around and available to you.)
- It can disrupt traditional family roles.
- There is a loss of management supervision.
- There can be a diminution of corporate identity.
- There is less privacy of information. (The information must flow through an extended network.)
- The data bases may create fantastic mazes, and heavy record-keep-

ing burdens may fall on the backs of the information workers.

An Energy Saver

Teleworking can certainly meet some pressing needs and solve some critical problems. These solutions deal primarily with fuel savings and travel reduction. For example, the experts predict that the "energy crisis" will not abate and that fuel conservation will continue to be a high priority. Teleworking can be a very important factor in energy conservation.

Teleworking has tremendous energy advantages over commuting. A team sponsored by the National Science Foundation and led by Jack Nilles, director of the University of Southern California's Information Technology Program, calculated that the relative energy consumption advantage of teleworking over commuting is at least 29 to 1 when

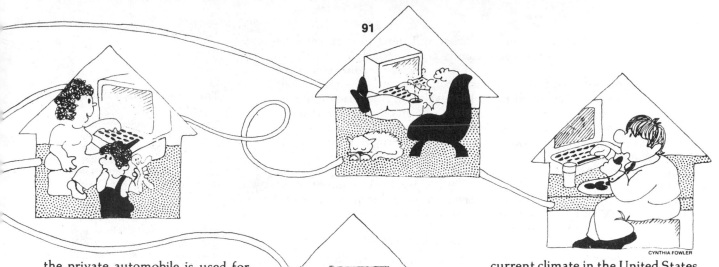

CYNTHIA FOWLER

the private automobile is used for commuting, 11 to 1 when normally loaded mass transit is used, and 2 to 1 for 100% utilized mass transportation.

A report in *Transportation Quarterly* last year forecasted that substituting 20% of U.S. domestic business travel could save 190,000 barrels of oil per day by 1985 and that if half of all U.S. office workers worked in neighborhood office centers, 238,000 barrels of oil per day could be saved by 1985.

While there are already perhaps thousands of teleworkers in the United States, forecasters have estimated that by 1990 this number will have increased to 10 million. Whatever that fraction of America's 100 million commuting workers will actually be, substantial savings will occur in energy consumption and in the time people currently devote to getting to and from the office.

An Electronic U.S.

The United States is already an electronic nation; the technology needed for teleworking is either already here or on the way. Today, 98% of U.S. households have television sets. More than 180 million telephones, over which Americans place more than a quarter of a billion phone calls per day, link the nation. The country has five million computers, and that number is growing by 25% per year. More than a million computers are being manufactured per year at an average cost of $300 or less, and that cost is on a continuing decline.

Fortune magazine reported last year that one in five American white-collar workers has an electronic keyboard device. By 1986, only one in five will *not* have a device, an increase from 10 million key-

boards to 40 million in just five years.

Fortune also reported that fewer than one in five desk-top, or "home," computers is used exclusively in the home. Half are used both at home and work. Perhaps the "home" computer is better named a "swing" computer, since many workers carry their terminals to and from the office.

With continued stress on increased productivity, American business will serve as a driving force to provide the tools and skills a worker will need to "produce" electronically and remotely.

Substantial growth rates are also projected for the interactive (two-way) electronic media. Marketing and trade publications are filled with optimistic forecasts. For example, *Broadcasting* magazine reports that while in 1982 videotex users in the United States probably numbered about 10,000 (and the great majority of them were involved in trials and tests), by 1990 45% of all U.S. homes will probably be served by videotex and teletext, which will become a $5 to $10 billion business.

Will Society Accept It?

While the technology already exists, the acceptance of teleworking will depend upon the social climate of the 1980s. Social researcher Florence Skelly believes that the

current climate in the United States is favorable to the acceptance and adoption of teleworking. In an address to the World Future Society's 1982 assembly, Skelly discussed the evident adoption of a new set of values in the 1980s that point toward the emergence of an interactive communications society. She identified a series of "discontinuities" now occurring—ways in which society is changing from the sixties and seventies. Skelly sees the eighties as characterized by:

- A re-emphasis on the home.
- A return to faith in technology.
- More focus on the future.
- More concern for the quality of life.
- A resurgence of Americans' historical pioneer spirit—their willingness to experiment with new things.

These new attitudes and goals held by the American public are quite consistent with the emerging world of teleworking and the electronic cottage. For instance, the re-emphasis on home life fits in well with working at home, as does greater faith in the technology needed to do so.

Despite its advantages, however, there will be many problems to consider and overcome for teleworking to succeed.

Technological Problems

While there seems to be general agreement that the hardware needed to perform remote office work via telecommunications offers no barriers, this is less true of software.

The lack of appropriate software programs has already slowed the acceptance of personal computers. Many of the software packages available today are far from user-friendly. They presuppose a skill and analytical ability many computer novices lack.

But new computer stores are opening at a rapid rate, as much to sell software as to sell computers. (Programs Unlimited, for example, today markets about 600 programs for top-selling microcomputers.)

When a microcomputer has been on the market for some time, third parties begin to produce software packages for it. VisiCalc™, the first "gold record" in the software area (with more than 30,000 copies sold to date), is believed to be directly responsible for the sale of more than 20,000 Apple computers.

But the current lack of user-friendliness is further complicated when the work-related usage requires access to the data bases of a firm. Using various data bases can often be quite complicated, as on-line data bases are intangible and heterogeneous, with different subject coverage, access languages, and structures.

One can imagine the greater needs of the teleworker—often removed from instructions and reference resources, and even from the company's computer experts, who can simply answer the worker's questions. This is but one example of the special support the tele-

worker will need to perform efficiently and effectively.

Other problems connected with the technology might include complex legal issues. Information providers, system operators, and users will have to anticipate questions of liability for information they handle and ensure that their contracts include adequate indemnity. For many issues, the legal environment is uncertain. Many of the questions being raised are brand new.

Societal Barriers

There can be a wide range of problems with setting up a home office. These problems may be simple—such as finding adequate room for the worker's electronic tools—or more difficult—such as changing family roles when both parents are home full time or when the father works and parents at home while the mother works out-of-home.

For example, a recent *New York Times* article identified the dangers of what it called "the electronic sweatshop." The article dealt with how the new telecommunications technology is eroding the bargaining power of white-collar workers because their work can be more easily transferred elsewhere—a phenomenon already dubbed "tele-scabbing." And although computer

The Quest for Computer Literacy

The quest for computer literacy is, and will continue to be, the main impetus behind the explosion in home computer sales, says a new report from International Resource Development, Inc., a market research firm based in Norwalk, Connecticut. While many are buying home computers to play video games or to provide their children with the newest learning tool, the study estimates that from 50 to 80 million people will purchase home computers this decade for the sole purpose of learning to use them.

Importing Workers by Satellite

New communications technologies mean many jobs can be performed virtually anywhere, and the implications of this development are just beginning to unfold. Workers can now even be imported—and jobs exported—without the need for anyone to cross national borders. Satellite Data Corporation in New York City is now offering clients the services of experienced data-entry and word-processing personnel—in Barbados. The company can do so by transmitting handwritten, dictated, and other documents via satellite, using compressed audio tapes and facsimile machines that can reproduce the documents virtually instantaneously in the West Indies—where workers, inexpensive by U.S. standards, type or key the data into computers. The keyed data is then returned via satellite to its source, in a form that can be used in computers or printed out.

U.S. DEPARTMENT OF ENERGY

The rush of traffic in and out of the city is repeated twice a day in many countries. Teleworking can reduce traffic and fuel consumption. One study found that the relative energy consumption advantage of commuting by telecommunications rather than by car is at least 29 to 1.

work can be praised for the flexible work-at-home hours it offers operators, some unions are damning it as a convenient way for companies to avoid paying benefits, since they can treat at-home workers as part-time employees.

Worse still, critics say, is that some work can be (and already is being) transported outside the United States to workers in Caribbean countries—workers who operate at well below U.S. wage scales.

Office workers in general are less organized than factory workers and are largely unaware of many management practices that can be counterproductive to employment and wage increases. Working at home may increase their isolation.

Before instituting teleworking, many firms will want to study how ideas develop and how this process will change in the work-at-home environment.

An in-depth review in the *AIA Journal* (July 1982) examined the change in operations created by electronic information. The authors found that when people no longer have to expend the time and effort to come together in a central place in order to work cooperatively on a project, the chances for gain in individual efficiency and quality are tremendous, but the risk of loss of overall organizational effectiveness is even greater.

The authors went on to postulate that few large complete ideas are the product of a single brain. They are more often the accretion of many smaller ideas that are combined, modified, and shuffled to become the great idea that brings about new products, improved products, and new uses of existing products. The many small ideas that grow into a major concept are not those that come from outside consultants, but those that result from communication between fellow workers involved in the same and allied projects.

One could argue that computer conferencing might provide the necessary collegiality, albeit remotely. But the long-term consequences of using teleworking to separate "thinkers" are perhaps considerable, and the potential impacts should be carefully studied.

Marketing Problems

Today's information explosion is aptly labeled. An ever increasing amount of office time is spent in collecting, processing, writing about, or verbalizing information. Effective handling of this load demands increasing productivity, which can be achieved by applying technology to the office environment. Automated offices using telecommunications media, data processing, and computers will conserve resources, improve reliability and consistency of the product, and increase productivity.

Brian Carne of GTE Labs discussed the expected rates of adoption of information-processing technology at the World Future Society's 1982 conference, "Communications and the Future." Carne pointed out that "market pull" drives the development of the automated office. However, business's interest in conserving funds and manpower does not apply in the home. The "wired household," according to Carne, is currently driven by "technology push," and its adoption is therefore not expected to keep pace with the development of the automated office. Marketers will have to be convinced first of the size and potential of the market. Then they will have to discover how to position their products and services and determine what benefits will convince decision-making managers of the advantages of teleworking. At the same time, the marketers of the equipment and services will have to begin to convince the workers themselves of the benefits of teleworking. Carne forecasts that without "market pull," the wired household will trail the wired business by more than five years. And even in business the move to automation still is not substantially established, according to Carne.

These barriers—in technology, in society, and in marketing—support my view that the adoption of teleworking will be more gradual than the optimistic forecasts that seem to receive banner notices these days suggest.

A Scenario for Teleworking

Regardless of the pace of its introduction and the problems surrounding its development, there will probably be a great deal of teleworking over the next two decades, involving a sizable portion of the 100 million commuting Americans.

The pattern of teleworking will be flexible rather than rigid. The majority of teleworking will not be a full week's activity. Teleworkers will probably work two or three days at home and the balance of the week in the office or at regionally located work centers. (Depending on the nature of the work, or the worker's habits, the pattern might be two or three weeks a month divided in the same fashion.)

Not all workers will become teleworkers. Certain industries and certain functions within a firm will be more conducive to teleworking conversion. Certainly information

ELLEN DUDLEY

Futurists Buckminster Fuller, J.C. Kapur, and Edward Cornish (left to right) converse before the opening ceremony of the World Future Society's 1982 General Assembly. Such a "meeting of the minds" stimulates the production of new ideas; teleworking—which keeps colleagues physically separated from each other—may not be as productive of new ideas.

Work in the Information Society: What the Experts Say

By the year 2000, about one-third of the work force in industrialized countries will be teleworking—using telecommunications rather than transportation to link themselves with central worksites—while half of all managers and executives will use electronic work stations themselves.

These predictions for an increasingly electronic work force were among those made by a panel of 16 of the world's leading futurists at the close of the World Future Society's Fourth General Assembly last July.

The international panel, which included such well-known futurists as Yoneji Masuda, one of Japan's leading futurists; Marvin Cetron, author of *Encounters with the Future;* and Barbara Marx Hubbard, president of Futures Network, predicted that 71% of the labor force in industrialized countries will work in the information and communications sector of the economy by the year 2000, a large increase from the estimated 50-55% today.

Contributing to the move toward the information society will be a more computer-literate population, who will increasingly use electronic devices to conduct financial transactions such as banking and shopping.

This shift is likely to cause some trauma, however, as the panel predicted that more than a third of the work force will experience significant disruptions of their jobs due to the increased use of robotics.

The panelists used the Consensor to make their predictions before a large audience at the Assembly's closing ceremonies. The Consensor allows each panelist to "vote" privately using hand-held terminals; it then gathers and averages the votes and immediately displays them on a screen in the form of a bar graph, permitting the audience to see the average or consensus prediction and the degree of agreement among the panelists.

The Consensor showed that there was little agreement among the panelists on some issues affecting the future of work in industrialized countries. For example, although the consensus prediction was that there is a better than even chance of a severe worldwide depression by the year 2000, four panelists believed that it is a virtual certainty while three felt there is very little chance. On the question of the likelihood of a breakdown in the international monetary system, panelists' predictions ranged from no chance to a 90% chance.

Panelists were more certain of the companies that will lead the way into the information society. AT&T was voted most likely to succeed in the battle over the office of tomorrow, followed by IBM and "Japan, Inc." The futurists did believe, however, that there was a 58% chance that the new, smaller communications companies will cause severe problems for AT&T, and that Japanese companies will have as enormous an impact on communications and computer industries as they have had on automobiles and TVs.

workers, who have grown from a small 5% of the work force in 1860 to 47% of the work force in 1980, will be teleworking oriented. This will also probably be true for the service-sector workers, who will have been conditioned to working with keyboards and screens and will accept more readily the idea that since their information sources are most often remote, their work can be done as effectively out-of-office.

Other patterns will develop as teleworking is incorporated into new functions. There will be those who will be able to work remotely with little need for face-to-face interaction or direct supervision. There will be others whose tasks will be enriched by live, personal interaction. And this pattern will be further affected by the use of tele-conferencing and computer conferencing, which provide still more options.

I do not expect teleworking to explode in the United States; rather, it will probably evolve at a pace determined by a host of interrelated factors. Generally, conditions are right for that growth to occur. Some of the factors that will favor the growth of teleworking are:

• Further increases in the number and percentage of information workers.

• The increased use of and familiarity with computers, which are becoming more user-friendly, and software that is more available, affordable, and understandable.

• The maturation of the telecommunications and microelectronic industries.

• The continued crisis in energy supplies.

• A continued resurgence of the home as a focal point for activities of all kinds.

As I have tried to illustrate by the use of a few examples, many problems and critical issues will arise with this growth and in many instances be unique to teleworking. These issues and others will have to be dealt with—by courts, by corporations, by management operations, by communities, by family structures, and by individuals. Their resolution may be simple or extremely costly and complex. Surely they will affect the speed and the extent of the spread of teleworking.

Information is indeed becoming available "in all places at all times." As Nobel laureate Herbert Simon recently wrote, "We've moved from a world in which information was very scarce to one where information is abundant. What is scarce is not information, but attention to information." Telecommunications and computational power may help to establish this universal availability. But to get to it, society must adjust to and accept changing roles and modes of living.

About the Author

Peter F. Eder is director of marketing communications for GTE Corporation, One Stamford Forum, Stamford, Connecticut 06904.

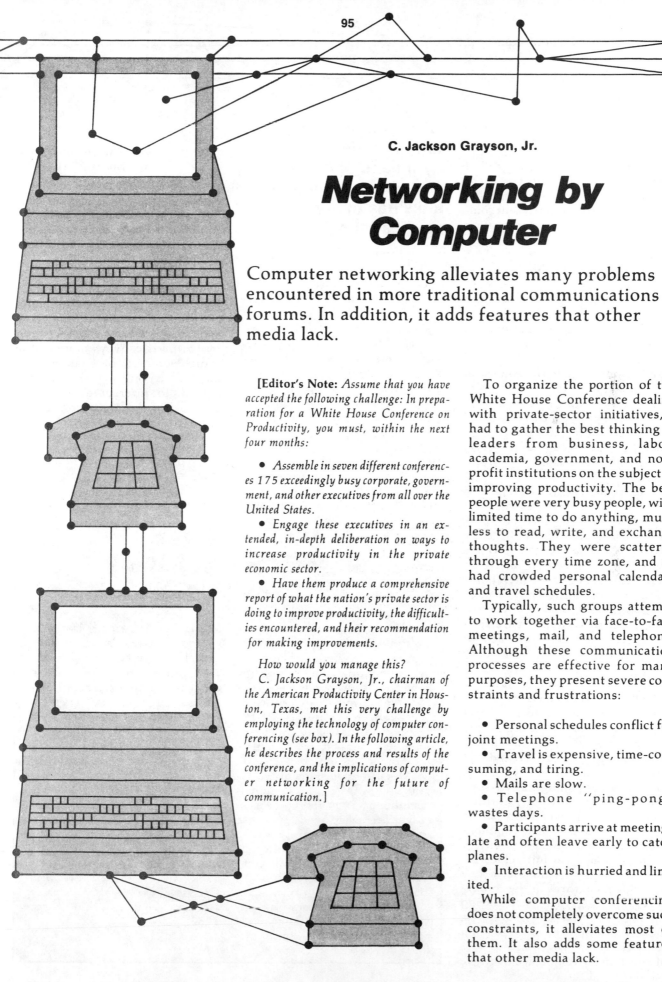

C. Jackson Grayson, Jr.

Networking by Computer

Computer networking alleviates many problems encountered in more traditional communications forums. In addition, it adds features that other media lack.

[Editor's Note: *Assume that you have accepted the following challenge: In preparation for a White House Conference on Productivity, you must, within the next four months:*

• *Assemble in seven different conferences 175 exceedingly busy corporate, government, and other executives from all over the United States.*

• *Engage these executives in an extended, in-depth deliberation on ways to increase productivity in the private economic sector.*

• *Have them produce a comprehensive report of what the nation's private sector is doing to improve productivity, the difficulties encountered, and their recommendation for making improvements.*

How would you manage this?

C. Jackson Grayson, Jr., chairman of the American Productivity Center in Houston, Texas, met this very challenge by employing the technology of computer conferencing (see box). In the following article, he describes the process and results of the conference, and the implications of computer networking for the future of communication.]

To organize the portion of the White House Conference dealing with private-sector initiatives, I had to gather the best thinking of leaders from business, labor, academia, government, and non-profit institutions on the subject of improving productivity. The best people were very busy people, with limited time to do anything, much less to read, write, and exchange thoughts. They were scattered through every time zone, and all had crowded personal calendars and travel schedules.

Typically, such groups attempt to work together via face-to-face meetings, mail, and telephone. Although these communication processes are effective for many purposes, they present severe constraints and frustrations:

• Personal schedules conflict for joint meetings.
• Travel is expensive, time-consuming, and tiring.
• Mails are slow.
• Telephone "ping-pong" wastes days.
• Participants arrive at meetings late and often leave early to catch planes.
• Interaction is hurried and limited.

While computer conferencing does not completely overcome such constraints, it alleviates most of them. It also adds some features that other media lack.

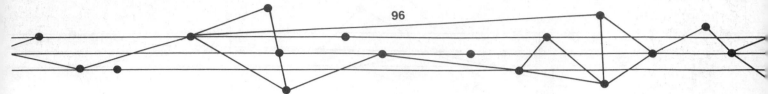

Via the Electronic Information Exchange System (EIES) based at the New Jersey Institute of Technology, the 175 participants were organized into seven different computerized conferences: cooperation in the workplace, health care, information workers, quality, reward systems, technology, and training. Most of the conference members had no prior experience with a computer. They had never "keyboarded" inputs, manipulated disks, or operated a printer.

Initially, therefore, almost all participants came to the American Productivity Center in Houston to set their computer-conference discussion agenda and to be trained on the computer and the conferencing system. A computer system was then made available to each of them.

The conferencing system was "on line" seven days a week for about 23 hours a day, with the bulk of its use occurring in the early morning and late evening. Some participants "signed on" daily—as many as three or four times. Some used it every other day, others several times a week. Only a few never used the system at all, effectively dropping out for lack of participation. For most, the amount of "connect" time was unusually high, given their demanding schedule of other activities.

Every conference had a moderator whose role was to stimulate the group, to help set the initial agenda for discussion, to guide and direct the discussion as it moved along, to synthesize thoughts, to keep participants mindful of priorities, and—finally—to act as ramrod and slave-driver to get the recommendations out and the report written.

In addition to the initial face-to-face meetings in Houston, a few participants in three of the conferences met together once during the process to discuss issues. The moderators met once in Houston to assess their progress. But 95% of the activity took place over the

"Bringing people together electronically by means of computers and communication links has many applications."

electronic network from computer terminals, most of which were located in the participants' homes.

Those who began with the terminals in their offices soon took them home. A few who traveled borrowed terminals of friends in other cities or carried portable terminals to remain in daily communication. Some even took their terminals overseas.

In 100 days of electronic dialogue, the seven conferences generated 2,170 conference comments, 12,700 private messages, and 177,335 lines of communica-

tion, all of which were condensed into a 150-page final report.

More Than Conferencing

The term *computer conference* implies that the only purpose of linking people via this technology is to conduct a conference. This is not so. Bringing people together electronically by means of computers and communication links has many applications. Hence, the term *computer networks* conveys more of the actual potential of enabling numerous busy individuals, widely dispersed, to interact over an extended period of time for a variety of purposes:

- To exchange information.
- To generate and exchange ideas and innovations.
- To work together on a common project.

What Is Computer Conferencing?

Computer conferencing is a system for linking people together, using personal computers, communication technology, and conference software. Office or home terminals are connected through telephone lines to communications satellites, which in turn are linked to a central computer.

Messages are transmitted via the computer to the terminals of other participants. These messages are displayed on video screens and may be reproduced in hard copy on a printer. A cumulative record of all communications is available for review at any time.

Computer conferencing differs significantly from "real time" audio or video conferenc-

ing, since participants can take or add messages at their individual convenience. It also differs from electronic mail, since conferencing software facilitates group "dialogue" via message storing, search and retrieval, editing, cross-referencing, and report writing.

Three resources on the subject of computer networking are: *The Network Nation* by Starr Roxanne Hiltz and Murray Turoff (Addison-Wesley, 1982); *Computer-Mediated Communication Systems* by Elain Kerr and Starr Roxanne Hiltz (Academic Press, 1982); and *The Network Revolution: Confessions of a Computer Scientist* by Jacques Vallee (And/Or Press, 1982).

NETWORKING

- To disseminate information rapidly and receive feedback.
- To exchange opinions and interact.
- To unite in seeing a common goal.
- To learn.
- To search for compromise, consensus, and majority positions.
- To obtain commitment.
- To improve decisions.

Computer networking is not a complete replacement for the more traditional methods of face-to-face meetings, mail, telephone, telegram, telex, and publications. Often, in fact, it can be used more powerfully in conjunction with many of these. But neither is computer networking a mere extension of older methods—any more than the impact of airplanes is limited to "getting there faster."

Most people presume that the ultimate and best form of meeting is face-to-face. While this unquestionably has advantages that can never be duplicated, there are also some disadvantages that people often forget:

- Typically, a small group of people dominates the discussion.
- Only one person can speak at one time. Others are reduced to passive states, often thinking other things.
- Crowded agendas usually cause some items to be dropped out, especially near the end of the meeting.
- Verbal people tend to dominate the discussion, and persons with senior rank are typically deferred to.

Similar disadvantages can be named by almost everyone for the other traditional forms of communication and linkage: "telephone tag," mail delays, and unread stacks of publications.

Computer networks are not The Answer either, but they can overcome or mitigate some of the deficiencies of some of the other methods, and they have some dis-

"The conference structure, in its simplest form, can be learned in several hours."

---

tinct advantages because of both the hardware and software:

- Reduction of travel.
- Reduction of telephone tag.
- A permanent written record of all discussions and convenient, quick access to prior comments.
- "Asynchronous" communication, meaning that people can use the system at a time convenient for them.
- Increased group resources (more people are available who otherwise could not participate).
- Different communication linkages—cross-groups, and more lateral links within and outside organizations.
- Increased equality of participation.
- Increased ability to collect quick information, data, group opinions, and surveys.
- Faster dissemination of news, data, updates, abstracts, etc.
- Increased quality of participation due to time for reflection and some research before response.
- Greater sense of community with people even though geographically widely dispersed, or even in different fields and institutions.
- Tailoring of the communications process to meet a group's particular characteristics, project goals, and types of participants.

Contrary to some common assumptions, the barriers to the use of computer networking are not those most commonly presumed:

- It is not necessary to understand anything about computers to learn and utilize the system.
- A person does not have to be an expert or even a fast typist to use the system.
- The conferencing structure, in its simplest form, can be learned in several hours.

As with any form of communication, there are also shortcomings and disadvantages:

- Computer networking can never entirely replace some face-to-face functions: eye contact, non-verbal communications, instant response to comments, press-the-flesh emotional contacts.
- People can more easily fail to respond to someone's comment or question.
- Dialogue among participants can drift more easily.
- Some can just "drop out" of the conference with little effect.
- Electronic communications have a greater chance to be misunderstood than face-to-face dialogue.

However, for many group activities, computer networking can be useful and productive in the accomplishment of their task. Usage is already expanding as more people experience the process, and several forces are accelerating this trend:

- Declining cost and widespread use of personal computers.
- Declining cost and increased availability/reliability of communications networks.
- Increased sophistication of computer networking software.
- Growing "user friendliness" of computers and communications.
- Increased time and travel demands on overworked executives.
- A growing recognition in the notion of the need for integrative, team-oriented work relationships.

Possible Uses of Computer Networking

- Applications are growing. And more are being added. The following are some suggestions as to possible uses of computer networking by various institutions.

Industry Associations

- More closely connecting key members of their association (board members, committee members, study groups).

• Carrying out committee project assignments.

• Conducting surveys for guiding association work, and for giving information to policy makers.

• Collecting quick guidance/data from members on special issues or projects.

• Disseminating selected publications and data to members.

• Collecting financial and productivity information, analyzing, and disseminating to members on an index basis.

• Responding to members with on-line requests for information, data.

Firms

• Linking corporate officers with divisional managers (beyond electronic mail).

• Linking plant managers/foremen across plants to share common problems and disseminate ideas.

• Facilitating the work of a task force or company project.

• Linking technical people together across plants and divisions.

• Providing a network relationship among members who share the same function in different company divisions (e.g., personnel, quality, marketing, etc.).

• Linking members of productivity committees, councils, and involvement teams.

• Linking corporations to associations, legislative services, data bases in an interactive mode.

Professional Societies

• Planning quarterly and annual meetings.

• Joining professionals together (as ARPANET has done) to have geographically dispersed groups function in a tightly knit professional relationship.

• Holding some "meetings" via computer network, including some

"As more groups use computer networking, more applications are found. The challenge is to fit the medium to the particular need."

participation from international members.

• Manuscript collection, editing, discussion, review, and dissemination.

• Special conferences and sub-conferences on knowledge areas, research topics, and public-policy issues.

• Membership contacts and services.

• Dissemination of data, professional society news, legislative reports, abstracts, etc.

Governmental

• Elected officials communicating with geographically dispersed constituents on a regular or continuing basis.

• Conferences on special topics for mayors, governors, city managers to share ideas, data, develop recommendations.

• Opinion surveys and referenda on issues.

• Shared productivity-improving information among public officials across the nation in departmental lines (e.g., sanitation, environmental agencies, welfare agencies, police, fire, transportation, etc.).

Education and Training

• Productivity courses: short intensive courses, semester-long courses, or a year-long series of courses.

• Networks among teachers to exchange ideas, techniques, data.

• Conferences among school administrators: citywide, statewide, or national.

• National educational data bases—on line.

• Linking of training directors in firms, together with others—academics, union leaders, government officials.

As more groups use computer networking, more applications are found. The challenge is always to fit the medium to the particular need. This is best done as a participatory process of communication between those who design network systems and those who use them.

Two researchers in this field (Peter and Trudy Johnson-Lenz) use the phrase "groupware" to describe this process. It begins with the group making known its purposes, process, outputs, and barriers to be overcome. Then the computer network systems designers suggest specific structures and procedures. As Murray Turoff, designer of EIES, has observed. "We are now beginning to realize that when we design a communication structure to operate within an interactive computer system for a group of humans, what we are really designing is a human system."

About the Author

C. Jackson Grayson, Jr., is chairman of the board and founder of the American Productivity Center. He has a doctorate in business administration from Harvard Business School, has been dean of the business schools of Tulane and SMU, and served as chairman of the President's Price Commission from 1971 to 1973. His address is 123 North Post Oak Lane, Houston, Texas 77024.

The Electronic Investment System:
Making Money with Your Computer

As computer investment systems become more widespread and more sophisticated, stock and commodities brokers may find themselves on the endangered species list. One such system is described here by its creator.

The Quotrader Investment Center, developed by author Grant Renier, consists of an Apple II computer equipped with a special set of computer boards, a monitor, and a printer.

by Grant J. Renier

Until recently, a person could not hope to participate successfully in stock or commodities trading without actually being on the floor of the exchange almost constantly, ready to react quickly to sudden shifts in the direction of the market.

Today, however, thanks to the computer revolution, it is possible to make (or lose) large sums of money in commodities or stocks while sitting at a computer console. Automated investment systems are becoming so advanced and process data so quickly that they may make the advice and expertise of brokers obsolete, relegating them to the cler-

ical function of simply buying and selling. Since investors will be able to personally supervise their funds, the new technology could put brokers on the endangered species list.

There are two basic approaches to trading in commodities or stocks. One approach, called "trading on the fundamentals," focuses on the analysis of external factors (wars, droughts, political events, etc.) that either affect the market or are perceived to affect it. The other approach, called "technical trading," looks at the market itself—how many shares were bought and sold, price variations, etc. The technical

trader assumes that there are so many outside factors that it isn't very useful to try to analyze them.

The technical trading approach, with its emphasis on sophisticated statistical analyses, is ideally suited to today's high-speed "number-crunching" computers, which can handle the great masses of data so rapidly that intra-day trading (in which you buy something and sell it later the same day) has at last become feasible for anyone with access to such computer power.

The Quotrader System

Over the last several years, I have been developing a personal investment center that combines this advanced computer technology with absolute ease of operation, so that people can handle their own market operations at home with maximum convenience and efficiency.

The system, called the Quotrader Investment Center, has two key elements: an ordinary Apple II desktop computer and a set of computer boards that can be simply and easily installed in the Apple II housing. Receiving raw market data from telephone lines, cable TV, or directly from a communications satellite, it provides the user with continuous market price quotes, up-to-the-minute bar charts, automatically generated buy and sell orders, and dynamic accounting. Quotrader is at present only equipped to deal with the commodities market, but in the near future will offer the same services to stock traders.

One of the primary objectives of the Quotrader system is to plug the user directly into the action at the various exchanges on a "real-time" basis. To have this on-the-spot capability, the private trader must be linked to a computer that, under the guidance of well-designed trading systems, can react instantaneously to changes in the market.

This whole approach marks a significant departure from the routine

use of computers in trading in the markets. Up to now, computer programs have been designed to analyze daily price fluctuations after the markets have closed, generating stop orders to be placed in the market for the next trading day. (A stop order is an order to sell if a stock or commodity goes down by a certain amount; for example, you may buy stock at $10 a share and instruct your broker to sell if the stock drops to $8 a share.) By contrast, the Quotrader system is interactive with the market; because it continuously tracks and analyzes price changes as they occur, stop orders are no longer needed as protection in the market. Instead, stop prices are handled as part of the internal functioning of the computer, which automatically generates market orders for you at the appropriate times.

This swift, highly responsive trading has two major advantages: first, you no longer risk publicizing your planned trades through the use of stop orders; second, the computer power of electronic trading systems can spot the early phases of any trends that may develop each trading day.

A Good Trading System

An essential component of any successful investment plan is a good trading system. One of the many features of the Quotrader system is the Technical Trading Program (TTP), which is one of a library of trading systems available in the form of silicon chips to be inserted in the Quotrader computer boards.

There are two main types of technical trading systems:

Projective systems try to analyze current price data in order to predict what price a commodity or security will reach in the future—days, weeks, or months ahead. Using this analysis, the investor decides whether to buy, sell short, or obtain an option to buy at a later date. (To sell short means to borrow stocks or commodities from your brokerage firm and sell them in anticipation that the price will be lower by the time you have to buy them back and return them to the broker.)

Reactive systems, on the other hand, try to react to changes in the market as they occur, developing a set of protective price limits ("stops")

The floor of the New York Stock Exchange may become less frantic, thanks to the sophisticated computer investment systems now becoming available that allow a trader to react immediately to changes in the market as they occur—without leaving his home.

that will be in effect for a short period—a week, a day, or even less than a day. A reactive system is normally a very fast way to trade. For readers who are unfamiliar with the fine points, here is how the stops work:

Taking a long position (with the object of buying low and selling high) in a commodity (or stock) means you are anticipating that the commodity will go up; therefore the two protective stops that a reactive system generates for you can be thought of as a double floor. As long as the price keeps going up, you do not care about the floor; but if it goes down, it will hit the first (and maybe the second) of these protec-

tive stops, triggering some action. At the first such stop, Quotrader will beep to alert you and then display a sell order on the CRT screen. If the price keeps dropping to or through the second stop, Quotrader will alert you again with an order to sell short.

Conversely, when you start out with a short position in a commodity (or stock), the two protective stops that a reactive system will generate for you can be likened to a double ceiling. If the price goes up enough to hit the first (lower) stop, it will trigger a buy order to cover your short position. If it keeps on going up to hit the second "ceiling," it will trigger a second buy order and put you "long" in the market. The speed with which these things happen will depend on the "fine-tuning" of your reactive system. In the third situation—where you are out of the market for a particular commodity—a reactive system will still generate two stops, but the stops will bracket the current price. Thus, price movement can trigger either a buy order or a sell (short) order to get you into the market, depending upon which way the commodity moves.

When people criticize technical trading methods in general, they are usually talking about projective systems, noting quite correctly that past zigs and zags in a price curve offer no solid basis for predicting future zags and zigs. It is my firm conviction that most of the successful technical trading systems are reactive.

One concern that critics sometimes express is: "What if a great many traders use these systems? If too many people got identical buy or sell signals from electronic trading systems, could the brokers be swamped by orders all at the same price, and would this affect the normal operation of the market?" If you have wondered about this, you can relax. It is not going to be a problem, no matter how popular such systems become, because the systems can be "customized." With Quotrader, for example, you can select a time interval for managing each commodity in your portfolio—anywhere from one minute to 225 minutes. This interval determines the rate at which price data is fed to the trading systems. The chances are remote that more than a few other users will ever choose exactly the same time (such as 87 minutes) for the same contract (or securities).

Capital Management

Once you have a good trading system, the second requisite for successful investing in the market is proper administration of your funds. The Money Management Program (MMP) contained within the Quotrader system is an important part of this administration, which also must include attention to important details such as "coverage" and taking money out of an investment program for other uses.

"Coverage" refers to the amount of cash in your program in relation to the margin requirement for commodities. (The margin requirement is the "down payment," usually 5% for commodities, that you have to pay your broker in order to gain control of a much larger investment.) To start off, not more than one-third of your total equity should be margined (or invested, in the case of stocks). Keep the rest liquid at first, perhaps in money-market funds. There are two good reasons for this:

• From time to time, you will be getting recommendations from the MMP to increase your position in a given commodity, so you will need ready cash to take advantage of those recommendations.

• You must have cash on hand to meet margin calls. (A margin call is when the value of a stock or commodity decreases and your broker calls on you to put up more money; for example, if you buy stock for $10,000, you pay $5,000—a 50% margin—and borrow the other $5,000 from the broker, with the stock serving as collateral for the loan; if the value of the stock drops to $8,000, the broker may call on you to come up with another $1,000.) Research by the Trenomics Corporation indicates that a two-to-one coverage (cash to margin) is appropriate.

This guideline is not engraved in stone, but given the leverage inherent in futures trading, it can produce outstanding returns from a relatively low-risk investment.

Many investment plans forget that the goal of investing is not to blindly keep on amassing capital forever. After all, you never see a Brinks truck in a funeral procession. We believe that profits are to be enjoyed, and the MMP is designed to signal you at the opportune moments to remove profits from the system, just as it will signal you at the advantageous times to increase your position in a particular commodity or security. When the MMP gives you the chance, you should skim off some of the gravy—once a quarter and, perhaps, even more frequently.

How do you recognize signals from the MMP, as distinct from the regular trading recommendations from Quotrader?

• MMP recommendations to increase your position are identified on the hard-copy printout of a buy order (or sell-short order) as coming from the MMP.

• MMP recommendations to remove profits (by selling if you are long, or buying if you are short) are also identified in the printout as coming from the MMP.

Discipline is the final aspect of effective investing. In this regard, the secret of success is to learn to detach yourself emotionally from the market. It is difficult, if not impossible, to preserve your objectivity and good judgment if you become overly emotional about your investments.

Once you have a good investment plan, a balanced portfolio, and a reliable trading system, detachment will help you to stick with them faithfully. In terms of Quotrader operations, this means following through on the recommendations from the trading system—not trying to second-guess it. By all means keep your records up-to-date on a daily basis, but do not agonize over the morning news; do not spring into action every time you see a little jump in prices; and do not read the *Wall Street Journal* from cover to cover, anxiously scrabbling for nuggets of financial wisdom. "Hang loose" and give the system a chance.

Conceivably, the only further need the users of the available computer technology will have for stock or commodities brokers is simply executing the computer-generated order to buy or sell—a purely clerical function. Want to know a secret? We are working on that!

About the Author

Grant J. Renier is president of Trenomics Corporation. In addition to developing the Quotrader and several other stock and commodities systems, he has lectured around the world concerning commodities and commodities trading systems; is a feature-article writer for *Commodities* magazine; and writes a quarterly newsletter for his clients. His address is: 257 North Greene Street, Greensboro, North Carolina 27401.

STEVE POSTMAN

Jim Rubens

Retooling American Democracy

> The American system of government has an unhealthy tendency to perpetuate the status quo well beyond its useful life, changing only in response to crisis. An improved form of democracy could be created— one that would be more responsive to the will of the people and more efficiently administered.

The two-centuries-old system of American democracy has become a victim of its old age. Public alienation and disenfranchisement from and mistrust of the national government have become recurrent themes of the past decade. The federal government is essentially a patched-up antique sputtering and creaking with increasing difficulty through a highly complex, fast-paced, and often erratically changing world.

Consider the American political system's inordinate difficulties with the Social Security system. After a year of study, a presidential commission finally determined the obvious—that Social Security payments will exceed revenues by up to $200 billion over this decade. Immediately prior to this finding, politicians could garner both respect and votes by claiming that no problem existed. The possible solutions floated out have proven deeply upsetting to large segments of the population. Debate and decision have therefore been bottled up until crisis backs American democracy into a corner. And action during that crisis will probably not be optimal.

But Social Security is only one example. Government is being progressively crippled by a syndrome of persistent political paralysis and lurching change in response only to crisis.

The proposed remedies for this outmoded governmental system usually rely on patchwork and new, but not materially different, faces. Even public-interest organizations such as Common Cause, which recognize the need for structural changes, limit their recommendations to incremental tinkering.

As American Telephone and Telegraph used to advertise, "the system is the solution." But with American government, it is also the problem. The system's problems are fundamental; so must be the solutions. Democracy itself, like the American auto industry, is due for a retooling to function in a different world.

A better-designed democracy would end the present system's unhealthy tendency to prolong the status quo well beyond its useful life. A redesigned democracy would yield speedier, more timely decisions by reducing the power of elected representatives who are excessively motivated by short-term political considerations. A better-designed democracy would not frustrate citizen initiative.

A better system would recognize that government activity consists of two major functions—policy-making and the administration of policy—that should remain relatively independent. Improving the two functions requires different approaches and different goals.

The standards for improved *policy-making* should be timeliness, responsiveness to change, and neutrality in effects other than those intended. *Administration* of policies should become far more efficient with respect to both public and private money and resources.

Two New Ways to Make Policy

To formulate better policies, decision-makers need to be better apprised of both public opinion and technical fact. Many public policy questions, such as abortion rights, legalization of marijuana, regulation of roadside billboards, or handgun control, relate directly to people's moral and aesthetic sensibilities. Too often, as has happened with these four issues, the will of the public has been badly diluted and distorted by elected representation. Such value-laden questions would be best decided by direct public referenda.

Fortunately, electronic referenda are already possible with present technology. Within 10 to 20 years, almost all American households will be linked into a two-way video/communications/computer/text printing network. Electronic, computer-assisted referenda would be easy to run and would become quite inexpensive. Computer referenda could be used frequently to make fine policy distinctions.

In such a system, citizens would petition electronically for a referendum. To attract sufficient petitioners, individuals or interest groups would use person-to-person persuasion or the media, exactly as they build constituencies at present. Petitioners would be required to convince some minimum percentage of the electorate, in the vicinity of five to fifteen percent, to sign up.

A successful petition would be followed by a period of public debate. For complex or ill-defined questions, successive options or issues focusing votes could be taken. Various interest groups would write position papers for distribution through the electronic network. The democratic network would provide automatic alerts to voting timetables, availability of position papers, or opportunities to engage in or witness public debates.

Bibliographies, abstracts, and libraries relating to questions at hand would be available through the network to anyone at any time. To the

How did Reagan's speech leave you feeling about economic recovery?

1. Optimistic 79%
2. Neutral 14%
3. Pessimistic 7%

WARNER AMEX QUBE POLL

QUBE/WARNER AMEX

Results of an interactive cable TV poll gauging public response to a State of the Union message by President Reagan flash on the screen. Cable systems, which allow the public to express its opinions instantly, could be used for electronic referenda that would allow direct democracy on heavily value-laden questions, says the author.

fullest extent of their capabilities and interests, citizens could easily participate in all phases of a referendum process. If political decisions were based more on the persuasiveness of the groups involved, the system would attract outstanding advocates. This better talent would then lead to better policy. (For a number of successful examples of electronic referenda, see "Teledemocracy: Bringing Power Back to People" by Ted Becker, THE FUTURIST, December 1981.)

Value-Free Decisions

Referenda, though well suited to value-dependent questions, are entirely unsuited to scientific and technical questions of fact. Experts, representatives of countervailing bodies of thought, and affected parties are the ones who should participate in the decision process on technical questions. How to control acid rain, what methods can control interest rates or inflation, which new energy forms are likely to yield returns on taxpayer research and development subsidies, or what strategic minerals to inventory are examples of primarily, although not wholly, technical questions.

A model for an improved value-free or technical decision-making process is the environmental impact review procedure mandated by the National Environmental Policy Act of 1969 (NEPA). NEPA requires that all major federal actions potentially affecting the environment be preceded by an alternatives-finding and analysis exercise. It guarantees opportunities for public comment and requires substantive government responses to the comments. The flaw in the NEPA process is that the government agency often ignores ultimate factual determinations and makes decisions heavily biased toward its original plans.

An improved value-free decision process could also be modeled generally after the "Science Court," an institution first proposed 15 years ago by an engineer and National Academy of Sciences member, Arthur Kantrowitz.

The Science Court has been used to defuse scientific controversies by having a panel of impartial mediators consider all sides of a question as presented by opposing advocates.

A good value-free decision process must break issues, insofar as possible, into a hierarchy of discrete and relatively independent components. A complex question, such as deciding which, if any, energy forms should be encouraged by tax or other subsidies, would be the product of a succession of underlying value-free and value-laden decisions.

Once an independent value-free question has been identified—whether by Congress, by separation from another poorly defined question, or by citizen petition—a decision timetable would be publicized in the media, by word of mouth, and over the electronic democratic network. Citizens could participate directly in decisions relating to their specific interests.

As a first step, major parties to the value-free process would come forward and jell around various groupings of opinion. These parties would include experts, affected and involved interest groups, and voluntary activists. To ensure credibility and acceptance of the final decision, it is important not to restrict participation.

Congress and the advocates would nominate an ad-hoc panel of mediators who would ultimately be responsible for making decisions. Mediators would be certified by Congress as knowledgeable concerning the issue at hand, yet impartial and free of conflict of interest (i.e., free from association with or bias toward any of the parties or toward any anticipated decision). Mediators would then be approved or rejected by the advocates in the manner that attorneys select among jurors.

As the advocates prepare and present their positions, the mediators may determine that the question at issue requires further refinement or isolation from related questions. Advocates and mediators would subject the various advocates' testimony to detailed and unlimited scrutiny. They would identify areas of agreement. The mediators would make determinations only when the advocates could not reach agreement. The mediators would be allowed to prepare minority or dissenting reports for inclusion in the text of the majority decision.

Some decisions would not be simple positive or negative determinations, but would consist of a choice among policy options to be later decided by value-laden referenda, or of determinations of relative certainties of various outcomes. Both value-free and value-laden processes would yield decisions with the force of law.

All parties to the process would be funded by the federal government to the degree necessary to adequately prepare and present their cases. The entire process would be open to the public and the media. All groups and individuals having unique knowledge about or having a stake in a question would be guaranteed the opportunity to participate.

The Science Court Experience

From those few times it has been tested, the Science Court has shown that when divisive issues are subjected to sophisticated, open-ended scrutiny, diverging viewpoints tend to depolarize, with many points of unsupportable disagreement quickly

"The exaggeration and eventual compromise inherent to politics force positions to extremes, but in a depoliticized decision structure where the advocates' credibility is at stake, agreement becomes less difficult."

evaporating. Controversies and ranges of options tend to narrow and decisions automatically to distill as a result simply of the structured, rational process itself. The exaggeration and eventual compromise inherent to politics force positions to extremes, but in a depoliticized decision structure where the advocates' credibility is at stake, agreement becomes less difficult.

Attempts to use the Science Court to resolve technical disputes have met with varying degrees of success. The Energy Research and Development Administration used the institution successfully in 1977 to select among 11 fusion energy research concepts competing for limited development funds.

In a more highly charged issue, the Science Court was used to modify public health policy concerning the use of X-ray examinations for detecting breast cancer. John Bailar, then of the National Cancer Institute, had been conducting a campaign to reduce mass breast cancer screenings for women under age 50. He reported that some medical organizations refused to consider the possibility that the practice may do more harm than good. Bailar found that simply announcing his intention to subject the dispute to the examination of a Science Court caused the medical establishment to drop its intransigent opposition to his proposals.

Most political questions are complexes of value-free and value-laden decisions. Resolving the problem of acid rain in Canada and the northeast U.S., for example, requires that the independent components of the decision first be segregated. Value-free questions include those of determining present and expected environmental and health effects (and their costs, where quantification is possible), and the costs and effectiveness of various control strategies. Although there would undoubtedly be vigorous disputes over these value-free questions, a techni-

cal consensus would ultimately emerge in answer to each.

However, the value-free process cannot determine the public valuation of the intangible costs of acid rain. How important is the loss of fish in the Adirondack Lakes to fishermen, to non-fishing residents of the northeast, or to midwesterners who benefit from acid rain through lower electricity costs? Random interviews relating to the issue could be used to assay and describe public opinion. More formally, a succession of issues-focusing referenda could be taken. A value-laden decision process based upon these groupings of opinion might show a majority of Americans to be appalled with a regionwide deterioration of the general environment. Or Americans might express an acceptance of the present trade-off of cheaper energy for environmental effects that don't intrude noticeably into everyday life, much as the cutting of trees and paving of earth are accepted consequences of a public preference for roads rather than footpaths.

The public will be qualified to create public policy—but *after* value-free determinations make credible and complete information widely available. The value-free decision process will keep the public continuously informed on relevant issues.

Acid rain control is one of many issues for which the needed resolution has been delayed because of the high political costs of alienating one or another interest group. When some resolution is finally reached, too many people feel that these same interest groups have exerted excessive influence.

When all parties to a question feel that their viewpoints have been adequately articulated and understood, they can better accept the ultimate decision. Alienation from government could be reduced, and minorities who do not "win" would no longer be disenfranchised.

Decisions would be more credible and would suffer fewer reversals.

"Congress and the president would play different roles in a more direct democracy. Congress's main duty would be to oversee the decision process."

Policy determinations, although always subject to change, would become more durable foundations to a more efficiently and rationally run government. Poorly-made decisions sometimes have staggeringly costly side effects—in wasted government, wasted citizen and business initiative, and wasted societal resources. Well-framed decisions and decision questions would result in policies whose effects are neutral except where intended. A well-designed process can avoid societal waste and directly boost personal wealth and national output.

These redesigned processes embrace citizen participation. Interest groups, although their participation would be fully encouraged, would not have inequitably advantageous access to the reins of government. The particular knowledge, expertise, or insight of each participating individual would be available for the nation's full benefit. Active citizens, knowing that their involvement would be welcomed, would special-

ize as voluntary government watchdogs in their fields of expertise or interest. The quality of government would rise.

Congress's Role

Congress and the president would play different roles in a more direct democracy. Congress's main duty would be to oversee the decision process. Congress would present issues for consideration by the voters, separate issues into components, and retain a veto power over what it considered to be bad decisions (with a 60 to 70% majority of both houses required for an override). Congress would require that decisions specify policy, results, standards, or goals, but leave administrators to determine methods.

Assuring that questions are precisely formulated would be Congress's most difficult and essential task. Congress would separate issues into value-free and value-laden components. For example, in making energy policy (which the present

system has been unable to accomplish despite eight years of effort), a value-related question such as whether electricity should be generated in large centralized plants or decentralized facilities would be isolated from technical questions such as costs and methods of cleaning up air pollution from coal burning. A new agricultural chemical would be licensed for use only after several independent questions had been answered. A value-free question would concern potential effects of the chemical on humans. Another would be a value-laden question fundamental to all safety regulation, but never yet posed by the current democratic process: what is the public's willingness to tolerate given levels of passive risk (for example, in the form of increased incidence of a particular type of cancer)? What is the public's valuation of an individual human life or an impairment such as loss of a leg or one's vision or hearing? Quantification of these values (as made by courts in personal injury liability cases) may allow direct comparison of total costs to total benefits. Desired levels of public safety can then be achieved in a rational, least-cost manner.

Congress would also ensure that decisions are made in a proper hierarchical sequence. Fundamental deci-

U.S. DEPARTMENT OF ENERGY

Smoke billowing into the atmosphere dramatizes concerns about pollution. In author Rubens's retooled democracy, the decision-making process would separate issues such as how to deal with pollution into value-laden questions—such as whether and how much pollution should be cleaned up or controlled—and technical questions—such as determining the costs and efficiencies of methods of pollution control.

sions and factual determinations would be completed before more detailed or dependent questions are posed. The courts would continue their present function of interpreting and reconciling laws and decisions that prove imprecise or contradictory.

National security considerations and the need to respond quickly in emergencies dictate that Congress and the president must retain exclusive powers over matters of national defense and during emergencies. However, citizens would contribute to the formulation of defense and emergency policy much more than at present.

The all-important budget-making function would continue to be the responsibility of Congress and the president. However, budget-making would no longer be the time-consuming political spectacle it is at present. The budget would no longer be government's central policy instrument. Policy would control budgets. Budget-making would consist of revising cost estimates and adjusting necessary tax receipts within some democratically determined bandwidth of acceptability. Rational government would do away with routine fiscal and monetary crisis.

Even Efficient Bureaucracy?

But government has all too often been clumsy at implementing even well-crafted policy. A second major essential for successful democracy is competent, efficient administration. Efficiency demands that intended results be generated at least cost to taxpayers and society at large. Government restrictions on and intrusion into private activity should be kept to the minimum necessary. The present lack of administrative elegance often leads to harmful side effects that outweigh desired benefits. The new 10% interest and dividends withholding tax will likely cost as much to administer as the government will gain in revenues. The American economy would benefit greatly from a government that no longer practiced such management indiscretion.

Despite its admitted defects, the best method yet demonstrated to allocate scarce resources—the free enterprise system—would be the model for an efficient administra-

"Despite its admitted defects, the best method yet demonstrated to allocate scarce resources—the free enterprise system—would be the model for an efficient administrative system."

tive system. In a classical capitalist economy, individuals seek to maximize their personal gains. Where buyers have access to full and accurate information about competitive products and where competing products are supplied by non-monopolistic sellers, prices are automatically driven down and product quality is driven up.

A "capitalist" administrative agency in a retooled democracy would have substantial latitude to select methods to achieve a clearly defined policy. Consider an agency charged with training and getting jobs for the unemployable. "Profit" for this jobs agency in a capitalist bureaucracy would not be money, of course, but permanent job placements.

Employees of the job placement agency would be hired, fired, and rewarded on the basis of demonstrated ability to create "profits." As in a well-run private business, pay scales and promotions would be granted for productivity, not longevity—results, not effort. Agency employees and management would be given freedom to experiment and innovate to find continuously improving methods of achieving "profit." As seeds sprout in moisture, entrepreneurial initiative would flourish in government bureaucracies in response to a market structuring.

Agencies may choose to contract out portions of their work to private organizations. Vermont's state employment agency, for example, contracts with private firms eager to make job placements at lower cost than the agency can. Private day-care centers and fire and police protection services have proven less costly than their public counterparts. These positive results, however, do not depend upon private contractors, but upon incentives.

In some cases, huge increases in agency productivity would be possible if proper incentive systems were put into place. Marva Collins, prin-

cipal of Chicago's highly publicized West Side Preparatory School, has proven that public school problem learners and troublemakers can be consistently transformed into highly self-motivated scholars. In Philadelphia, Falaka Fattah's Malcolm X Crime Prevention Institute has substantially reduced the city's juvenile crime and murder rates, where two decades of massively funded federal programs have achieved only marginal results. In both cases, these startlingly positive results were achieved without *any* public funds.

If such innovators in human service delivery were encouraged nationwide, an upwelling of human capital would result. "Profits" would soar. An administrator's task would be to identify and duplicate the successes of these innovators.

Agency directors would be attracted to their positions by fully competitive pay scales and professional recognition. Top pay for agency administrators at the federal level must reach levels competitive with private industry—$200,000 and even $500,000 for outstanding operating or entrepreneurial performance. Many superbly qualified managerial candidates have an altruistic desire to serve the public and would accept somewhat lower pay than for private industry, provided that professional working conditions could be guaranteed.

The President As CEO

The president's role would be adjusted to that of chief executive officer of the federal administrative system. The president's primary responsibility would be to find superior candidates to fill top government jobs. The president would promote, hire, or fire agency heads on the basis of their productivity. The president's office would provide the interface between policy and administration and would oversee long-range interagency planning.

The president's office would report to Congress and the public any flaws in and needed remedies to existing policy, along with cost and benefit estimates for major goals being considered by the decision process.

Less of a political figure and more of an administrator, the president would have a longer—perhaps even indefinite—term of office. In parliamentary fashion, a new election could be called at any time, if requested by a suitably large number of petitioners over the democratic network.

Better government would have lower thresholds of change and adaptation than does the present overly rigid American democracy. In far too many important policy matters, today's government reaches only gridlock and stalemate, often harmfully perpetuating the status quo. A more highly evolved form of democracy would react like a biological system, being driven continuously and automatically toward equilibrium with a changing environment.

The high levels of talent and ingenuity that Americans apply to art, business, technology, and science are not applied consistently enough to government. American genius is available to drive government to far higher levels of performance and achievement than at present, but only if given opportunity and rewards. A better form of democracy will avail itself of this genius. Today's challenge of leadership is to guide the necessary structural changes, avoiding the eruptive lurches that grow likely as change is deferred.

About the Author

Jim Rubens has been a citizen activist in the areas of environment, energy, and government reform for the past decade. He is a small businessman, entrepreneur, and investor. He is a public affairs columnist and radio commentator for New Hampshire Public Radio. His address is Etna Highlands Road, Etna, New Hampshire 03750.

ROGERS & COWAN, INC.

A forger may be able to copy the way a signature looks, but not the unique way in which it is written.

Forgers, Beware!

A new method of detecting a forged signature may help stop credit-card fraud. Instead of examining the way the signature *looks*, the computerized system verifies signatures by *how* they are written. Upon receiving a credit card, you would "enroll" your signature in the company's computer by signing on a template that records the speed at which you write, when your pen leaves and returns to the writing surface, and whether you dot your *i*'s and cross your *t*'s as you write them or at the end of the signature. Since a thief who tries to use your credit card will only be able to copy the way your signature *looks*—and not the unique way in which you write—the store's computer will immediately identify the attempted forgery. The system was developed by researcher Warner Scott of Texas Instruments.

James S. Albus

Robots and the Economy

Robots perform many tasks far more efficiently and economically than humans. But people will never run out of things to do, and in the "robot economy" of the future, they could receive income from stock ownership of robots and automated manufacturing systems.

Spectacular advances in microcomputers are forging new technological frontiers in robotics. It has now become practical to dedicate as many as 10 powerful computers to the control of a single robot. Robotic devices can now be made that are highly intelligent, adaptive, skilled, dexterous, and, most important of all, economically practical.

Most of the robots used in industry today are simple-minded machines that can neither see nor feel. They are typically programmed by recording each task as a series of points in space. This recording is then simply played back whenever the task is to be performed.

But the day is rapidly coming when robots will be equipped with a multitude of sensors such as vision, touch, force, and proximity. They will be able to react to sensory input and adapt to changing or unexpected conditions. And their memories will store drawings or parts and plans for assemblies, which will enable them to perform complex tasks with a minimum of instruction or supervision from humans.

During the remainder of the 1980s, robot perception and decision-making capabilities will increase many times over. The use of robots to perform a wide variety of manufacturing and assembly tasks will become commonplace. By the early 1990s, mobility systems will enable them to move about freely in unstructured environments such as shipyards, construction sites, and even natural environments such as fields, forests, air, and water.

With plans stored in their computer memory, robots in factories and construction sites will know how to cut and fit materials, how and where to construct walls, weld plates, lay pipes, paint, pour cement, and so on. These developments will dramatically lower the cost of both manufactured goods and fabricated structures.

But the most economically important development will be the to-tally automated factory. There are already a number of computer-controlled flexible manufacturing systems, which can operate overnight and on the weekend with little or no human supervision. Before the year 2000, robots and computer-controlled machines working together with computerized planning, scheduling, materials transport, inventory control, and tool management systems will be able to perform many, if not most, of the manufacturing operations that now require human skills. This could double productivity, for totally automated factories will be able to operate the equivalent of four shifts a week rather than only one or two shifts.

Automatic factories will even be capable of a significant degree of self-reproduction. Once automatic factories begin making the components for other automatic factories, each generation of machines will produce machines less costly and more sophisticated than the last. This could lead to an exponential decline in the cost of manufactured

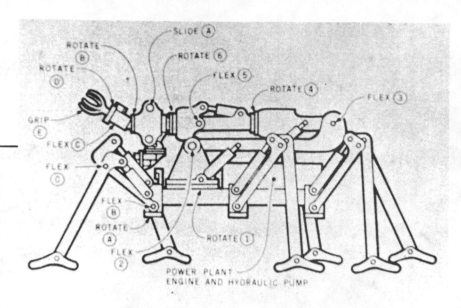

goods similar to that which has occurred in the cost of computing power over the past 30 years.

To appreciate what this might mean, consider that in 1953 a computer with 64K bytes of memory cost more than $1 million. Today, you can buy a machine with similar capabilities for around $1,000. That is a three-orders-of-magnitude decrease in cost in three decades over and above inflation.

If a similar cost reduction had occurred in the manufacturing industries, the world would be a very different place today. In 1953, a Buick automobile with the whole luxury package of options cost about $3,500. If the cost of manufactured products had followed the cost of computers, an equivalent American automobile today would retail for $3.50.

Computers are used to design, manufacture, and test other computers. In other words, computers have a degree of self-reproduction, and this accounts for, at least in part, the dramatic cost decline in computing hardware. A similar regenerative effect may occur in manufactured goods once the automatic factory becomes a widespread phenomenon.

The High Stake

This technology has far-reaching implications. The prospects for improving productivity, reducing inflation, improving economic growth, and enhancing a nation's international competitive position vis a vis its trading partners are enormous. On the other hand, the potential threat of competition from automatic factories in other places is equally important. It may be extremely difficult for industries using conventional manufacturing techniques to compete successfully with industries that are totally automated.

Some have suggested that the introduction of the computer into the manufacturing process and the spectacular and steady decline in

the cost of computing power are historic events that will someday rank with the invention of the steam engine and the discovery of electricity. Many believe that robots and automatic factories will lead to a new industrial revolution.

The first industrial revolution substituted mechanical energy for muscle power in the manufacture of goods and the production of food. This brought about an enormous increase in productivity, put an end to slavery, and freed a great mass of human beings from a life of poverty, ignorance, and endless physical toil. It also brought about profound changes in the distribution of economic and political power in the world.

The next industrial revolution will substitute computer power for brain power in the control of machines and industrial processes and will be based on robot labor. The next industrial revolution—the

Robot grips empty cola can gently, without crushing it. Industrial robots are becoming increasingly dexterous and "intelligent," says author James S. Albus.

Design for a robot construction apprentice of the future. The author predicts that, by the early 1990s, robots could have mobility systems allowing them to move about freely in construction sites, shipyards, and factories.

Robot welder at work. Spectacular new developments in robotics will help to lower manufacturing and construction costs, often more than doubling the productivity of human workers.

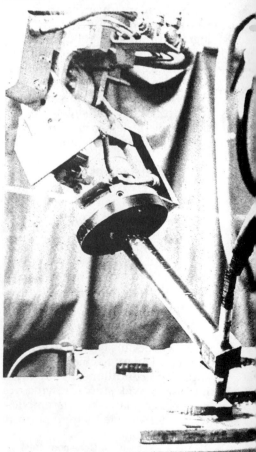

Astronauts performing tasks aboard space shuttle get help from robot arm.

NATIONAL AERONAUTICS AND SPACE ADMINISTRATION

robot revolution—could free the human race from the regimentation and mechanization imposed by the requirement for manual labor and human decision-making in factories and offices. It has the capacity to provide us with material wealth, clean energy, and the personal freedom to enjoy what could become a golden age of mankind.

Fear of Unemployment

Unfortunately, there exist major barriers to this new industrial revolution. There remain formidable technological problems that will slow the rate of implementation of robotics and automatic factories, though these technical problems are surmountable.

We have not yet come up with a good answer to the question "If robots do all the work, how are people going to get an income?" The question of unemployment, and of competition for jobs between robots and human workers, is so far unanswered. I believe this is the single most important barrier to the new industrial revolution.

The fundamental problem is that income to the average family is distributed primarily through wages and salaries. The income distribution system in America—and indeed in the entire industrialized world (including socialist and communist countries)—is based on the labor theory of value. Income is primarily determined by employment (that is, the sale of labor). This is a serious structural flaw, for it works against policies designed to upgrade productivity in the industrial system. It means that rapid increases in productivity produce, or at least are widely perceived to produce, unemployment.

Just one example of the problem is the lawsuit recently brought by the agricultural unions against the state of California because of the state university's research on automated farm machinery. The complaint was that the state was supporting the development of technology that will put farm laborers out of work.

But the problem is not isolated to farm workers—or to California. Practically anywhere you go today, robots are a frequent subject of conversation, and the discussion seldom goes for more than two minutes before someone asks, "What will I do if a robot takes my job?" The fear of robots is pervasive.

There are several reasons for this. First of all, practically everyone has been imprinted by a science-fiction literature that has consistently portrayed robots as hostile machines with irresistible strength that are

"The new technologies of robotics and computer-integrated manufacturing will create entirely new industries, employing millions of people (and robots, too) in jobs that don't exist today."

programmed by evil or misguided masters. Few of us have not read at least one book, or seen one movie, in which robots were portrayed as destroyers of cities and menaces to civilization as we know it.

Secondly, even the serious literature about the future has been almost uniformly pessimistic about the prospect of advanced automation. The nearly universal opinion expressed is concern about robots producing massive and intractable unemployment.

The Reality of Unemployment

The threat to employment is vastly overrated. The number of robots is growing at less than 35% per year, and there is little historical evidence to suggest that robots have ever caused a net increase in unemployment. The Japanese, for example, have more robots than all other countries put together, and they have the highest productivity growth rate in all industrial nations. Yet the unemployment rate in Japan is less than 3%.

The current high rate of unemployment in America is not because robots are putting people out of work but because American industries are becoming obsolete. The United States is finding it increasingly difficult to produce goods and services at competitive prices on the world market.

The massive loss of jobs in the textile, shoe, camera, consumer electronics, steel, and automobile industries is not because of automation but because of lack of modernization to meet and beat competition from foreign manufacturers. In fact, unless the nation increases productivity through greater use of automation, it may soon become impossible for U.S. industries to make enough profit to pay for the high salaries and benefits, generous vacations, and comfortable retirement programs that Americans have come to expect.

It is also wrong to assume that a human job is lost for every robot installed. The new technologies of robotics and computer-integrated manufacturing will create entirely new industries, employing millions of people (and robots, too) in jobs that don't exist today. Robots will make possible new methods of manufacturing, construction, tunneling, and deep drilling. They will be used for undersea mining, man-

ufacturing in space, and farming of the oceans, all of which would otherwise be impossible or impractical. Robotics could make solar and geothermal energy sources economical and may substantially reduce the hazards of nuclear power.

Of course, there will be many new human jobs created just in the industries that manufacture, sell, install, and maintain robots. A re-

COURTESY OF JAMES S. ALBUS

Author James S. Albus programs vision robot. Since robots can produce many things profitably below market prices, they "could make us all rich," says Albus.

At this computer-aided design workstation, geometric characteristics of parts are entered into a factory's data base. In the "robot economy," factories using such modernized equipment would begin producing cheaper and longer-lasting products.

cent study done for the state of Michigan predicts that by 1990 the number of jobs created in the robot-manufacturing industries alone will be between 35% and 75% of the number of jobs lost in the robot-using industries. And if the increased productivity resulting from more efficient production technology makes American products more competitive on the world market, the net effect on employment will be overwhelmingly positive in almost all sectors of the economy.

Many occupations will survive and prosper even in the most advanced robot economy. Doctors, nurses, teachers, entertainers, social workers, psychologists, and religious counselors will continue to be required as long as there are humans with needs for such services. A robot-based economy should produce sufficient material wealth to increase the demand for health, education, recreation, and social services by making them available to more people. Occupations in leisure industries, the arts, and many types of personal services would then abound. Scientific research and exploration of the oceans and outer space will offer unlimited opportunities for many types of fascinating careers into the indefinite future.

We can, of course, always spread the available work around. A shorter workweek of 20 hours, or perhaps eventually 10 hours, may be possible. Longer vacations, sabbatical leaves, and increased adult education all have the capacity to raise the number of jobs while reducing the amount of work.

In addition, we must never underestimate the capacity of our politicians, labor unions, and bureaucrats to generate make-work. Remember Parkinson's Law: "The amount of work always expands to fit the number of workers assigned to do it." Both government and business bureaucracies have accumulated a great deal of experience in holding committee meetings, sending memos, and issuing regulations and directives that can occupy an indefinite number of executive personnel and office workers for an arbitrary length of time. There is no question that we will find something to employ as many people as necessary for as long as is necessary to create a rationale for passing out paychecks every two weeks. We have both the technological means and the political will to create work in whatever quantities are deemed fit by the voting public.

The problem is not in creating enough jobs to keep everyone employed. The problem is in generating enough real wealth to meet the payroll. This generation is in no danger of running out of things that need doing. The world is filled with need. It is premature to worry about robots eliminating work as long as there exist such overwhelming problems as providing food, clothing, shelter, education, and medical care for millions of people living in desperate poverty.

The Purpose of an Economic System

We often forget, in our preoccupation with unemployment and job security, that the fundamental purpose of an economic system is not to create work but to create and distribute real wealth.

Anyone who can produce goods and services that can be sold for a profit at, or below, current market prices almost always becomes rich. The fact that so few of us are rich should tell us something about how hard it is to create real wealth.

But hear this! Robots can create real wealth. Robots, and the associated technologies of automated manufacturing, can produce goods and services that humans want and need. Robots can produce clothing, homes, autos, furniture, appliances, entertainment, education, medical care, and so on, and they will eventually be able to produce these things on a massive scale at a profit below current market prices. In short, robots could make us all rich.

All that is needed is a mechanism that can distribute the wealth that robots will create to those of us who need it. Fortunately, there is a mechanism available—it is called ownership—and there are many forms of it. Stock in robot manufacturing or leasing companies, and private ownership of individual robots, are just two.

"One possible solution to the problem of wealth distribution in a future robot economy might be to make it easy for people to become robot owners."

An industrial robot typically produces about $30,000 per year in product value added. This means that each individual who owns an industrial robot gets $30,000 of income per year whether or not he or she is otherwise gainfully employed.

Possible Solutions

One possible solution to the problem of wealth distribution in a future robot economy might be to make it easy for people to become robot owners. There are, in fact, some efforts currently under way in the U.S. Congress to do just that. There is a bill now working its way through the legislative process that would sell stock to the public. Such stock would pay dividends and be issued at a price that would encourage the widest possible distribution.

Another, more comprehensive, approach would use credit issued by the Federal Reserve System to finance investments in development and construction of robots and automatic factories. Dividends on the profits from those investments would be paid to every adult citizen on an equal per capita basis.

To be more specific, a semi-private investment corporation, which we might call a National Mutual Fund, could be created for increasing productivity in private industry. This investment corporation would be authorized by Congress each year to draw funds (up to a specified amount) from the Federal Reserve, which it would use to purchase stock from private industry. This would provide equity financing for the modernization of plants and machinery and the introduction of advanced computer-based automation.

Profits from these investments would then be paid in the form of dividends by the National Mutual Fund to all adults equally. By this means each citizen would receive income from the industrial sector of the economy independent of employment in factories and offices. Every adult citizen would thus derive substantial income from invested capital.

The National Mutual Fund would begin with a modest sum and increase the amount every year until the investment rate for the National Mutual Fund equaled the total private investment rate.

Of course, simply doubling the nation's investment rate through newly created money would be inflationary in the short term. Thus, in conjunction with (but institutionally separate from) the National Mutual Fund, a mandatory savings bond program could be instituted to restrain short-term demand. In order to share the pain of saving fairly, savings would be withheld as surcharge on individual income taxes. In order to assure that these savings do not simply end up as a tax in disguise, these bonds would bear interest at 4% above the prevailing inflation rate and be redeemable after five years.

The key idea in this plan, which might be called an Industrial Development Bond program, is to index the mandatory savings rate to the leading indicators for inflation on a monthly basis. If inflation is predicted, mandatory savings

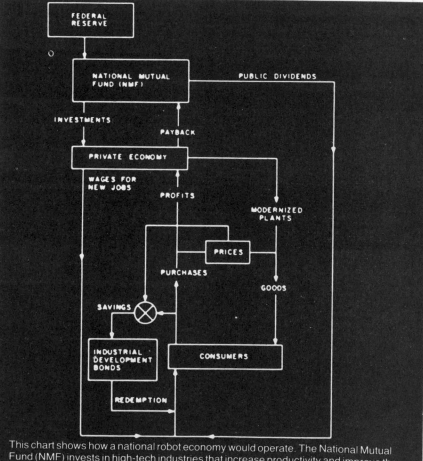

This chart shows how a national robot economy would operate. The National Mutual Fund (NMF) invests in high-tech industries that increase productivity and improve the quality of products at a cost below current market prices, thus creating real wealth. The fund pays dividends equally to every adult, regardless of employment. To control inflation, the amount of mandatory savings (Industrial Development Bonds) is adjusted from month to month. Income is derived both from the NMF dividends and from the interest received on the Industrial Development Bonds (which can be redeemed after five years).

CINCINNATI MILACRON

Wielding a laser, robot trims plastic automobile parts in shielded booth. The "robot revolution" will free humans from repetitious, difficult, and hazardous work in factories, says author Albus.

would go up for the next month to reduce consumer demand. As soon as prices stabilized or declined, mandatory savings would be reduced. This policy would effectively divert short-term demand from consumption into savings to compensate for increased investment. At that same time, it would assure that the purchasing power to distribute the fruits of investment in highly productive technology would be available once the new plants and modernized machinery began to produce increased output.

The National Mutual Fund would draw money from the Federal Reserve Bank where it was created. It would invest in highly productive robot industries and eventually pay dividends from profits in those industries to the general public. Industrial Development Bonds would regulate the amount of money in circulation and hence the demand for goods and services. The price index would be the controlling function on the rate of withholding for the bonds. When cheaper, more reliable, and longer lasting products began flowing out of the robot factories, mandatory savings would be reduced, and the bonds being redeemed would increase demand

to consume the increased productive output.

Of course, the difficulties in creating such a system would be enormous. It would involve a significant new method for the financing of industry and for the distribution of the wealth that it creates. There are many questions of how such a system would be controlled and protected from abuse. Certainly, it is an unconventional proposal, but the wealth-producing potential of robot technology is unprecedented.

There will also be problems in overcoming the fear that surrounds the subject of robots: a fear in part born of the science-fiction literature of malevolent robots; a fear in part born of the prospect of monopoly control of robot technology by the large corporations; and a general fear of the unknown, a distrust of modern science, and a feeling of powerlessness of the individual in a society dominated by machines.

But there are other things more deserving of our fear than robots. As the world population grows and conventional resources become more scarce, increased productivity and new technologies that substitute new resources for old offer the only real alternative to economic decline.

Without rapid productivity growth, a world of growing shortages will become an increasingly dangerous place. Nations competing over a shrinking stock of wealth and resources will inevitably come to military confrontation. The world's best hope is a great surge of industrial productivity that can outstrip the present population explosion and give us another chance at stabilizing human population into an equilibrium with the finite living space aboard the planet earth.

Robots could make us all rich. Wealth is the only known cure to poverty, and robots have the potential to create enough real material wealth to provide everyone with plenty of material goods. The only problem is whether we humans can create the mechanisms to distribute this wealth so that everyone gets a fair share. What we do with the new technology of robotics could be a matter of life and death for the coming generation.

About the Author

James S. Albus is chief of the Industrial Systems Division, Center for Manufacturing Engineering, National Bureau of Standards (Building 220, B-124, Gaithersburg, Maryland 20899), where he is responsible for robotics and automated manufacturing systems interface standards research. He is the author of *Brains, Behavior, and Robotics* (BYTE/McGraw-Hill, 1981) and *People's Capitalism: The Economics of the Robot Revolution* (New World Books, 1976). His previous article for THE FUTURIST was "Robots in the Workplace: The Key to a Prosperous Future," February 1983.

This article represents the author's personal opinion and does not reflect the position or official policy of the National Bureau of Standards, the Department of Commerce, or any other branch of the U.S. government.

MAPS
of the Future
by Hollis Vail

Tomorrow's maps may be very different from today's, thanks to new technological breakthroughs in surveying, aerial and satellite photography, and the processing of cartographic information. The following article describes how maps are changing and describes how they may be used in the years ahead by motorists, foresters, fire-fighters, engineers, urban planners, fishermen, and pilots.

Maps are one of man's great inventions. Originally people could not venture into lands outside their home areas without traveling blind or relying on people from that area to lead them. Then, at sometime in prehistory someone drew a map. It may only have been some stick lines on the ground, but it did three things:

- It depicted earth features on a small surface.
- It symbolized the earth features (e.g., a line to represent a river).
- It showed a selection of features rather than trying to show everything.

Later, man had to add another quality—proportions. He needed to know not only that there was a route through the mountains, but how far it was. A notation indicating "two days travel" was helpful, but not everyone traveled at the same speed. So another concept was invented:

- The location of earth features and consequently their general size, was related to a reference system (such as the system of latitude and longitude).

These basic concepts made maps possible. Later, the printing press made it possible to produce many copies of the same map. Today, because of technological developments such as aerial photography and high-speed presses, maps have become a routine, almost unappreciated item in our lives. We pick them up casually at the corner gas station as an aid for traveling. Planners sketch great visions on them with a hope that some of their markings will become reality. And the news media use them to show where world events are happening.

A New Image for Maps

Maps have become so ubiquitous and easily available that most people never stop to consider what a map really is. For many people a map is simply a piece of paper with lines on it. They might worry about the accuracy and "completeness" of the map, but seldom do they associate maps with their basic underlying concepts. But that could change in the next few years, because the field of mapping is undergoing a revolution that will thoroughly shake up conventional ideas as to what a map is. Here are some of the possibilities:

- Instead of getting a stock road map at the service station, you may have one printed to your specific needs. You will "tell" a special computer your destination, desired layover points, type of interest ("I want to fish and take pictures of old churches."), and modes of travel (plane, car, hiking). A computer-assisted machine will then print a special map showing your best route, picture-taking and fishing points, and other information needed for your trip.
- A rancher may order a map that looks like an aerial photograph except that it is corrected to remove scale distortions and has additional data printed on it, such as property lines, wells, and other special features.
- A forester may order a "spectral image" map that will be a reading of the heat radiated from the forests and will enable the forester to locate diseased trees. Quick action can then be taken to prevent a disease from spreading.
- A researcher will sit in a theater observing how cities have grown. Through sequential maps developed from aerial photographs taken at intervals over a number of years, the researcher will study urban growth generated by significant events, such as the development of shopping centers. His "movie map" will show roads being added, buildings going up, services being developed, and other developments affected by the shopping center.
- A firefighter who learns that a brush fire has broken out will dash to a computer terminal, enter the fire location, wind, temperature, and other conditions, and have the computer project on a map the fireline location six hours away. On

seeing the fireline projection, the firefighter will then determine the threat to homes and other valuable properties and plot strategies for fighting the fire.

- A truck dispatcher, on learning that his company has to transport a heavy wide load, will contact the appropriate computer, give it the load characteristics and destination, and get back a printout listing the routes to be followed and setting forth any special conditions, such as permits required, or bridge and underpass dimensions that require attention.
- A pilot, upon deciding on his flight plan, will obtain a computer tape containing a digitized model of the terrain the aircraft will be flying over. This tape will go into a small computer on the plane. Coupled to the computer will ·be an inertial guidance system which will monitor at all times the exact position and altitude of the aircraft. As the plane takes off, this inertial guidance system will read its elevation into the computer and the computer will check the aircraft altitude continuously against the elevation of the ground below and ahead of the plane. If at any time these threaten to come together, except at airports, the. computer will warn the pilot.

These map users may or may not hold in their hands a map as we think of it today. Some will indeed have a piece of paper with markings on it that looks much like today's map. But others may have what looks like a photograph or a series of strangely colored images. Some users, such as the truck dispatcher, may receive a computer printout listing routes and giving written instructions or information. And others, such as the pilot, will never see the "map" because it will be in a form that only the computer can read.

> *"Instead of getting a stock road map at the service station, you may have one printed to your specific needs."*

All of these "maps" will grow out of the revolution now taking place in mapping. They are possible, in part, because new technology is introducing

Author Hollis Vail says that the field of mapping is undergoing a revolution that will thoroughly shake up conventional ideas as to what a map is.

new opportunities and enabling cartographers, or map makers, to reconsider what is possible. The new technology has also made it possible to develop a national cartographic data bank, a step that could move the United States well along toward an integrated system of national mapping.

The Revolution in Technology

Today we expect a map to be a true representation of the area it depicts. Maps showing limited access highways, for instance, should show where the exits are, and *not* show exits that do not exist. I recently drove twenty miles extra because the road map I was using showed an exit that was not there.

We expect reliability in maps because it has been possible for many years to locate and represent earth features with substantial accuracy. Aerial photography has enabled cartographers to depict much more precisely the relationships and size of features on the ground. Today we use the photographs in accurate, efficient stereoscopic plotting instruments to produce most of the detail shown on modern maps.

Not evident on maps are the limits of the existing technology. Even with such modern equipment as electronic distance measuring devices (EDM's), it has not been practical for certain kinds of surveys in the United States to be related to each other. It has been too expensive for most local surveys to be tied into the nation's geodetic networks and to establish points in the survey with the accuracy sufficient to the needs of a national cartographic data system. Thus, property corners and many other positions usually are established without reference to the national geodetic network.

In recent years, technology has offered some ways out of this condition. One of the most exciting is the development of inertial-surveying systems. These devices couple space-age technology with small but powerful computers to make it possible for two men in a vehicle to proceed from point to point and, from the readings on their meters, tell their geographic location and elevation. Today these survey vehicles can continually read their geographic location to one-meter accuracy. In a few years, the accuracy should be within 30 centimeters, which with smoothing can be improved to 15 centimeters. Currently these systems are exceedingly expensive. In a few years, however, as costs come down, inertial-surveying devices mounted on ground vehicles or helicopters could make it feasible to tie most surveys into the national geodetic network and thus enable such data to be related to a national data system.

Changes Coming in Aerial Photography

Aerial photography has been a mainstay in mapping for many years. Indeed, most of the data on maps are derived from aerial photographs. Yet photography, like surveying, is on another threshold.

One of photography's limitations has been the absence of an integrated national system of aerial photography. Most aerial pictures are taken on an "as needed" basis to meet localized requirements rather than to supply nationwide coverage. Until recently, the lack of an integrated national system of aerial photography was unimportant, because there was no way to process and utilize effectively such a vast body of photographs even if they had been available. New technology coming on the market today, however, is capable of handling the massive processing task.

Another development in aerial survey is multispectral sensing—the use of radiometers sensitive to different wavebands of the electromagnetic spectrum. Objects on the earth reflect different amounts of solar energy at different wavelengths. Trees, for example, reflect strongly at different spectral wavebands than water or wheat. It is therefore possible to identify and map vegetation and other features of the earth's surface from the air, using special films, such as infrared, and special filters. Thus aerial survey becomes an amazing means for monitoring what is happening in the world.

Jeep equipped with an inertial navigation system for surveying on land. The system, which includes gyroscopes, accelerometers, and a small computer, provides a continuous record of the position and elevation of the vehicle as it proceeds along its course.

Photo: Litton Industries Photo Lab., Woodland Hills, California

Remote-sensing practitioners still have much to learn about translating data gathered by their instruments into meaningful information, but the effort often pays off. Take the researcher who wanted to study the habits of bears. His first task was to discover where in the mountains he could find bears, so he turned to remote sensing. A first run of the remote-sensor data gave him a map that showed features such as rock outcrops, trees, grass, and brush. He had to make a field trip to verify the information and gather additional clues for the multispectral analysis. But the final results were gratifying because the computer, using the multispectral data, was able to identify the areas the bears favored and even the location of their favorite berries.

It is possible that in a few years we will cease to refer to aerial photography, calling it instead aerial imagery. "Pictures" in the future may be taken through imaging systems capable of scanning the earth to a resolution finer than is possible in today's photographs. These "pictures" would be digital readings, such as are being obtained by the LANDSAT satellites, taken through selective wavelength filters.

The advantages of the image approach are numerous. The images become fully manipulable by computers so that it is possible to control the contrast and enhance the image. In addition, pictures can be composed using data selectively drawn from new data and prior data. Thus clouded areas can be "filled in," roads and buildings made more visible, crop areas identified and measured, and many other special treatments carried out.

Satellites Aid Mapmakers

The discussion of aerial imagery leads naturally to the subject of satellite imagery. At the present time, it does not appear likely that imagery from satellites will have the resolution needed to differentiate objects as small as one meter on a side. But that does not mean that satellite imagery will not contribute to mapping in the future. Two exciting potentials of satellite imagery are:

- *Time-lapse mapping.* The regular and frequent passage of a satellite such as LANDSAT over an area of the earth makes possible sequential photographing of a flood, from the time it is a quiet river, through its crests, to the time it has returned to being a quiet river (with some possible changes in its riverbed).

- *Synoptic imagery.* Until the advent of satellites, it was impossible to see and photograph large areas of the earth in a single exposure. Aerial photographs could be assembled in a mosaic, but it was not until satellite imagery became available that we discovered the difference between an aviator's-eye view and an astronaut's-eye view. Today we see—through satellite pictures—fault lineaments, and other features not evident even in the most carefully assembled plane's-eye mosaic.

New Equipment Speeds Mapmaking

Transferring data from the sky to the map has been another big step for technology. For years, photographers in airplanes have taken pictures quickly, but cartographers on the

A modern image-correlator mapping machine. This system uses electronic correlation of images to produce orthophotos, contours, and digitized terrain models. Operator communicates with equipment by means of console, which displays the image on a cathode ray tube, and a manual editing device. The main elements in the system consist of a twin scanning device (left), an electronic image correlator, a computer, and a magnetic tape input/output device. Not shown in the picture is the printer, which is located in a separate darkroom. The cost of such a system approaches one million dollars.

Photo: U.S. Geological Survey

ground have processed them slowly. Even with the most advanced equipment, cartographers have had to trace manually the visible features on the photographs to make their maps. Manual tracing is fairly easy and fast for roads, rivers, and shorelines. But elevation of the land surface is quite another matter. Cartographers have had to draw the countless miles of contour lines very laboriously by viewing projected photographs stereoscopically.

This tedious task is likely to be eliminated during the next few years by automatic image-correlation instruments that compare the stereophotos electronically to determine elevations. These instruments scan the photos in closely-spaced straight lines, much like the light beam in a TV tube. The instruments take thousands of closely-spaced readings of the elevation of the earth in each photograph. A computer can use the readings to produce a digital model of the terrain in the photographed area. While taking the elevation readings, the instrument also "photographs" each tiny area of the picture. These tiny "pictures," known as differential images, are likewise put on tape for the computer to process. The computer then analyzes the data on the tapes according to a predetermined program, which calculates the

effects of elevation and the earth's curvature, and then determines the coordinate location of each elevation and each differential image.

Once processed by computer, the terrain data can be used by many people for many purposes. Contour lines, if desired, can be computed and plotted automatically. Maps can be created that show the slopes, allowing the viewer to quickly determine whether the countryside is flat, gently sloping, or craggy and steep. Special users, such as foresters, may work just with the elevation data in the computer to determine such things as what areas in the forests can be seen from a heavily-traveled highway. Knowing this, they then can avoid clear-cutting which would be visible to people on the highway.

The differential images are later reassembled into a large photograph in which they are correctly positioned according to a reference system. The corrected photos, called "orthophotographs," may then be "assisted" by adding information such as contour lines, or by classifying roads, setting down boundaries, and adding names. These orthophotographic or picture maps can then be used like conventional maps: a scale provides a measure of distances on the map and a number of

maps can be fitted together to show larger areas; the roads, boundaries, and other features all fit nicely together.

Do-It-Yourself Mapping—Present Style

Today a great deal of mapping is done on a "do-it-yourself" basis. Anyone can make a map by taking an existing map of the area, putting some tracing paper over it, and tracing off the features that interest him. Some extra work is required if the mapper needs to update portions of the data. New roads can be shown, or buildings added or deleted. The mapper also can add his own special data, such as where the fish are biting. Once the drawing is complete, all he needs to do is have the local print shop run off as many copies as he wishes.

A more ambitious mapmaker can buy special equipment and do a more professional job, but even professional mapmakers do essentially the same things as the ordinary person who makes a map. The professional gets someone else's maps, utilizes the parts he needs, and adds whatever special information is desired. Since U.S. government maps are not copyrighted, they provide an exceptionally rich source for mapmakers, both professional and homegrown.

A few mapping agencies, such as the U.S. Geological Survey, do not copy someone else's map, but gather original data directly from the world itself by means of surveys, aerial photographs, and field investigations. The mapmakers of these agencies develop their maps from photographs by means of ingenious plotting instruments and add other locally gathered data. Then they make finely scribed plates and print thousands of copies for the public, including other mapmakers.

The U.S. national system of mapping, in which a few mappers gather the basic information and other build on it, makes sense because it is very expensive to gather basic map data and comparatively cheap to copy it. In copying what is on a single seven and one half minute quadrangle map, produced at a scale of 1:24,000 by the U.S. Geological Survey, a mapmaker is taking advantage of data that cost $10,000 to $20,000 to gather. Each of these maps covers about 50 square miles, which may seem a lot until one learns that it takes some 55,000 seven and one half-minute quadrangle maps to cover the conterminous U.S. A state the size of Ohio requires 780 of these maps.

One major complication in the system is the fact that the entire U.S. still has not been mapped at that scale. The Geological Survey, the country's primary civilian mapmaker, has been concentrating on seven and one half minute quadrangle maps since about 1950. These maps now cover only about 65% of the country. Other areas are covered by maps at a scale of 1:62,500 (one mile to the inch), but the only complete coverage of the United States is at a scale of 1:250,000 (four miles to the inch), a scale too small for many purposes.

Another complication arises as the data are processed to produce the map. The original agency cannot put all the data it gathers on the map, especially if it is a small-scale map, so the data are edited. Much valuable information may be lost on the cartographer's "floor." Small streams particularly experience this treatment. A stream may run past your country cabin, but the cartographer may edit it out to simplify the detail on a small-scale map.

The new technology coming into the mapping field promises to help correct some of the problems, because data can be processed much faster and fewer details will have to be omitted. The new technology is more expensive initially but, viewed in a multiple-use and life-of-the-data sense, the cost of the data to the mapmaker should be much lower.

A National Cartographic Data Bank

The new technology may speed up the availability of the data and reduce its overall costs, but a central problem still remains: The data are still available to most mapmakers only on the maps produced by the primary mapmakers.

One way of resolving the problem is to make the data available at an earlier stage in its processing. Instead of letting the cartographer edit the data, the larger mass of data could be made available to mapmakers. Perhaps a national cartographic data bank could be set up to provide the data to the mapmakers in whatever forms they wanted it.

If the formation of a cartographic data bank seems an obvious step, why hasn't it been done? The answer can be attributed in part to a lack of suitable technology, but that is not the full answer. Ironically, a larger deterrent to the formation of a national cartographic data bank has been the map itself.

Government agencies that made maps were slow in recognizing the extent to which cartographic data gathered for maps could be very useful to other agencies and the private sector. For example, the Geological Survey, the federal agency most active in gathering the basic data needed for mapmaking, collected cartographic data for many years as a part of its program to produce the National Topographic Map Series and the other maps for which it is responsible. But the Survey made little effort to supply the original information, collected at great cost, to other agencies that could use it for making their own maps or for other purposes.

The drawback of focusing on the map is that the area to be covered, the scale used, the data to be edited out, and the schedule are all keyed to the specific map being produced. Other mapmakers have to accommodate themselves to the decisions of the original mapmaker, who may have omitted buildings, stream beds, and other features that other mappers desperately need to show on their maps.

The move to end the "map fixation" came when the Office of Management and Budget (OMB) set up an interdepartmental task force to take a look at federal mapping, charting, and geodesy. The task force found much duplication and loss or inaccessibility of data and concluded that the country needed a better way of gathering and dispensing cartographic data. OMB logically assumed that some federal agency ought to have as its *mission* the gathering and development of a national cartographic data bank.

The logical federal agency to do this would seem to be the Geological Survey, since it already gathers basic land data for the entire United States. But setting up the national cartographic data bank is not easy, because of differences between the processes whereby maps are produced and those needed to provide data to users. To provide both the new and old services, the Geological Survey needs to reexamine its basic data-gathering procedures and revamp—or completely overhaul in some cases—its methods of gathering and processing cartographic data.

In 1975, after a painstaking examination of both the OMB report and existing procedures, the Geological Survey's Topographic Division, under the direction of its Chief, Robert H. Lyddan, decided to undertake the development of a national cartographic data base which will be built on the body of data already in the Survey's files.

As a result of this decision, the Topographic Division will have to make many operational changes and will have to move from its present non-digital processes to the new technology. The new technology represents almost a quantum jump in equipment costs as well as in capability. A modern image-correlation digital-mapping system, for instance, costs about a million dollars a unit, and a number of units are needed. The older "expensive" stereoplotting instruments cost $25,000-$100,000.

The ability of image correlators to process aerial photographs, the availability of higher-resolution lenses and high-altitude aircraft, and the development of multispectral

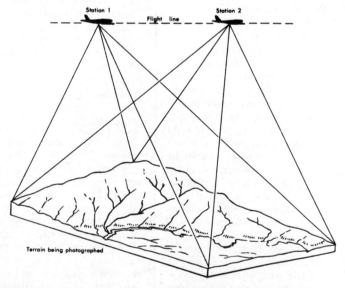

Overlapping aerial photographs provide stereoscopic coverage of area to be mapped.
Photo: U.S. Geological Survey

sensing devices also called for another operation entailing a high-capital investment—a program to photograph the United States completely every five years.

The National Mapping Program

To address the many problems involved in establishing a national cartographic data bank, the Topographic Division of the Geological Survey instituted The National Mapping Program, which will have as one of its primary missions the development of a cartographic data bank that initially will contain 11 types of land data (see box). These data are essentially the data already gathered for the production of the National Topographic Map Series. The availability of these makes possible the immediate establishment of a sizable data bank, although the information cannot yet be withdrawn without some difficulty.

Making the data bank responsive will require some sizable efforts, including:

- The development of methods for storing and accessing the existing body of data.
- The establishment of the program to obtain aerial photographs of the entire United States at least once every five years.
- The acquisition and utilization of image-correlation systems and other advanced techniques.
- The development of a national system for digitizing cartographic data so that the data can be gathered and manipulated to respond to a wide variety of needs.

Input from Other Agencies Welcomed

In formulating the National Mapping Program, the planners recognized that other federal agencies gather data useful to mapmakers. Some agencies gather soil data; others assemble specialized information such as population distributions and the location of radio stations.

The National Mapping Program will not interfere with such data gathering by other agencies, but will propose to them that they make the data available through the outlets of the National Mapping Program. The Program will also provide a working arrangement with these agencies to secure such changes in their gathering and handling processes as are necessary for their data to be compatible with the other information in the data bank.

A Data Bank for Cartographic Information

In the years ahead, people will likely have ready access to increasingly precise and complete knowledge about the world they live in. In the United States, for example, the Topographic Division of the U.S. Geological Survey has established a National Mapping Program which has as its main goal the creation of a national cartographic data bank. The data bank will initially contain the following types of land data:

1. Reference systems—geographic and other coordinate systems except the public land survey network.

2. Hypsography—contours, slopes, and elevations.

3. Hydrography—streams and rivers, lakes and ponds, wetlands, reservoirs, and shorelines.

4. Surface cover—woodland, orchards, vineyards, etc. (general categories only).

5. Non-vegetative features—lava rock, playas, dunes, slide rock, barren waste areas.

6. Boundaries—portrayal of political jurisdictions, national parks and forests, military reservations, etc. This category does not fully set forth land ownership or land use.

7. Transportation systems—roads, railroads, trails, canals, pipelines, transmission lines, bridges, tunnels, etc.

8. Other significant man-made structures such as buildings, airports, and dams.

9. Identification and portrayal of geodetic control, survey monuments, other survey markers, and landmark structures and objects.

10. Geographic names.

11. Orthophotographic imagery ("picture maps").

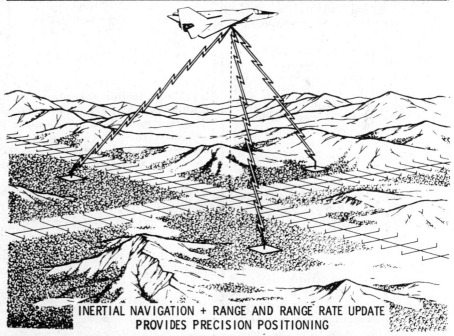

INERTIAL NAVIGATION + RANGE AND RANGE RATE UPDATE PROVIDES PRECISION POSITIONING

Modern surveying by inertial navigation and electronic ranging. Electronic signals to fixed ground stations plus inertial navigation equipment fix the position of the aircraft and provide a means of determining the exact position of any point along the flight path.

Photo: Litton Industries

The National Cartographic Information Center (NCIC) will serve as the contact and dissemination point. Established in 1974 as an arm of the Geological Survey's Topographic Division to succeed the old Map Information Office, NCIC now inventories and keeps track of thousands of maps, aerial photographs, and geodetic-survey points.

Do-It-Yourself Mapping— Future Style

The mapmaker is on the threshold of realizing a dream. Until now, he has been hobbled by many conditions that impeded his access to badly needed data. The ability of the new technology to gather and process data and the establishment of cartographic data banks will strike down many of the hobbling conditions. As this happens, the mapmaker and his new companions at the consoles of computers will begin to live their dream.

Here are some examples of what will be possible in the future:

- A national association of hikers decides hikers need a map specifically tailored to their needs. This map should show special items of interest on the trail as well as the location of rest and camping places. To make this map, the association needs basic data such as terrain elevations and the location of trails, roads, and vegetation lines. The association contacts the National Cartographic Information Center and asks for a computer tape containing the basic data for the area their map is to cover. Then they take the tape to their local computer center, where the basic data is plotted out by the computer, the association adds its special information, plates are made, and the printer produces a few thousand maps that will guide hikers through the countryside.

- A regional flood-control agency decides it needs to study the flood potential in a particular river basin. Agency officials want to know what might happen if rain fell all over the upper basin rather than in spots as it normally does. The flood agency calls the National Cartographic Information Center and obtains a tape containing the terrain of the river basin. The programmers then use the computer to simulate wild, heavy storms in the upper basin and watch the computer printout as the drainoff crests at various points along its channel. The programmers then put breaks in levees, or create debris jams that cause the river to crest over banks and levees. The computer simulation then applies the forces of the flood to objects in the river's path, destroying bridges, flooding homes and businesses, and forcing hundreds to abandon their homes. Finally, the computer tallies up the potential costs of flood damages.

- A developing country needs to assess the impact of damming a river in one of its remote unmap-

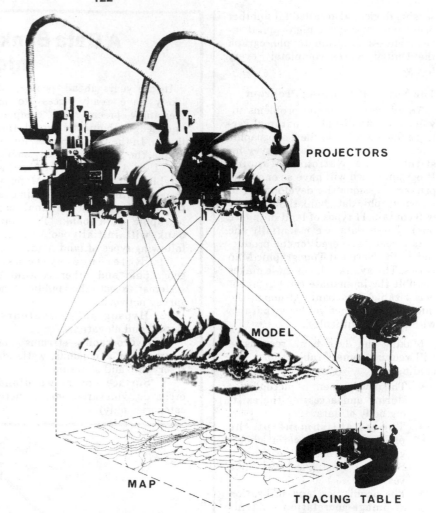

Double-projection mapping instrument. Transparent prints of overlapping aerial photographs are placed in the projectors in the same orientation they had when the pictures were taken. The projected images are viewed stereoscopically on the surface of a tracing table, giving a three-dimensional impression of the terrain. Map features and contour lines are traced in the stereoscopic model and reproduced on the map sheet.
Photo: U.S. Geological Survey

This surface relief model was developed from a digital terrain data base (Vancouver area, British Columbia).

Photo: Harvard University

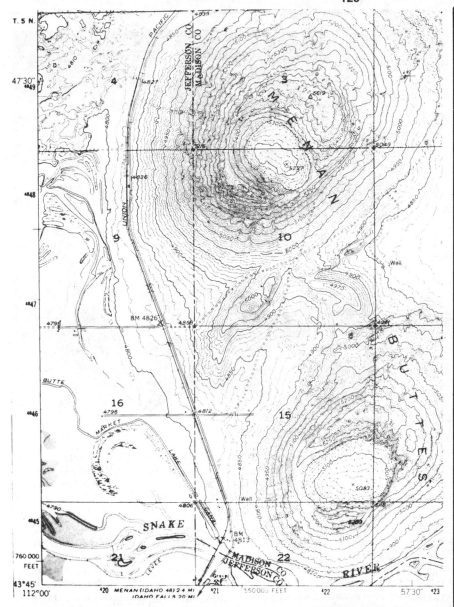

Portion of a standard U.S. Geological Survey topographic map. The contours show craters of two extinct volcanoes (Menan Buttes, Idaho). Other features shown include a part of the Snake River, a section of the Union Pacific Railroad, swamps, land-section lines, and political boundaries.
Photo: U.S. Geological Survey

How To Order Maps

The National Cartographic Information Center (NCIC) is the best central source of information about U.S. maps and charts, aerial photographs and space images, land use data, and other cartographic data. NCIC provides a direct inquiry and ordering service for aerial photographs and space images from the EROS Data Center; provides information and accepts orders for advance material from topographic mapping and map separates held by the Topographic Division of USGS; and refers orders for Geological Survey maps to the Branch of Distribution Offices. NCIC also sells reproductions of out-of-print USGS topographic maps.

For more information, contact: National Cartographic Information Center, U.S. Geological Survey National Center, STOP 507, Reston, Virginia 22092 (Telephone: 703-860-6045).

To order topographic maps of areas east of the Mississippi River (including Minnesota, Puerto Rico, and the Virgin Islands), contact Branch of Distribution, U.S. Geological Survey, 1200 South Eads Street, Arlington, Virginia 22202 (Telephone: 703-557-2751). For areas west of the Mississippi River (including Alaska, Hawaii, Louisiana, Guam, and American Samoa), contact Branch of Distribution, U.S. Geological Survey, Box 25286, STOP 306, Denver Federal Center (Building 41), Denver, Colorado 80225 (Telephone: 303-234-3832). Photos are available for the cost of reproduction. A large lithographic copy of a satellite image mosaic of the conterminous United States is available from the Arlington Branch for $1.25.

If you would like to obtain an aerial photo showing your own house, these are available for many parts of the United States. Simply write to NCIC, identifying the location as specifically as possible (give latitude and longitude or enclose a map with your area marked) NCIC will let you know if any photos are available, and, if so, will send you an order form and price list.

ped areas. High altitude photographs of the area along the river are sent to a data processing center that has an image-correlator mapping system. There the photographs are processed, yielding both digital terrain data and orthophotographs. The engineers of the developing country then project various reservoir elevations in their computers and get back plotted shorelines that can be laid on the orthophotographs. They then can study visually the areas that would be submerged by the reservoir. And this can be done in a few months instead of the

few years the older processes took.

The foregoing represent only a sample of the mapmakers' dreams that will become realities in the near future as the new capabilities of mapping are developed. In the years ahead, we will have increasingly precise, accurate, and timely information about our planet, and this should enable us to make wiser decisions about what we want to accomplish and how to go about it.

Hollis Vail is the Departmental Mapping Coordinator in the Department of the Interior, Washington, D.C. 20240. □

Mapping the Earth from Satellites

Two satellites now are selectively monitoring the world's agricultural and forestry crops from orbits 570 miles above the earth.

Data gathered by the satellites will help provide a more complete and up-to-date picture of the world food situation than is possible by other means, thus providing an "early warning system" that will give the world's governments time to minimize the ill effects of food shortages. By monitoring water distribution and vegetation patterns, these satellites can also measure the effects of droughts. Satellite imagery is now being used for evaluating range conditions over vast areas of the western United States.

The two satellites, called LANDSAT-1 and LANDSAT-2, circle the earth approximately 14 times per day and can map the entire earth (with the exception of the extreme polar regions) every 18 days. Because they can simultaneously photograph an area 115 miles on a side, the satellites are particularly

EROS Data Center, located on a 318-acre site 16 miles northeast of Sioux Falls, South Dakota, is operated by the U.S. Department of the Interior through the Geological Survey. Photo: U.S. Geological Survey

Precision photographic reproduction laboratory at EROS Data Center processes photographic products ranging from 16 millimeters to 40 inches square in a variety of formats. Personnel are clad in protective clothing to maintain the clean, dust-free laboratory environment. Photo: U.S. Geological Survey

This satellite (LANDSAT-1) was launched in 1972 and is still functioning. Circling the earth 14 times every 24 hours, it continuously monitors earth resources by remote sensing devices and also relays data collected by widely scattered ground-based instruments. Photo: NASA

useful for mapping large regions. Repetitive mapping is helpful in studying the effects of floods and monitoring seasonal changes in vegetation, snow, and ice. The boundaries of urban growth can also be systematically recorded.

Geologists are using LANDSAT imagery to learn more about the structure of the earth. Satellite imagery, for example, can help pinpoint geologic structures which, in turn, assists geologists in their search for undiscovered natural resources such as oil, gas, and minerals. Hydrologists use satellite imagery to assist them in the discovery and development of water resources.

Repetitive satellite imagery has also proved effective in monitoring strip mining and reclamation of strip mines and will play an important role in assessing the environmental impact of the Alaska pipeline.

LANDSAT has also made it possible to map areas that have

never before been mapped, such as parts of Antarctica and shallow seas such as the Indian Ocean, where previously uncharted reefs and other areas of shoal water have been revealed.

In addition to its global repetitive mapping capability, LANDSAT has several other advantages over airplanes: For one thing, satellites are not subject to the atmospheric turbulence which affects the quality of aerial photographs. In addition, the narrow-angle mapping done from satellites produces a geometrically correct two-dimensional rendition of the earth (the orthographic view). Aerial photography, taken from a much lower altitude, provides three-dimensional information which must be processed into a two-dimensional map, which is a costly and complex process. On the other hand, LANDSAT cannot do topographic mapping, which would show, for example, contours of mountainous regions.

Satellites can also operate for periods of years, whereas an aerial mapping flight usually lasts only a matter of hours. LANDSAT-1, originally called the Earth Resources Technology Satellite (ERTS), was launched on July 23, 1972, and is still functioning today.

A third satellite, LANDSAT-C, is scheduled to join the other two in orbit in September, 1977. LAND-SAT-C will have two capabilities not possessed by its predecessors: a thermal channel which will measure temperature variations on the earth's surface and the ability to uniquely record an area as small as 40 meters on a side, compared to an 80-meter minimum for the others. Even the 40-meter image element, however, is inadequate for recording cultural details, such as most roads and buildings, which are shown on the larger scale maps.

The EROS (Earth Resources Observation Systems) Data Center was established in 1971 by the Department of the Interior to reproduce and distribute as sale items copies of imagery, photography, electronic data, and computer products collected by 16 different organizations, including the U.S. Geological Survey and NASA. In addition to the LANDSAT data, the EROS Data Center serves as the primary repository for aerial photography acquired by the U.S. Department of the Interior and for photography and imagery acquired by the National Aeronautics and Space Administration (NASA) from high altitude research aircraft and from Skylab, Apollo, and Gemini spacecraft.

Descriptions of products available from the EROS Data Center, order forms, and price lists can be obtained from the EROS Data Center, Sioux Falls, South Dakota 57198 (Telephone: 605-594-6511). Information about satellite imagery can also be obtained from the National Cartographic Information Center, U.S. Geological Survey National Center, STOP 507, Reston, Virginia 22092 (Telephone: 603-860-6045).

(Portions of the preceding information were excerpted from the U.S. Geological Survey Annual Report, Fiscal Year 1975 and from other USGS publications. The Annual Report is available for $3.40 from Branch of Distribution, U.S. Geological Survey, 1200 South Eads Street, Arlington, Virginia 22202.)

Orthophotograph of U.S.-Canada border near Lake Champlain. Vermont is in lower right of photo, New York at lower left, and Quebec at top. The border, marked by a fence, can be seen running in a straight line across lower center of photograph. (The border fence is most visible where it crosses wooded areas.) This orthophoto is one of a series being produced by the U.S. Geological Survey at the request of the U.S. Customs Service to help analyze increased border activities in connection with the 1976 Summer Olympic games in Montreal. This orthophotograph is shown in black and white, but the image maps delivered to the U.S. Customs Service are in full color, produced by a new process combining panchromatic and black-and-white infrared photography.

Photo: U.S. Geological Survey

MASSACHUSETTS   Boston   Cape Cod

Oneida Lake

RHODE ISLAND

Mohawk River

Providence

Syracuse

Narragansett Bay

Hudson River

Montauk Point

NEW YORK

Long Island

New York Metropolitan Area

PENNSYLVANIA

NEW JERSEY

Philadelphia

Pennsylvania Dutch Farming Region

Delaware River

Susquehanna River

Wilmington

Beaches

DELAWARE

MARYLAND

Baltimore

Delaware Bay

Cape May

Delmarva Peninsula

Washington

Potomac River

Chesapeake Bay

Rappahannock River

VIRGINIA

York River

Richmond

James River

Norfolk

This photo mosaic of the northeastern United States, which is shown in color on the cover, was assembled from 16 images taken from a LANDSAT satellite. The mosaic shows a 100,000-square-mile area extending from Boston, Massachusetts, to just above Norfolk, Virginia. Crops and forests show up as bright red due to the infrared nature of the photography. Bare fields, road networks, and cities and towns appear in various shades of white, gray, and light blue. The dark gray coloring of much of the New York metropolitan area is due to the higher shadow content caused by the density of tall buildings in the area. Central Park can be seen as a small red spot in the middle of the city. In the rural areas, unplowed fields are whiter than plowed fields. Clear water shows as dark blue, while silty, turbid, or polluted water shows as lighter blue. Deep water is generally darker than shallow water. The lighter blue areas in the Delaware Bay denote pollution. On the other hand, the light blue coloring of the Potomac River near Washington, D.C., is largely the result of turbidity caused by a major storm shortly before the picture was taken. A line of reefs shows very clearly off the New Jersey coast. Just inside the reef line is a wetland area which consists of water, marshland, and bogs. The white formations over Long Island are clouds. The mosaic was assembled by the General Electric Company Photographic Engineering Laboratory, 5030 Herzel Place, Beltsville, Maryland 20705. In addition to mosaics, the photo lab maintains an extensive library of individual LANDSAT color images covering locations throughout the world.

Cellular Radio

First Step in the Personal Communications Revolution

The revolution has begun.

As *Megatrends* author John Naisbitt explained in a recent speech, the development of an international personal communications network will lead to communications directly between individuals, bypassing the national communications networks completely.

"In effect," Naisbitt said, "this new multinational satellite-based individual-to-individual communications system will break down the last of the national barriers. That is extraordinarily important. People will be connected as individuals regardless of where they happen to be physically located at any one time."

The coupling of modern communications satellites with personal communications devices such as cellular radio "might help fashion us into some sort of global family,"

Cellular radio is already revolutionizing the mobile telephone industry, but it is actually only the first step toward something far more important—an international person-to-person communications network.

Naisbitt explained, "It will have social and political implications that are as profound as those which came with the introduction of the telephone itself to our society."

Dick Tracy would feel right at home in the personal communications revolution. After all, he has been carrying his own personal communications device on his wrist for almost 40 years. The wristwatch telephone is not quite here, but a completely self-contained portable cellular telephone that weighs just 28 ounces and fits inside a man's jacket pocket or a woman's purse has already been introduced. An even smaller, lighter model should be on the market within two years.

The cellular radio telephone isn't just a "cordless" telephone; those are simply extension phones without wires. They will operate effectively only up to about 750 feet from their "base station." By contrast, the cellular radio phone can operate without wires throughout an entire metropolitan area, and it can make long-distance and international calls through the existing wired telephone network.

STUART CRUMP, JR.

David Meilahn (left), an insurance agent who is a cellular customer, places the first commercial cellular phone call in the United States on October 13, 1983, in Chicago. With him are his wife, Gail, and Jeff Benuzzi, a technician with Chicago Communication Service.

"The coming of an inexpensive, practical, and totally portable wireless telephone will at last bring us to the era of personal communications— a revolution in which cellular is the first step."

Bell Telephone, through its Advanced Mobile Phone Service Inc. (AMPS) subsidiary Ameritech Mobile Communications, put the first commercial cellular telephone system on the air in the United States on October 13, 1983, in Chicago. More than 6,000 users—most with cellular telephones mounted in their cars—are already on that system, and more are being added daily.

The only thing preventing faster growth is the lack of available user equipment and service shops to install the mobile cellular phones in cars. At last count, more than 26 companies were selling cellular car phones in the Chicago area, and more companies are being added each month.

Washington, D.C., and Baltimore became the second and third cities to go on the air with cellular service when the Cellular One non-wireline system began operation in December 1983. Washington also became the first city in the world to have competing cellular systems when the AMPS subsidiary Bell Atlantic Mobile Systems wireline system went on the air on April 2, 1984. By mid-July 1984, 13 U.S. cities had at least one cellular system operating.

If all the cellular systems planned for the United States meet their announced start-up dates, more than two dozen cities will have fully operating commercial cellular systems before the end of 1984.

The Importance of Cellular Radio

Before cellular radio came along, car telephones were primarily an overpriced luxury service. Because of a limited radio channel availability, only a few hundred people in a given city could own car phones using today's conventional equipment—and only a dozen or so of them could place a phone call at the same time. Today's pre-cellular mobile telephone service is over-subscribed in most major cities. In

MOTOROLA

A cellular radio phone can operate without wires throughout an entire metropolitan area and can make long-distance and international calls through the existing telephone system.

How Cellular Telephones Work

To understand how cellular telephones work, it is helpful to start with the conventional "improved mobile telephone service" (IMTS) system, the type of pre-cellular car telephone system found in most areas today.

The heart of an IMTS system consists of a powerful two-way transmitting system that feeds directly into a large antenna located somewhere near the center of a city. The telephone's signal is transmitted between a car's antenna and the large central antenna. A car phone works within a radius of 25 or 35 miles from the tower.

Because the signal from the tower blankets the entire city, only one car telephone can use a single frequency in that city at any one time. And because only about 12 to 24 channels are allocated to each urban area by the Federal Communications Commission, only one or two dozen car-phone calls can be placed at a time.

By contrast, instead of one large antenna in the center of the city, a cellular system divides the city into a number of smaller segments or "cells" (hence the name "cellular"). Each cell has its own antenna, with the cells spaced throughout the city so that their signals overlap slightly.

When a call is made using the cellular system, the signal is fed into the cell that is nearest the phone. If the phone is in a car, the signal will eventually begin to fade at that cell site. A central computer—the "Mobile Telephone Switching Office," or MTSO—constantly monitors the strength of the signal not only in that cell site but also in adjacent cell sites.

At some point, the computer determines that the phone is leaving or has left one cell and is traveling into another, so the computer sends out a data signal to both cells, instructing them to "hand off" the signal from one cell to the other. This "hand-off" takes place in a fraction of a second. The central computer also routes cellular phone calls into the conventional landline telephone network. This interconnection allows cellular phones to place calls anywhere in the world.

Because the cell sites have low-powered transmitters, the same frequencies can be reused at other, non-adjacent cell sites elsewhere in the city. Thus the same frequency can be used and reused several times throughout the city, allowing an almost unlimited number of phone calls to be placed from cellular phones at the same time without the limits inherent in conventional IMTS systems.

Later on, as the number of subscribers on the system increases, the cell channels will become crowded. When that problem arises, the cells can be "subdivided" into a series of smaller cells, thus increasing the number of available channels.

A portable telephone is especially useful for construction sites and other locations where hard-wired landline telephones are difficult to install or are nonexistent.

most cities, if you call the phone company or a mobile telephone service and ask for a mobile telephone, you will be put on a 5- to 10-year waiting list—an indication of the market for more mobile telecommunications.

The development and widespread use of cellular radio, however, will eventually make the car telephone available to almost anyone who wants one. Cellular radio will allow thousands of people to own car telephones in any city.

The first cellular phones will be expensive—about $150-$200 a month (not including equipment), but that price is expected to drop dramatically within a few years. Cellular is, however, only the first of the new "personal communications" technologies.

The cellular radio as we know it today is actually a rather primitive instrument. In another two or three decades it will appear, in retrospect, to be about as advanced as was the crank telephone. Today's cellular radio is only the first step in the development of the totally wireless telephone of the future, which in turn is just part of the developing personal communications industry—a much larger industry than cellular alone.

Future Applications

Lighter, portable cellular phones that can be carried everywhere are expected to eventually replace the bulkier car phones that are perma-

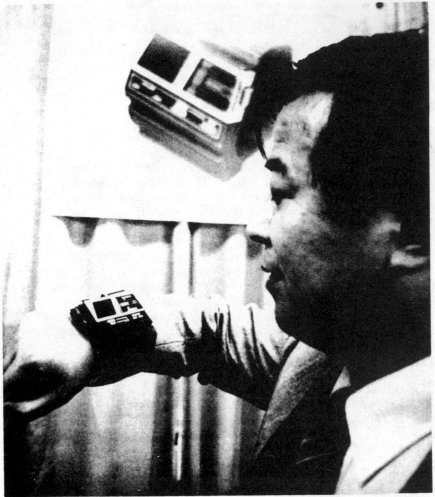

STUART CRUMP, JR.

Masashi Kuroyanagi, a Japanese electronic engineer, shows the two-way wrist radio that he designed. The device has a range of only about one-half mile, but it suggests what the two-way wrist radiotelephone of the future may be like.

nently mounted inside the car and can only be used when you are in your car. A self-contained portable phone that will work on the cellular system has already been developed, but it has only a limited range because its batteries provide less transmitting power than is available with standard mobile units.

The result is that the portable may not be usable everywhere in a city during the early phases of cellular implementation. Very few portable units currently are in use in Chicago because the system was not designed to accommodate the lower-powered portable units. However, several hundred portables are operating on the Washington/Baltimore system, which was designed specifically to accommodate the portable telephone.

The coming of an inexpensive, practical, and totally portable wireless telephone will at last bring us

to the era of personal communications—a revolution in which cellular is the first step. Cellular by itself constitutes a significant step forward in the development of wireless, portable personal communications devices. Those companies that manage to win cellular franchises in the larger cities will find that they have a valuable license, which explains why so many people have been applying for cellular licenses in hopes of getting a piece of the cellular "pie."

During its early years of operation, the high price of cellular service will put the cellular phone beyond the reach of the average consumer. But, as with every new electronic technology, the price of cellular service should begin to tumble as the systems come into more general use and manufacturers gear up to meet the demands of competition.

At least 28 companies have already announced their intention to supply a variety of cellular equipment for this new market. It is obvious that there will be tremendous competition for business. Users will be in the enviable position of being able to select from a variety of options the ones that best suit their needs.

The importance of cellular as the first of the new breed of telephones without wires is likely to be overlooked because the importance of most revolutionary new inventions is generally underestimated during their infancy. When Alexander Graham Bell demonstrated his early model telephones, few people appreciated just how radically different his device was. Many viewed it as a "toy." A member of the British Parliament, upon seeing the telephone for the first time, is reputed to have commented, "This may be well and good for our American cousins, but we shall have no need of it because we have an adequate supply of messenger boys."

In reality, the coming of cellular radio—with its possibilities for revolutionizing the personal communications industry—is one of the most important communications developments since the invention of the telephone itself.

About the Author

Stuart Crump, Jr., is the publisher of *Cellular Radio News, Personal Communications Magazine,* and *SMR News,* which are published by FutureComm Publications Inc., 4005 Williamsburg Court, Fairfax, Virginia 22032.

Robert S. Block

A Global Information Utility

High-powered satellites, along with other existing technologies, make possible a World Information Utility that could distribute virtually limitless information to every point on earth.

In a few years, a small antenna on your rooftop could give you access to hundreds of millions of pages of information every day. The amount of information that could be delivered by high-power satellites to homes and businesses is virtually unlimited.

The high-powered multi-channel satellite technology needed for direct broadcast satellites will be available by 1986. An information utility could be launched in the United States within a few years; by the end of the decade, the utility could operate worldwide.

Most of the technologies needed to operate an information utility in the United States already exist in one form or another. They are to be found in satellite communication systems, telephone-based data networks, teletext, videotext systems, pay television networks, teleconferencing and interactive media networks, personal computers, videotape recorders, video-game technology, security systems, and electronic billing systems.

What an Information Utility Could Do

By combining video, audio, and data, a utility could distribute an enormous amount of information for business, government, education, and entertainment. To illustrate an educational application and the incredible capacity of a utility, suppose an information utility offered a full-semester chemistry course. Using less than 35 ten-thousandths of its capacity for a single day, the utility could transmit a burst of information adequate to fill more than 100 hours of interactive education.

The course material could be recorded on a videotape and consist of 50 hours of audio lecture; 10,000 color slides; 4,000 graphs; 100 interactive videographic experiments; and 6,000 pages of text, reference material, workbook exercises, and exams.

The course would be equivalent to three lectures a week, plus two lab classes a week, for 13 weeks. Students would listen to a lecture while viewing the appropriate slides and graphs, read the assigned text and reference material, and then do workbook assignments. Using sophisticated branching techniques, the system would automatically refer students to appropriate parts of the lecture, text, reference material, slides, or graphs, depending on the response to the workbook exercises.

At one point in the workbook assignment, two beakers might appear on the screen in the form of an interactive videographic display. Students would then conduct an assigned chemistry experiment by selecting and mixing chemicals and monitoring the result.

If the experiment was not understood, or was done incorrectly, ad-

KATHLEEN GAMMON/SEATTLE PACIFIC UNIVERSITY

No place like home to work with a computer! An information utility makes it easier for people to work or study in their homes—or anywhere they choose. For example, the utility could provide a student with an entire 13-week chemistry course, including lectures, homework, lab experiments, and exams.

ditional reference materials would be cited and the experiment redone. Upon completion of the workbook, students would take an examination. When completed, the test would be scored immediately and the students would be told their grades and what sections to read or review. The scores would be encrypted for transmission to the educational institution.

Students could be required to provide the test score or be barred from further class participation until it was provided. If tuition were charged, students would have to pay on time or lose access to the system.

The security system of the utility, plus that of the user terminal, would prevent unauthorized persons from gaining access to or tampering with grades or payment records. It would also keep students from changing their scores or say-

ing they paid the bill when they had not.

How the Utility Would Work

As envisioned, an information utility would not be a storage center for information. Instead, it would be a distribution center for information received from suppliers. Suppliers would provide information in a standardized format at the appropriate time. The utility would label and encrypt the information, then transmit it up to the communications satellites for distribution over wide geographic areas. Utilities would use satellites because of their low cost, high efficiency, and large capacity.

Some users would receive the information directly from the satellite, while others might receive it after redistribution by cable, broadcast, master antenna systems, microwave, etc. Two-way com-

munications could be established by telephone, two-way cable, microwave, return satellite transmission, or other means.

Receiving antennas (dishes) would be from two to four feet in diameter, perhaps smaller, depending on receiver location and satellite power. Equipment capable of receiving, decoding, and displaying data, slides, sound, and full-color motion on standard TV sets will cost less than $500, based on current technology. In the next few years, an additional $500 may also buy data processing, storage, and printing capability.

A utility would probably find it best to own and operate the satellites itself. Assuming a $100 million cost for an eight-transponder high-power satellite, and a life expectancy of 10 years, the $10 million a year cost breaks down to $145 per hour (or $2.43 per minute) for each

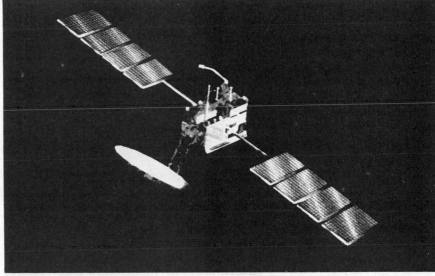

COURTESY OF TELEASE, INC.

Communications satellites such as this could deliver vast amounts of information to any point on earth, says author Robert S. Block.

transponder, which carries one full TV channel. Even if two satellites are used to cover the continental United States (so people wouldn't need such big antennas) full coverage would cost less than $300 an hour.

One-Way vs. Two-Way Transmission

A utility would be designed to provide both one-way and two-way communications links between a vast information base and a dispersed network of users. The relative use of one-way and two-way techniques would depend on many factors and would probably change over time.

● **One-way transmission.** An information utility will most likely begin mainly as a one-way system. Some information would be transmitted continuously, with access time measured in seconds or fractions of a second. Other information would be available in minutes, hours, days, or weeks. Obviously, it is more efficient to transmit the Super Bowl game on national television (one-way) than to have 50 million viewers call in to the network to order the game on their picture phone (two-way).

Even for information that is specific to individuals, it is often more efficient to use one-way techniques for the distribution of a large volume of information and employ two-way to handle the exceptions.

For example, it is better for banks to mail checking account statements to their customers at the end of each month (one-way) rather than to have customers call all month to ask about bank balances (two-way).

"Smart" user terminals with inexpensive mass storage memories and the huge transmission capacity of a utility should make it possible to provide most services in the one-way mode. The utility would continuously provide the schedule of information transmission so that users could program their terminals to automatically capture and store needed information. At a convenient time, the user could interact with the stored information base. The result would be similar to "on line" interactivity with any stored information base.

● **Two-way transmission.** A user might need information before the next scheduled transmission. In that case, it could be requested from the supplier directly. The information could be provided immediately on the two-way link or through the utility, depending on the nature and the amount of information requested.

The User Terminal

Several models of information terminals may be offered. The simplest system would consist of a receiver/decoder and a display device to display information in real time. This could include such services as electronic newsletters, stock and commodity prices, world

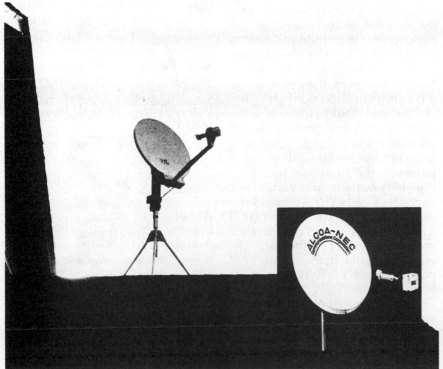

PHOTOS COURTESY OF TELEASE, INC.

Satellite receiver on housetop collects a wide variety of information signals sent via satellite. A World Information Utility could be launched with existing technologies such as teletext, videotex, satellite communications systems, and so on, says author Block.

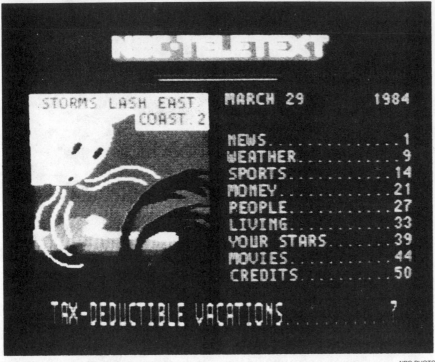

NBC PHOTO

Teletext service offers menu of information to choose from. Although it is a one-way transmission, this system allows users to select and store blocks of information to be read or processed at a more convenient time.

weather, sport scores, and paging services.

A more complex information center might consist of a receiver/decoder, a videocassette recorder, and an audio cassette recorder, plus components very similar to those found in any good personal computer: a central processing unit, a keyboard, main memory, disk or diskette memory, a monitor or TV set, and a printer.

Tape recorders could act as a mass storage medium for data and to store video and audio. Video and audio could be viewed and reviewed, while data and programs could be downloaded to the computer's main memory or diskettes for processing.

Access to certain information could be restricted to specific groups such as doctors, police, union members, or other subscriber categories. To control access, a utility would encrypt the information and assign it an identification number, authorization codes, and a cost. Terminals could gain access only to "authorized" information and would accumulate a record of usage and costs for all services purchased. Each month the terminal would print (or dis-

play) a detailed bill. When paying, subscribers would send along a copy of the bill, so that the utility could distribute the payment equitably among the information suppliers.

To assure the accuracy of received billing information, the utility would transmit a detailed bill back to the user terminal, which would compare the information with its secure stored purchase record. In the event of a discrepancy, the terminal would notify the subscriber and could cease to work until the bill had been properly paid and a matching signal sent from the utility. To further assure payment and minimize bad debt, the utility could require an advance deposit or establish a maximum credit limit for each subscriber. If a subscriber's remaining deposit/credit reached a zero balance, the terminal would stop working until payment was made or the credit limit increased.

Electronic billing techniques would permit a utility to operate in a one-way mode, eliminate the need to mail bills, reduce losses associated with nonpayment, increase the speed of payment to information suppliers, and give sub-

scribers continuous information on their bill—i.e., they would not have to wait until the end of the month to find out how much they had spent.

The Future of a World Information Utility

The establishment of one or more satellite-based information utilities in the United States is likely to occur in the next few years. There are no technical, regulatory, political, or economic roadblocks to such a service. Indeed, it is merely an extension of existing services.

Creation of a World Information Utility requires the solution to nontechnical problems far more complex than the technical ones. Issues such as cultural, religious, and political censorship; cross-border data flow; language barriers; and copyright and patent protection would have to be negotiated with governments throughout the world.

Even so, because a utility would have the technical ability to provide or deny access to specific information on a subscriber-by-subscriber basis, the system could operate within almost any established government or nongovernment policy. That flexibility, along with very substantial benefits to every society, may lead to a World Information Utility—and that, to a better world.

About the Author

Robert S. Block is founder and president of Telease, Inc., a California-based company that develops applications of high technology for communication and information systems. He is an inventor, holding seven patents and three patents pending for television, computer, and telephone technologies. He spoke on the World Information Utility at the World Future Society's Fifth General Assembly, "WorldView '84," in June. His address is Telease, Inc., 1875 Century Park East, Suite 930, Los Angeles, California 90067.

Cartoons by Computer

A cartoonist finds that the computer is no joke as an artist's tool.

SPYDER WEBB

Thomas Alva Edison and his groupies.

Artist Spyder Webb has made the jump from hand drawing to creating-by-computer.

With his Apple Macintosh personal computer, he explains, "I draw with a 'mouse' rather than with a pad/stylus arrangement. The results in black and white are excellent, and, by printing onto watercolor paper, I can paint color in the traditional manner, blending the most ancient and the newest technologies to produce something that for me is more comfortable, natural, and aesthetically pleasing than either alone."

Webb doesn't see computer-aided drawing as a substitute for the "real" thing. "Creating art with a personal computer is not better or worse, faster or slower, than drawing with conventional media," he says. "Neither should it be approached as a means of imitating traditional media. It is something different."

Once mastered, a computer can make the creative process less tedious. "I can try a series of steps, and if I am displeased with the result, I can revert to an earlier version of the drawing, which I've saved in the computer's memory. I can try several versions, all branching from a particular point in the development of the drawing, and save

each version, without having to do the entire thing over again each time."

Webb doubts that computer-drawn art will replace art drawn with traditional tools; rather, it will add to the methods available to artists to create images. "Is it the wave of the future? Well, it's at least *a* wave of the future," he says. "One thing is certain, at least for me—it's not just a new way of doing old things, it's a way of doing new things."

Source: Spyder Webb Cartoons, 8637 Liberia Avenue, Manassas, Virginia 22110.

George Bugliarello

HYPERINTELLIG

The Next Evolutionary Step

Hyperintelligence—a dramatic extension of the power of the brain—will be made possible by global computer networks. Hyperintelligence will help to create a new and better global society.

Global networks offer us the possibility of expanding our biological intelligence to form a hyperintelligence—an intelligence operating on a global scale and representing a major evolutionary step for our society and our species.

To understand the significance and potential of hyperintelligence and how it may come about, we need to look at the parallels between biological and computer evolution.

The practical use of computers started in 1945 with the ENIAC machine—the first electronic computer. From that time until the mid-1970s, computers were used primarily by themselves, as isolated and generally very expensive machines. But in the last few years the explosive growth in the number of computers—due to dramatic cost reductions and the great advances in telecommunications exemplified by optical fibers and satellites—has made possible extensive and far-reaching networks of computers connected to other computers, to data banks, and to other devices.

In the United States, there are now millions of personal computers, several hundred thousand larger computers, and well over a thousand large data banks. It will not be long before the majority of households and businesses in the United States have a computing device of some sort, such as a personal computer or an intelligent terminal. A very large number of these devices will be interconnected. The same developments are occurring in Japan and, at a slower pace, in Western Europe and other parts of the world.

The emergence of computer networks interconnecting millions of computers and their users can be viewed as the most recent step in the development of our ability to sense, to reason, to remember. This development started within our own bodies but is now being carried out at an accelerated pace by societal and mechanical devices. It has become what I call for short biosomic, that is, driven by an increasingly indissoluble combination of biological organisms, social organizations, and machines (or artifacts).

In evolutionary terms, language is a product of the last purely biological evolutionary step that led to the emergence of modern man some 50,000 years ago. It gave us the ability to conceptualize and to communicate with precision with each other.

Writing was a subsequent evolutionary step, but a biosomic rather than a purely biological one, because it required artifacts such as pencil and paper. It expanded the reach of our communications beyond the range of our voice and beyond the strictures of biological "real time" communications, thus giving us memory more lasting than the biological one.

The reach of our mind was further extended by printing and then by telecommunications, both exquisitely biosomic activities, as they involve complex machines and sophisticated social organizations.

Marshall McLuhan perceptively saw telecommunications making the earth into a "global village." But in reality it is the current biosomic evolutionary step—the extended symbiosis of telecommunications and computers—that is making the global village truly possible in a technical sense and is endowing it with global intelligence. The immense potential power of a global computer network to extend our brain is obvious if we consider that, while in the brain every node is a neuron, in a computer network every node is a human brain augmented by a computer.

The power of a computer network to extend our brain increases with the number of nodes. Every quantum step in the dimensions of the network provides a quantum step in its capabilities, in the same way that every evolutionary increase in our brain size has added to the capabilities of our species.

Specialized Networks and Free-Association Networks

The size of a computer network is not its only relevant parameter, any more than the brain is just a collection of neurons. Structure and organization are equally important. Thus, we must differentiate a general node (represented by an ordinary citizen with a personal computer) from a data bank, or from a specialized node (represented by a professional or specialist, often able to utilize more powerful computers).

We also need to differentiate run-of-the-mill local networks, such as an office network or expert networks, where the key nodes may be teachers, doctors, or other experts, from what I like to call free-association or "affinity" networks, linking general users. While local area networks and expert networks are bound to be relatively small,

ENCE

usually involving no more than a few thousand nodes, affinity networks are virtually unlimited in their growth potential and could ultimately interconnect hundreds of millions or even billions of people.

The significance and impact of local area networks and expert networks are relatively easy to perceive, since a number of them—however embryonic and unsophisticated—are already in existence. We can, for instance, envision the improvement in the quality of health care if doctors were able to make frequent "electronic rounds" of patients at home or in the hospital via a network. A terminal at the patient's location—personal computer or other device—could be endowed with sensors to monitor temperature, pulse rate, blood pressure, or other vital signs and programmed to call attention to abnormal readings.

Similarly, we already see improvements in teaching through an "electronic classroom," consisting of teachers and students communicating with each other, with the library, and with data bases via a computer network. For example, at my university—the Polytechnic Institute of New York—each freshman is given a compact computer that can be connected via a modem to a computer network and operated either at the university or at home. The computer can also be carried in a briefcase and operated while commuting. At other universities, networks of less portable but usually more powerful personal computers are being established in student dormitories.

The "electronic classroom" can be expanded to include students from other courses, from other institutions, and even from other countries. A broad array of data bases can be utilized, and classes can be taught by several teachers from different disciplines and locations, thus providing the students with broad interdisciplinary and

"With appropriate programming, a network becomes a sensing device, not only for physical but also for social, political, economic, or other issues."

cross-cultural experiences. These are not dreams; they are reasonable and even conservative expectations of the revolution in education that will be brought about by the computer networks now in the process of development.

The Impact of Free-Association Networks

Free-association networks—those whose nodal points are computing devices operated by ordinary citizens—will have a far greater and more fundamental impact. The biosomic amplification of our brains embodied in these networks will make possible a series of progressively more complex and significant activities bound to revolutionize our society and propel it to higher levels of achievement and humanity.

Two examples are greater awareness and sensory capacity and greater problem-solving ability:

● **Awareness and sensing.** Those connected by a computer network—however extensive the network may be geographically—will be able to get to know each other. They will also be able to form, through their interactions, groups having affinities of interest, such as people living near a volcano, gourmet cooks, people having parents with Alzheimer's disease, teachers of Ottoman history, or people seeking a market for their skills. The possible subgroupings in a free-association network are almost infinite, and so are the options for a network member to participate in them.

The network will also have the potential for knowing the environment, both physical and social, surrounding each node—that is, surrounding each member. The aggregate of such knowledge can provide members of a cluster and of the entire network with an awareness of that environment. For instance, if the cluster is one of people living near a volcano, it can keep them abreast of changes in

temperature, of unusual animal restlessness, or of any other physical phenomena that may have a bearing on their safety. This could give the members of the cluster a better knowledge of how to help each other in case of an emergency. In turn, the network can tell the rest of the world of the perceptions, concerns, and needs of that group of dwellers near the volcano.

With appropriate programming, a network becomes a sensing device, not only for physical but also for social, political, economic, or other issues. Such a device can be more comprehensive, far more sensitive, and far abler to respond quickly than anything available today through mass media, traditional polls, or electoral mechanisms. If the nodes of a network are also equipped with physical sensors, the sensing capacity of the network can be further extended—to weather, to pollution, or to traffic conditions, as well as to providing fire alerts or pinpointing crime.

● **Problem-solving.** The combined brain and computer power of an entire computer network can be mobilized to solve some of the problems of concern to members. The more extended and diverse the network, the greater its problem-solving potential.

A network of millions of nodes turned to problem-solving represents a large quantum step in the problem-solving ability of our species. For instance, the over 500,000 engineers and scientists involved in research and development activities in the United States are currently able to interact only to a limited extent—and slowly. They are geographically scattered. When they want to communicate with each other, they can do so by telephone or via meetings that rarely exceed an audience of a thousand. They also communicate—but more slowly and with more limited feedback—through professional associations, which seldom exceed 100,000 members,

or through publications, where the feedback is even slower and more constrained.

Under these conditions synergism is quite limited. Much greater power could be achieved by interactions via a computer network to which each researcher had access through his or her personal computer. Even greater problem-solving power could be achieved by a network encompassing the roughly 3 million engineers and scientists engaged in research and development worldwide.

The Importance of Language

Most computer users in the western world use English because it is the *lingua franca* of science—a situation reinforced by the numerical preponderance worldwide of the United States computer market and by the associated large investment in software written in English. With global computer networks, the user's language could be English or could be any other language. But it would in any case be greatly enriched by terms and concepts from other languages, such as *blitzkrieg* or *chic*—words not exactly translatable and thus best kept in their original language.

This could ultimately lead to a world language—a new hybrid English—offering access to worldwide computer networks, to data banks compatible with that language, to electronic newspapers, etc. Access could, of course, also occur in the user's native language rather than in computer English, but it would be much less efficient. A translation would be required, which engages a great deal of computer power and is far from being successfully achieved.

Hyperlanguage and Hyperintelligence

Access to the network and communication within the network is only the first step necessary in the development of a network lan-

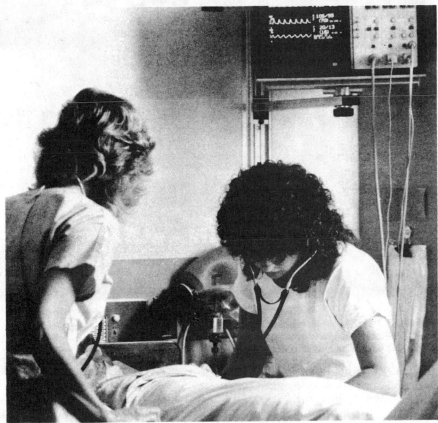

HEWLETT-PACKARD

A computer measures this patient's vital functions and notes hourly trends. Such a computer could be tapped into by doctors from their offices, allowing them to check frequently on patients.

MICOM SYSTEMS, INC.

Students use one of the computer terminals provided in every Union College dorm room, giving students access to the college's computer. Students at other institutions—even those abroad—could be hooked into the same computer.

guage. When that step is achieved, a second and far more exciting vista opens up: the creation of a new language for describing the large aggregate of knowledge and feelings embedded in a network. Such a network will "feel" in a different way than its component nodes—not in a way antithetical to them but more holistic, in the same way that a brain is more than just the sum of the processes in each of its neurons. The network will also "know" more comprehensively and in a more integrated fashion than just the sum of its nodes.

As the result of these feelings and knowledge, inevitably the network will generate new syntheses in all sorts of areas—from politics to art to science—and will provide a quantum expansion of our minds in the realm of thought and in that of action. The key to this is a language for conceptualizing and integrating the network "gestalt." We can envision that such a language—in effect a hyperlanguage—will emerge from a process not un-

like that which gave birth to human language.

Human language, we believe, has been shaped from the events and from the organization of human society. Similarly, the hyperlanguage of the network will have its start from the events and from the structure characterizing both the network and the environment with which the network interacts.

In other words, if we view the networks as an emerging new and fundamental form of human organization, as a new form of work organization, of educational organization, or organization for leisure and for other social interactions, then we can expect these new forms to give birth to a new hyperlanguage that will overarch our traditional natural languages.

The emergence of the network's hyperlanguage will make the networks as different from a mere interconnection of nodes—nodes satisfied only to communicate with each other to respond to their immediate needs—as humans are

from chimpanzees. The chimps have some ability to grasp new concepts but no language to formulate them unless that language—one of simple signs and instructions—is proffered to them.

Thus the hyperlanguage of the networks will be the expression of the hyperintelligence of the networks, and vice versa—as two interdependent and mutually reinforcing processes.

Hyperintelligence and a New Morality

The emergence of hyperintelligence should lead first of all to a new morality, because by definition it will put us in a broader context, more connected to each other across national and ideological boundaries and more connected to our environment, both on earth and in the rest of the universe. Furthermore, it should transform global computer networks into global action networks, integrating knowledge, intelligence, and the new moral sense toward the achievement of new goals for our species.

It is tempting to speculate, for instance, whether our present balance of nuclear terror or our inability to develop a decent standard of living for humanity or to resolve local conflicts are not the result of a lack of hyperintelligence to guide our actions.

Developing a Hyperlanguage

There are many ways we can approach the task of building a hyperlanguage. None are mutually exclusive, and probably each will have much to contribute to the others.

We could, for instance, systematically design a whole hierarchy of network functions somewhat analogous to those of the brain. We could look at reflexes, at the creation of network rhythms, and at the balance between stimuli and centrifugal signals, which is key to the crucial feedback process in the brain. The development of capabilities such as these for the network (by no means an easy task) would then give us the instruments for creating truly adaptive and intelligent computer networks.

Alternatively, a somewhat less structured approach is to study and further develop the social protocols for the interactions among the users of an existing network, such as a local area network. Just as the social interactions among human beings are believed to have given birth to our natural language, the necessity of the users of a network to develop (however informally at first) protocols for their interactions is a good starting point for a hyperlanguage. However, the genesis of the hyperlanguage is bound to be more complex.

Network Play

A very significant role in the genesis of the hyperintelligence necessary to create the hyperlanguage (or vice versa) is bound to be assumed by play, just as in the case of human intelligence. Play or gaming—the use of the network to create make-believe situations—differs from modeling and simulation only in purpose. By relaxing constraints rooted in reality, it gives free rein to imagination.

But play also has another very important function. It provides the members of the network with a sense of control over events and situations that is denied to them by

BRITISH INFORMATION SERVICES

Computerized radar tracks weather conditions. Networks utilizing similar equipment can monitor meteorological and geological changes and flash early warnings to network members who might be affected, says author Bugliarello.

the reality outside of play. That sense of control is believed to be a powerful element in the development of human intelligence. It can be reinforced by network play and used to enhance the intelligence of the network.

Furthermore, network play can also come to acquire a significance analogous to sports in channeling exuberant human energies. But a network "olympics" would be far more heady than traditional sports viewing because the games would be participatory, involving interactively all the members of the network. Such a network olympics could easily transcend geographical boundaries, giving rise to a new spirit of sport and games that would tend to counterbalance the growing nationalistic strictures of many of today's international competitions.

Other Consequences of Computer Networks

The emergence of a hyperlanguage and of hyperintelligence is but one of the consequences arising from the creation of extensive computer networks. There are several other significant consequences, including:

● **More powerful collective memories.** The first relatively mundane but important consequence will be the growth in number and

power of data banks—the specialized memories of the networks—to respond to the multiplicity of needs of the networks. The data banks will become increasingly interactive, able not only to supply information but also to cull information from the networks. (Of course, appropriate "information filters" will be required, to ensure the validity of the information fed to the data banks.)

The encyclopedia of the future will be a data bank—or better, a set of interconnected data banks—and the library of the future will offer as a major service the coordination and retrieval of data banks. The library can have a branch in every home and every office that is part of the computer network connected to it.

The very name "library," with its connotation of "book" as its primary function, may be replaced by a term more descriptive of its new function. But books as we know them today will continue to be very important, and to be collected in libraries, because browsing cannot quite be replaced by electronic means—although forms of electronic browsing will undoubtedly develop, with their own unique characteristics.

● **New forms of social organization.** A more far-reaching and truly revolutionary consequence of com-

"There will emerge a greater sense of community, thanks to the multiple, varied, and deep interactions that networks afford."

puter networks will be the development of new forms of social organization. There will be new forms of organization for the delivery of services, for domestic activities, for designing, for manufacturing, even for doing "network art" (for example, interactive artistic compositions involving many networks using computer graphics). There will be a real possibility of integrating the home and the workplace by placing them both as nodes of the same network, with potentially revolutionary consequences for the configuration of our cities.

There will also emerge a greater sense of community, thanks to the multiple, varied, and deep interactions that networks afford. The networks will also enable us to deal with greater sophistication with political questions, beyond the stilted confines of a simple "yes" or "no" decision—and will enable us to deal with the consequences of political decisions. It will be possible, for instance, to simulate and test decisions over an entire network before they become translated into action. This would be a major step in the evolution of democracy.

● **New professions.** New professions will emerge to manage the multiplicity of functions of computer networks—to manage, for example, data banks, the new libraries, or the new office-home interactions (responding to questions such as how to monitor network performance, how to bill, how to optimize interactions, and how to maintain and repair).

Dangers

Some of the very attributes and capabilities that make computer networks and hyperintelligence such a quantum step in biosomic evolution raise issues and entail dangers that need to be recognized and faced. Among these are:

● **The need to retain other forms of expression and communication.**

We must be extremely careful to avoid stifling or destroying other forms of expression, of communication and interaction, lest computer networks, rather than expanding our faculties, simply redirect them. Furthermore, although computer networks offer us the opportunity to advance evolution, we will need periodically to wean ourselves away from them, just as periodically we engage in camping, hunting, or other throwbacks to periods of more direct immersion in nature.

● **International tensions.** Nondemocratic societies will endeavor to control computer networks within their borders and to prevent the creation of computer networks that cross their borders, as networks can represent the most subtle menace to the survival of authoritarianism. This in turn may lead to heightened international tensions.

Eventually, however, nondemocratic societies will have to participate in some form of international computer networking if they want to avoid the penalties of being left technologically and scientifically far behind societies that encourage the free diffusion of networks. Thus, even in nondemocratic societies we can expect a moderate growth of those computer networks that exclude political expressions, such as networks for health care, science, or technical training. The difficult problem for authoritarian regimes will then be how to bar these systems from also being used for unauthorized communications.

● **Social inequities.** Inevitably, access to a computer network costs money, as it requires possession of or access to a personal computer or other form of terminal, as well as expenditures for long-distance communication. This is bound to exclude the poor and less-educated segments of the world population. It is an urgent responsibility of governments, both at national and in-

ternational levels, to see that these disparities do not result in permanently disenfranchised human beings.

● **Survivability.** The networks need to be protected against sabotage as well as against the possibility of a massive crisis such as an electromagnetic pulse created by a nuclear burst. Although complete survivability of all networks would be prohibitively expensive, selective survivability is achievable and is a must, lest the new biosomic brain of our society be destroyed.

The Hope for a New Society

It is easy to foresee a time when being plugged into a computer network will be as essential to civilized living as having access to transportation or being literate. If we are willing and able to pursue the great opportunities that the emergence of global computer networks offers us, and if we are vigilant about some of the associated dangers, then we can truly expect that hyperintelligence and a new and higher form of human society will emerge. This will be a society qualitatively and quantitatively far more aware of its potential. It will be, above all, a society both motivated and able to act. Hyperintelligence—and the global computer networks that make it possible, are the best hope that we have to create this new society—to *create* our future rather than just to accept it.

About the Author

George Bugliarello is president of the Polytechnic Institute of New York. He holds a doctorate from MIT and is a specialist in fluid mechanics, computer language, and biomedical engineering, with concern for the social implications of technology. His address is Polytechnic Institute of New York, 333 Jay Street, Brooklyn, New York 11201.

FOR FURTHER READING

The following annotated bibliography is selected from recent issues of FUTURE SURVEY and FUTURE SURVEY ANNUAL, edited by Michael Marien and published by the World Future Society.

This bibliography makes no attempt to be comprehensive. It is designed simply to suggest a few selected references for persons seeking information going beyond the scope of this book.

The source of each item is indicated by its number:

Numbers 1—1603 are from FUTURE SURVEY ANNUAL 1979
Numbers 1604—3090 are from FUTURE SURVEY ANNUAL 1980-81
Numbers 3091—4457 are from FUTURE SURVEY ANNUAL 1981-82
Numbers 4458—5597 are from FUTURE SURVEY ANNUAL 1983

The numbers beginning 84 or 85 are from monthly FUTURE SURVEY issues published during 1984 and 1985.

Readers seeking additional references may find them in these publications. To stay current with future developments in computers and related fields, readers may turn to forthcoming editions of FUTURE SURVEY ANNUAL and the monthly FUTURE SURVEY. An annual subscription to FUTURE SURVEY, including both the monthly and the annual, is $60 per year.

General

5364

Exploring the World of the Personal Computer. Jack M. Nilles (Center for Futures Research, USC). Englewood Cliffs NJ: Prentice-Hall, Jan 1982/234p/ $15.95;$12.95pb.

The big computer of today will be a personal computer in 5 to 10 years. The major uncertainty is not whether, but when and how the new computers will insinuate themselves into our lives. This introductory overview, based on a technology assessment of personal computers (**FS Annual 1979**) #14560, describes 1) capabilities and limitations of personal computers, present and future; 2) uses to which personal computers are being or will be put in the home and office, and for education, recreation, and health care; and 3) philosophical issues of presernt and prospective uses: privacy, equity, standards, consumer protection, crime and other misuse, effects on creativity and innovation, and the position of the US in the international economy. Concludes with a balanced summary of the computer as friend (offering a greatly increased set of options) and as foe (invading privacy, creating unemployment, etc). [NOTE: The use of nontechnical language in this book makes it appropriate for high school students and, perhaps, college underclassmen.] **(introduction to impacts of personal computer)**

4300

The Microelectronics Revolution: The Complete Guide to the New Technology and Its Impact on Society. Edited by Tom Forester. Cambridge MA: MIT Press, Feb 1981/608p/ $25.00;$12.50pb.

Essays on the origins and nature of microelectronics, the characteristics of the burgeoning micro-chip industry, the growing use of microprocessors in everyday products, automation in factories, the word processing revolution in offices, the consequences for employment and implications for industrial relations, and the problems of a microelectronic age or "information society." **(micro-chip anthology)**

5362

The Rise of the Computer State. David Burnham (*The New York Times*). Foreword by Walter Cronkite. NY: Random House, May 1983/273p/$17.95.

Computers and telecommunications enormously enhance the ability of organizations to collect, store, collate, and distribute all kinds of information about virtually all Americans. Computers have allowed far more organizations to have far more access to far more people at far less cost than ever was possible in the age of the manual file. The computer has thus wrought a fundamental change in American life by encouraging the physical migration of information about the most minute details of our personal and public lives into the computerized files of a large and growing number of corporations, government bureaucracies, and trade associations. Many computer scientists, government officials, and business executives take comfort in the observation that there has been little concrete evidence of widespread abuse of these interlocked systems. Because the changes have not kept pace with the most dramatic predictions, the apologists have been able to minimize the significance of those alterations that have undoubtedly occurred. The potential for abuse is considerable, and many more alterations are in store, such as fifth generation computers [see **The Fifth Generation,** above]. Since virtually all research funds to enhance the computer are provided by large organizations like the Department of Defense, AT&T, and IBM, it seems likely that the first applications of these new computers will be to assist these groups achieve their varied goals and not necessarily to nurture individual freedom. Many of the current areas of concern about the effects of the computer were identified decades ago, but the US has yet to work out a way to consider the merits and demerits of major new computer systems. For every new system whose development has been stopped, scores of other systems have been put in place with little or no examination of the questions that surround their operation [NOTE: Often causing economic hardship, not to mention social hardship. See item on "conspicuous computing," #5366.] As suggested by Senator Sam Ervin, the danger of massed data bases requires the creation of a permanent counterweight: a commission serving as ombudsman for both public and private computer systems. Concludes with a possible scenario of the US in 2020, showing a superficially glossy but limiting world of high technology alongside a despairing underclass. **(growing threat of computer abuse)**

2816

The Micro Millennium. Christopher Evans (deceased, 1979; formerly National Physical Laboratory, UK). NY: Viking, April 1980/255p/$10.95; Pocket Books/Washington Square Press, March 1981/$3.50pb. [published in UK in 1979 as **The Mighty Micro**].

The world is on the verge of a computer revolution which will be even more rapid, widespread, and overwhelming than the industrial revolution. After describing how computers operate, Evans considers four pathways of growth, ranging from immediate cessation to indefinite acceleration, concluding that growth will accelerate in the near future. Three stages of development are then considered.

In the short-term future (1980 to 1982), computers will continue to become dramatically smaller, the amount of information they can hold will continue to increase, and costs will decline. In the early 1980s, computers will become the leading industry in the world, and IBM will soon displace General Motors as the world's largest corporation. Bureaucracies will rely increasingly on computer modeling, and the public will gain greater awareness of computers. Employment patterns will change rapidly, but not precipitously.

In the middle-term future (1983-1990), books will be compressed into chip form, with the new computerized version of a book available at something like 20¢, as raw material and distribution costs reduce sensationally with miniaturization. Computer books will be mailed by the dozens in small envelopes, and, at a later date, be transmitted instantly by cable or microwave. "Smart" encyclopedias of the late 1980s will do their own research, acting literally as study partners. The power of the established professions (physicians, accountants, lawyers, teachers) will be eroded. With direct computer scanning of credit cards and automatic transfers of funds, cash will no longer be necessary. To guard against crime, credit cards will be equipped with a built-in computer chip which identifies its owner through fingerprints or some equally unique sign. Petty theft will decrease, as well as burglary (due to sophisticated security systems) and traffic accidents (due to "collision-proof" vehicles with batteries of microprocessors capable of detecting danger). Video conference systems will enable a decentralization of commercial and business life, and industrial robots will be in widespread use. In order to support a growing, increasingly more affluent civilization, and the complexity that it has spawned, people will turn to computers for assistance in managing.

The long-term future (1991-2000) will be dominated by the evolution of machine intelligence to the Ultra-Intelligent Machine: a computer programmed to perform any intellectual activity at least marginally better than man. This evolution can be expected because of great commercial forces coming into play, big budget research sponsored by government, and the temptation of creating an Ultra-Intelligent Machine. Indeed, the technology itself can be used to advance the pace of development. Some far-reaching political and social impacts include the possible decline of communism, as fantastically cheap devices make the dream of universal affluence and freedom from drudgery a reality; after this, even the most ardent Marxist would have to bow to the overwhelming testimony of the microprocessor. The increased affluence of the computerized world may also spill over into the Third World, and information between rich and poor nations will be widely exchanged. The working week will be down to 20 hours or less by the 1990s, with substantial increases in vacation time and much earlier retirement. Enormous advances will be made in home entertainment devices such as wall-size displays, which will increasingly shift the focus of attention to the home (with the risk of developing an introverted society, especially if the outside world becomes squalid or dangerous). New religions might have the computer at their center, either playing a Satanic role, or serving as a deity. Microminiaturization will have a profound effect on general health. For example, many wristwatches will incorporate minute computers which monitor body processes, or microprocessors might be implanted within the body to detect the first sign of malignant cells being generated. Computers might also act as a sounding board and confidant in psychotherapy. Increasingly, they will serve as intellectual and emotional partners, and it might be like having the wisest and most knowledgeable private tutors on earth: an Einstein to teach physics and a Freud to discuss psychoanalysis.

One of the main problems of the 1990s will be to find an outlet for human energy no longer channelled into daily work. Some of the problems of "enforced leisure" will be solved by an increasing preoccupation with sport and exercise, and by a flowering of culture and the arts. New global goals may be proclaimed, such as a vigorous thrust into space, or large expeditions under the oceans. The book is concluded by a discussion of the limits to growth of computers.

(computer revolution in next 20 years)

5366

Computer Choices: Beware of Conspicuous Computing. H. Dominic Covvey and Neil Harding McAlister (U of Toronto and Toronto General Hospital). Reading MA: Addison-Wesley, 1982/225p/$8.95pb.

The early predictions of the first computer prophets did not come true, and many businesses suffered rude awakenings as they realized that promised solutions would not be forthcoming. Here, the co-authors of **Computer Consciousness** (A-W, 1980) offer a weapon against "digital obfuscation": a survey of practical issues in the development or acquisition of any computer system, with a particular slant toward the computing neophyte. To a large extent, computers have been oversold by computer interests and some user advocates. The principle at work is "conspicuous consumption" —an irrational lust for the aura of sophistication and progress that a person, department, or institution can acquire by becoming "computerized." The techniques of consumer motivation have been just as effective in selling computing products as in selling automobiles. The result is that the remains of once grandiose computer schemes lie de-energized in many back rooms of our institutions. Chapters are devoted to consumer issues, technical issues (software engineering, security problems, economics of computing), and management issues. Concludes that the computer must be dragged from its pedestal and put in its proper place as an adjunct to human processes, where the human-machine interaction creates beneficial results. The enemy to be faced and conquered is not computers, but us: our perception of computers and the way we choose to use them. [NOTE: A popular guide raising intriguing questions about the degree of computer waste and misuse in society: is it a relatively small problem, or one that is large enough to be a major source of lagging economic performance?]

(dangers of "conspicuous computing")

4299

The Computer Establishment. Katharine Davis Fishman (NYC). NY: Harper & Row, Oct 1981/468p/$20.95.

A journalistic history of the growth of computer technology, how IBM came to dominate the field, and the upstart "dwarfs" who have dared to challenge the preeminent leader. The outcome of the massive IBM antitrust trial will affect the industry's future. Concludes with chapters on problems of privacy and on new technologies enabling home information systems, electronic banking, artificial intelligence, and medical applications.

(computer industry)

2817

Microcomputers: A Technology Forecast and Assessment to the Year 2000. Kensall D. Wise (U of Michigan), Kan Chen (U of Michigan), and Ronald E. Yokely (Bethesda MD). NY: Wiley-Interscience, Feb 1980/251p/$15.95.

Microcomputers (computers contained in a single slice of silicon) may well rank as the third great cultural invention of the 20th century, following the automobile and television. The technology is relatively new, and is making fast progress. Separate chapters are devoted to technology forecasts of microcomputer hardware, peripheral hardware, microcomputer architecture and software, and microcomputer systems. In Chapter 8, three scenarios are provided, reflecting descending degrees of microcomputer usage in society: 1) Expansive Growth: a highly technological society, with material affluence and leisure and microcomputers everywhere, e.g.: robots performing dangerous and boring jobs, personalized automated transportation systems; 2) Resource Allocation: a recycling and energy-conscious society where microcomputers would still be a major factor in the US economy and way of life, with major impacts on education, medicine (better diagnosis and record-keeping), law (geographically separated trials) and government (an increase in direct participation); 3) Muddling Through: a society which does not work well, with general hostility toward technology, a loss of glamour in the electronics industry, an increase in computer crime and the use of computers for political repression, and frustration resulting from information overload. Concludes with a chapter discussing the impacts of microcomputers on the national aviation system, and a chapter devoted to policy concerns such as monitoring microcomputer development, and the question of regulation vs. innovation.

(microcomputers in year 2000)

5369

Mass Producing Intelligence for a Rational World, Gerald W. Smith and Jerry D. Debenham (U of Utah), *FUTURES,* 15:1, Feb 1983, 33-46.

We can no longer afford haphazard, intuitive decision-making, but must develop comprehensive systems for rational decision-making that reflect the complexity of our world. Over the next 50 years, a variety of specialized mini-computers will change or even take over the role of marriage counselors, financial consultants, negotiators, tax experts, middle management, and teachers. Some possible implications include: 1) **Education:** reorganization of general education around life-decision skills, focus on information utilization and accessibility rather than memory; 2) **Industry:** intensive evaluation of products by consumers resulting in increased durability and quality, home teleshopping may dominate the retail market; 3) **The Family:** more successful marriages due to match-making computer decision systems, increased involvement of family members with one another as decision-making in the home increases; 4) **Politics and Democracy:** a more rational election process focusing on the voting records and experience of candidates, more effective government decision-making. Concludes that public accessibility to vastly more rational systems of decision-making in no way assures a sane society, but we should have a better society. [NOTE: Rather idealized and starry-eyed, especially in contrast with the more sobering "counter-intuitive" speculations by Mandeville in the same issue of *FUTURES.*]

(a better world from computer-aided decisions?)

2456

Microelectronics at Work: Productivity and Jobs in the World Economy. Colin Norman. Worldwatch Paper 39. Washington DC: Worldwatch Institute, Oct 1980/63p/$2.00. [Brief version, *"The Menace of Microelectronics,"* in *The New York Times,* Sun, Oct 5, 1980, F3.]

Examines the history of the microelectronic revolution over the past 30 years, the automated factory, and the electronic office. The new electronic technology promises an array of benefits, and the electronic age is well under way. It will lead to productivity improvements in factories and offices, alterations in the content of many jobs, and changes in the way information is processed, stored, and communicated. But, although technological advance has generally been accompanied by high rates of job creation, this pattern may not provide a reliable guide to the future. The transition to the electronic age will thus require policies to deal with technological unemployment: 1) advanced warning, consultation, and retraining of displaced workers when the new technologies are introduced; 2) greater industrial democracy to ensure that microelectronic technology is not used in a way that degrades jobs and deskills workers; 3) more concerted actions by both governments and industry in retraining; and 4) in a period of "jobless growth," attention to new ways to distribute the benefits of this growth and to share work in a high-productivity economy by reducing work hours.

Microelectronic technology is also likely to affect work in developing countries. The automation of factories in the developed countries may erode the comparative advantage held by developing countries with their lower labor costs; and if the electronics industry stimulates other industries, their concentration in the advanced countries is likely to increase the gap between rich and poor nations.

(microelectronics and employment)

1448

Running Wild: The Next Industrial Revolution. Adam Osborne (President, Osborne & Associates). Berkeley CA: Osborne/McGraw-Hill, Inc (630 Bancroft Way), Sept 1979/181p/$3.95pb.

As a result of the microelectronic revolution, perhaps half of all jobs in the industrial world will be eliminated in the next 25 years, and many remaining jobs will be changed. Any job requiring responses to information requests or executing routine orders will be eliminated. Any job that depends on human judgment will be safe. This new industrial revolution has been brought about by many small non-established companies, and there is no way to control or stop any aspect of the industry. The first computer store in the US opened in 1975; by the end of 1978 there were 700 stores, and by 1990, microcomputers sold by such stores will account for 90% of the computer market. Some future developments: 1) within 25 years, robots will be assembling autos and electronic intelligence will handle any manufacturing function that can be explicitly defined; 2) within 20 years, the post office as we know it will disappear; 3) within 20 to 25 years, film and film processing will be eliminated, with camera images stored in removable microelectronic clips which are inserted into color printers; 4) the elimination of programming jobs with the advent of self-programming computers; 5) a word processing system that can automatically transcribe dictation; 6) bionic people: prosthetic limb responses that are equivalent to those of a natural limb, normal hearing through electronics for the most profoundly deaf, and sight for the blind with electronic devices rivaling the retina of the human eye. There is also considerable opportunity for the misuse of computers, such as theft from banks, and Osborne urges legislation to outlaw electronic funds transfer until adequate safeguards are developed.

(microelectronic revolution)

1455

The Microelectronic Revolution: How Intelligence on a Chip Will Change Our Lives, Jon Roland (San Antonio TX), *The Futurist*, XIII:2, April 1979, 81-90.

The power of yesterday's large, expensive computers is now being packed into a single tiny chip of material smaller than a fingernail, which can be mass-produced for a few cents each. Pocket calculators and digital watches are only the beginning. Personal computers in homes, offices, schools, and factories are growing rapidly, and by 1985, pocket-sized versions should be available for less than $200. These portable personal devices will permit communication with other such devices, and systems could arise with a greater capacity than the telephone system. Even the Library of Congress may be available to anyone on personal microcomputers, with profound consequences for education. This will raise questions of user charges and payment of royalties on proprietary materials. Many occupations may cease to exist, while many others will be radically affected. Microcomputer technology will also make the cashless, checkless society feasible, and may answer the legitimate objections to electronic funds transfers [see #1453]. If so, banks as such will disappear, leaving one or more worldwide banknets.

(personal computers)

2842

The Computerization of Society: A Report to the President of France. Simon Nora and Alain Minc (French Ministry of Finance). Introduction by Daniel Bell. Cambridge MA: MIT Press, Feb 1980/186p/$12.50.

First published in January 1978, this report was a bestseller in France. The authors coin the word "telematics" ("telematique" in the original) to describe the growing connection between computers and telecommunications. The computer revolution is the common factor that will speed the development of other technological revolutions. Above all, insofar as it is responsible for an upheaval in the processing and storage of data, it will alter the entire nervous system of society. Telematics opens radically new horizons and will bring a substantial increase in productivity, particularly in the public service sector. It could allow the decentralization or even the autonomy of basic units, but it could also reinforce the mechanisms of rigidity, authority, and domination, making the *"Tout-Etat"* scenario plausible. Nobody in France would dare advocate such a scenario, but innumerable pressures lead naturally to it. The primary challenge of the years to come is to build a system of connections that will allow information and social organization to progress together. [An excerpt from this book appeared in *Society*, 17:2, Jan-Feb 1980, 25-30.]

(French report on social impact of computers)

2822

Portable Terminals. International Resource Development, Inc. Norwalk CT: IRD (30 High St), March 1980/168p/ $895.00. [sic]

The market for portable terminals has expanded ten-fold since 1970, and will see another expansion of more than ten-fold in the 1980s, perhaps growing past the $3 billion mark by 1990. The market seems likely to change its character significantly, with the portable terminal becoming a consumer product rather than exclusively a business or professional product. It will gain in "intelligence" through the incorporation of microprocessors, higher production volumes will bring falling prices, and the channels of distribution will change. The IRD report describes three major types of portable terminals: 1) computer terminals, and their applications in electronic mail, insurance, chicken feeding, newspapers, energy conservation, etc.; 2) hand-held terminals, and their applications in grocery stores, sales order entry, controlling processes, etc.;

and 3) mobile radio/computer terminals, and their applications in police work, fire prevention, highway maintenance, marine services, warehousing, etc.

(market expansion for portable computer terminals)

Jobs

2849

The Future With Microelectronics: Forecasting the Effects of Information Technology. Iann Barron (Immos Co, UK) and Ray Curnow (Science Policy Research Unit, U of Sussex). London: Frances Pinter Ltd, Fall 1979/243p/$17.50 (dist in US by Nichols Publishing Co, Box 96, NYC 10024).

A study of the technological implications of information systems and their consequences for government policy over the next ten years, sponsored by the UK Department of Industry. The Technology available within the next five years will be more than adequate to generate changes in the economic and social order. The sequence and timing of these changes toward an information society will be determined not by technological factors, but by social and economic factors. Microelectronics will soon make possible the electronic typewriter—a silicon replacement for the word-processing terminal and the visual display unit—which will be a key device in the office and will also extend into the home. The office will not be eliminated, though, since much interaction at work is not carried out on a written basis. The most immediate consequence of this technology will be the impact on employment: information occupations amount to about 65% of the labor force, and even moderate improvements in office productivity could bring about unemployment levels in the 10% to 20% range, unless offset by compensatory increases in demand for these other activities. The overall consequences must be seen as comparable with the industrial revolution of 200 years ago. Widespread use of microelectronics must be expected to lead to a general shake-up of industry, with a change in the relative competitive position of many companies. Economically, it is far more important that the UK use the new technology than that the UK should provide it. Use promotion must be the most important aspect of future policy, and much emphasis must be placed on adult education, and retraining. Unemployment and inequality in the distribution of benefits resulting from the expolitation of this technology will almost certainly warrant government recognition and action. **(effects of information technology; electronic typewriter)**

84-390

Computer Technology and Employment. Stephen G. Peitchinis (Prof of Economics, U of Calgary). NY: St. Martin's Press, Nov 1983/c260p/$35.00.

In the first of a three-phase evolutionary process, the last 25 years have seen free-standing instruments such as computers, word processors, and copiers expand employment. The merging of computers and telecommunication technologies into telematic systems, projected for the second phase, will also have a positive effect on employment. But the third phase, when telematic systems of separate businesses and institutions are linked together into a telematic network (similar to the telephone network), will have a problematic impact on employment. **(computers and employment)**

3908

Women and the Chip: Case Studies of the Effects of Informatics on Employment in Canada. Heather Menzies. Toronto, Ontario: The Institute for Research on Public Policy (PO Box 9300, Station A), April 1981/130p/$6.95.

Informatics involves the automation of all phases of information manipulation: gathering, integrating, storing, and disseminating. The jobs that it will render obsolete are concentrated in the service sector—jobs traditionally held by women. Unless policy-makers move to head off current trends, up to one million Canadian women could be unemployed by 1990. Women represent over 90% of bank tellers, telephone operators, and clerk-typists; yet automation is threatening to reduce employment by 30 to 40% in these occupations. Paralleling this trend, computer-based technology is upgrading and possibly increasing the more professional information work where few women are represented: analyzing, interpreting, making decisions, and otherwise responding to the information that is increasingly processed by the computer. Unless occupational mobility policies are implemented, women risk massive unemployment as they become increasingly redundant in the clerical-occupation levels. Women need training programs to gain the necessary computer skills and basic computer concepts, and occupational mobility strategies (such as occupational bridging and affirmative action agreements) to place women in occupations where the work is becoming more demanding and complex. If women are left in clerical job ghettos, they will fall further behind, perhaps finally becoming unemployable and raising the number of Canadian families living in poverty.

**(threat of unemployed women in Canada
as result of computer revolution)**

84-386

The Work Revolution. Gail Garfield Schwartz (Washington DC) and William Neikirk (*Chicago Tribune* Correspondent, Washington). NY: Rawson Associates, Dec 1983/255p/$14.95.

An economist and a journalist warn that a revolution in work, primarily driven by technology, is gathering force daily, and that conventional wisdom about the growth of jobs and improvement in quality of worklife cannot be upheld. The jobs of the future will be either "smart" jobs or "dumb" jobs, splintering the work force into two camps. The rapid upward trend in the creation of jobs is over; in the future, the trend at best will be modestly upward and, at worst, negative. If the economy does not create 20 million new jobs in the next seven years, enough to provide work for larger proportions of women and immigrants in the work force, there will be a sharp struggle over jobs. Worker displacement will be long-term phenomenon in many industries: many of these workers will only be able to find lower-paying dumb jobs—downward mobility at its most basic level. The key to job security in the future will be synergism: mastering two or more skills to enable flexibility. Overall, a national Jobs Declaration will be necessary to meet the challenge, where government insures that everyone who is able to work can do so. The cost of a Quality of Life public jobs program would be largely offset by the value added to the economy.

(work revolution)

84-258

High-Tech Will Hurt Women, Amy Dru Stanley (Yale U), *The New York Times* (Op-Ed), Monday, 19 Sept 1983, A19.

For wage-earning women, technological innovation means diminished requirements for skills, reduced opportunities for mobility, the loss of jobs, and greater vulnerability to union-busting. Computers and data processors have fragmented and simplified clerical and service work. Women's work in coming years will be more tedious, more specialized, more susceptible to technical monitoring, and accompanied by new health hazards (high stress, eye and back strain). Technology could be used to eliminate dull and arduous labor while enhancing creativity and autonomy, but no romance between women and high-tech is in the making.

(high-tech and women's work)

Office of the Future

4313

Computers and Banking: Electronic Funds Transfer Systems and Public Policy. Edited by Kent W. Colton (Brigham Young U) and Kenneth L. Kraemer (U of California-Irvine). NY: Plenum, 1980/326p/$25.00.

During the 1970s, the technology was developed for a major change in the system by which Americans make payments and transfer funds. But implementation of EFT systems has proceeded at a far slower pace than first anticipated. The vision of a checkless and cashless society has been met with suspicion and even hostility from some consumers and certain elements within the financial community. Today, the major emphasis of EFT technology has shifted from radical revisions to a modification of the existing system. The essays in this volume, developed through close interaction with the National Commission on EFT, consider the outlook for EFT technology, an agenda for research on EFT and the consumer, more social inequality as a potential impact of EFT, EFT and privacy, vulnerabilities of EFT to theft, national economic and monetary impacts of EFT, and problems and policies in making EFT available to the public.

(electronic funds transfer systems)

3918

Teleworking: Working Closer to Home, Jack Nilles (Center for Futures Research, USC), *Technology Review,* 85:3, April 1982, 56-62.

Telework—the use of computers as a primary communications tool in the workplace—implies decentralization. Telework and telecommuting are likely to increase at an accelerating pace over the next decade. By 1990, there may be as many as 10 million telecommuters (mostly part-timers), if the information sector continues to grow. If we replaced one-seventh of our urban community with telecommuting, the nation would benefit from no longer having to import oil, and air pollution would decrease. Many workers, however, complain of isolation in home workplaces; thus, there may be greater emphasis on local work centers in small cities. Another potential problem of telework at home is that it may exacerbate workaholism.

(telework; local work centers)

84-263

Online Communities: A Case Study of the Office of the Future. Starr Roxanne Hiltz (Prof of Sociology, Upsala College NJ). Norwood NJ: Ablex Publishing Corp, Jan 1984/261p/$29.50.

The office of the future should be thought of as a communications space created by the merger of computers and telecommunications, with workers and computers located in many different places. Most of the work performed will take place "online," mediated and supported by a computer network. This case history in social invention describes the nature and impacts of the Electronic Information Exchange System (EIES), which seeks to enhance communication and productivity within scientific research communities. The results of a survey of about 100 users indicated that using a computer-mediated communication system can result in significant increases in productivity. Also, those who use the system most tend to expand their use of other communication media, rather than to substitute for them. The productivity benefits of online work modes include exposure to a broader range of information than would otherwise be possible and access to an enlarged network of helpful people. But the key variable for increased productivity is not the technology itself, but whether the potential for increasing connectivity is realized. The high dropout rate among invited users, contrasted with the testimonials of the confirmed users, suggests that computer conferencing is like religion: it only helps if you have faith that it will.

(study of computer-mediated communications)

84-392

Release from High Data Dosage: The Office of the Future, Keith Thomas Brown (Managing Partner, Brown Weit Matarazzi), *Vital Speeches of the Day,* 50:13, 15 April 1984, 414-416.

The ideal office building in 1968 was a sleek, glass skyscraper. Today's ideal combines modernist sleekness with elements of classical and other past styles. There will be relatively little change in building exteriors in the next 16 years, but interiors will change substantially as high-tech electronic technology creates new high-touch needs: 1) buildings will be smaller, compatible with the trend to smaller work teams; 2) the need for interior space will fade, but there will be greater need for management spaces where data can be reviewed and decisions made; 3) due to the elimination of office clutter, traditional desks will be replaced by tables; 4) to meet the growing need for frequent organizational change, most offices will be constructed of prefabricated components for easy rearrangement; 5) there will be greater access to the outdoors via balconies and patios, and more suburban garden-type office structures close to nature and to parking lots; 6) controlled natural light will be considered a must, as a balance or relief from the glow of computer terminals; 7) the most prized ingredients of interior design will be warm and natural materials; 8) variety in the design of buildings and spaces should increase to offset the uniformity of the computer environment. In sum, we will see an increase in the importance of human interaction, comfort, and individuality, all serving as a release from high data dosage.

(trends in office interiors)

2850

Soon, "the Nil-Hour Day," Christopher Evans, *The New York Times* (Op-Ed), Saturday, Feb 23, 1980.

Author of **The Micro Millennium** (Viking, 1980) asserts that the whole pattern of industrial life and social interaction has been turned inside out by the computer, and the concept of jobs as essential ingredients of human life has vanished into the past. The impact of the Computer Revolution will be greatest in areas where high levels of skill and training are normally required. The changes to take place in the rest of this century continue an unvarying trend towards increasing world affluence in parallel with a decreasing requirement to work. Working days of 16 hours have given way to seven-hour days, which will become a five- and perhaps even a four-hour day in the next decade or two. Eventually the nil-hour day will arrive as we hand over the job of providing wealth to the computers. **(computer revolution and shrinking work day)**

Finance

84-267

Electronic Funds Transfer: The Creeping Revolution, R. T. Clark (Inter-Bank Research Organization, London), *Telecommunications Policy,* 8:1, March 1984, 29-43.

For more than ten years the heralds of electronic funds transfer (EFT) have trumpeted the advent of a revolution in banking, but many of today's forecasts are mere echoes of those made long ago. As with predictions that saw teleconferencing replacing travel and the home terminal replacing the office, it was firmly believed that what was technologically possible would inevitably come to pass (although over-simplified and glowing pictures of a bright tomorrow may be necessary to create the momentum to make any change happen). It now seems most likely that, in ten years, all the major elements of EFT will be in place in most countries, although not all will be operating on a national scale. It is unlikely that any of the major existing payments systems, including cash, will have disappeared or been reduced to vestigial levels within ten years by EFT developments. One major exception to this pattern is the automated clearing house, which is now in place and operating well in many countries. Their success is due to their potential to reduce bank costs and their principal interface with financial institutions. Other EFT developments to date have the common theme of self-service banking for the individual based on the concept of a plastic card as the key to the account. Such banking for a mass market seems inevitable, with personal service restricted to those who pay a premium for it. Consumer acceptance of self-service has been good when care has been taken to avoid any impression of railroading customers into change.

(EFT slowly developing)

4313

Computers and Banking: Electronic Funds Transfer Systems and Public Policy. Edited by Kent W. Colton (Brigham Young U) and Kenneth L. Kraemer (U of California-Irvine). NY: Plenum, 1980/326p/$25.00.

During the 1970s, the technology was developed for a major change in the system by which Americans make payments and transfer funds. But implementation of EFT systems has proceeded at a far slower pace than first anticipated. The vision of a checkless and cashless society has been met with suspicion and even hostility from some consumers and certain elements within the financial community. Today, the major emphasis of EFT technology has shifted from radical revisions to a modification of the existing system. The essays in this volume, developed through close interaction with the National Commission on EFT, consider the outlook for EFT technology, an agenda for research on EFT and the consumer, more social inequality as a potential impact of EFT, EFT and privacy, vulnerabilities of EFT to theft, national economic and monetary impacts of EFT, and problems and policies in making EFT available to the public.

(electronic funds transfer systems)

*84-268

Smart Credit Cards: The Answer to Cashless Shopping, Stephen B. Weinstein (VP for Technology Strategy, American Express Co, NYC), *IEEE Spectrum*, 21:2, Feb 1984, 43-49.

"Smart" cards with microchips that can compute as well as hold data may be commonplace in a few years and could open a new frontier to designers of information systems, distributing processing power directly into the hands of the general public. Such integrated circuit cards have unique advantages as identification and access passes, bearers of personal records, carriers of electronic authorizations and tickets, encryption devices, and electronic money. Cards now being tested in France appear to be working well, and there is little doubt that technical and cost barriers will be overcome by the end of the decade. To illustrate, a customer goes to a special pay phone and inserts her electronic communications services card, and enters a password. The telephone acknowledges that a central computer has validated her identity. As the phone conversation proceeds, a screen displays charges as they accumulate, and charges at the end of the call are entered into the "electronic receipts" section of the card's memory. The charge is automatically submitted to the payee of choice via the telephone network.

Business Management

4312

Management and the Microelectronic Revolution, Brian C. Twiss (The Management Centre, U of Bradford) *Long Range Planning*, 14:5, Oct 1981, 101-105; 14:6, Dec 1981, 83-89.

Part I offers brief, critical abstracts of 21 books on microelectronics published in the UK in the 1979-1981 period. Part II provides an overview of the literature. Some of the conclusions: 1) There is little support for the view that new technology will provide a significant number of new job opportunities; the major areas of job displacement will be those occupations with a high level of female employment (assembly operations in manufacture and offices); 2) A new social system will be created in the firm, with a heavy polarization between the highly qualified technicians and the unskilled; 3) All planners should be carefully analyzing the capabilities of this technology, which in many cases will pose a serious strategic threat to the technological base of their companies.

(microelectronics and management literature review)

84-494

Rationality Under Infoglut, Ray Jackson (Science Advisor, Science Council of Canada), *World Future Society Bulletin*, 18:3, May-June 1984, 19-25.

A first rough sketch of the problems of rational decision-making under the complicated and growing problem of information overload or "infoglut." Possible solutions are arrayed in two broad categories: 1) **Supply Side Solutions:** slow down production by changing academic values and priorities, eliminate redundancy by stricter refereeing, reduce the noise of advertising and propaganda, simplify the world we live in by breaking it down into smaller working systems, make knowledge more accessible and comprehensive; 2) **User Side Solutions:** constructing "expert" computer systems, new techniques of integrating knowledge, use of the whole brain to enhance learning capacity, and an evolutionary transition to new methods of knowing—direct understanding at some higher level. [NOTE: Also see *Non-Communication and the Future* by Michael Marien, in Howard F. Didsbury Jr (ed.), **Communications and the Future** (World Future Society, 1982), which introduces the notion of an Age of Infoglut.]

(coping with infoglut)

2851

Needed: A Computer Study Unit, Harlan M. Blake (Prof of Law, Columbia U) and Milton R. Wessel (Counsel to the Assn of Data Processing Service Orgns), *The New York Times*, Wed, Oct 22, 1980, A31.

America is well-advanced into the computer age. Momentous decisions are being made and large-scale investments planned for computer-related systems in communications, banking, and marketing that will deeply affect the nation's future. These giant new systems will profoundly change national and international economic relationships and performance. They will alter business decision-making and the structure of economic power. Moreover, there is an accelerating trend toward merger and acquisition in the computer-services industry, threatening the positions of independent firms engaging in less than all of the elements of the newly broadened and integrated products. The emerging systems are so complex and intertwined in all branches of the economy, and so enormously costly, that once the investments are made there is no turning back. Yet, the fundamental questions they raise have not been answered—or even asked. Similar to the Temporary National Economic Committee, which brought together the nation's best thinking on the key economic concern of the 1930s, we need a Temporary National Economic Committee on Computers in America's Future, to make an in-depth assessment of the effects of the burgeoning use of computer systems.

(national assessment of computer systems needed)

Automation and Robots

2458

Microelectronics, Industry, and the Third World, Kurt Hoffman and Howard Rush (Science Policy Research Unit, U of Sussex), *Futures*, 12:4, Aug 1980, 289-302.

As microelectronics revolutionizes production in the developed countries, the traditional export successes of the Third World are threatened. This trade, which has grown

*84-398

rapidly in the past decade, relies heavily on the comparative advantage of low wage labor. Microprocessors are now eroding that advantage. The magnitude of the potential changes, and the likelihood of their negative impact, suggest that action by Third World governments is necessary.

(microelectronics and the Third World)

2823

Next: Machines That Can Talk, Peter J. Schuyten, *The New York Times*, Thursday, Oct 30, 1980, D2.

Speech synthesis and its sister technology speech recognition represent a $3 billion market opportunity by 1990. This "talking chip" is expected to ignite a battle in the semiconductor industry that may rival those associated with the semiconductor memory chip. Three separate technologies are vying for the market: 1) phoneme coding, where speech sounds are stored in a computer memory chip and then, using a microprocessor, combined to create speech; 2) linear predictive coding, which stores not only the sounds, but a computerized model that mimics the process by which sounds are produced; and 3) waveform digitization, where the frequency or pitch of spoken words is broken down into digital pulses, compressed according to a complex mathematical formula, and stored in memory for later reconstitution (users report that this technology provides the most lifelike speech). By Christmas of 1981, talking toys and calculators will be on the market, to be followed by talking cars and appliances, automated office equipment, and industrial process control systems. **(talking chips)**

84-497

Reinventing Man: The Robot Becomes Reality. Igor Aleksander (Prof of Electronics, Brunel U) and Piers Burnett. NY: Holt, Rinehart and Winston, April 1984/301p/$17.95.

Aleksander is the head of the British Cybernetics Society and leader of the team that developed WISARD, a self-programming learning machine that abandons the traditional idea of programmed computers functioning according to sequential circuits; rather, it is made of unprogrammed silicon memory chips, randomly arranged like neural networks in the brain. The authors survey the history of fictional robots, from the *golem* to the electronic dictator. Despite the prevailing image of a walking, talking, mechanical man, robots are more accurately seen as a category of machines which are, in one or more respects, made in the image of man. The robot's progress to date has been to take over jobs that a human worker might describe as "so simple a machine could do them." After another decade and a half of development, *robot industrialis* will have become an extremely common and diverse object, with a great variety of shapes and uses. There is little doubt that silicon technology will continue to make more and more capable elements for information machines available at lower and lower prices, or that economic imperatives will impel us towards more widespread use of machines that replace men. Perhaps by 2000, roboticists may be contemplating the design of an electronic machine comparable to the human brain in its capacity, structure, and complexity. Enlarging the understanding of ourselves may be a purpose sufficient in itself to justify the cost of a millennial machine. **(future of robots)**

Not For Sale: Young People in Society. Benny Henriksson. Aberdeen UK: Aberdeen U Press (dist in US by Pergamon), 1983/204p/£10.50;£5.50pb.

Translation of the summary of a 650-page report of the Swedish National Youth Council, published in 1981, which criticizes commerce for exploiting children and youth. The young have no productive functions in the modern welfare state: they live in a period of waiting, a vacuum of leisure and consumption, which produces a lack of self-confidence and a negative belief in the future. As young people lose their functions and adults become distanced from them, the role of consumer becomes increasingly important. The market provides children with idols, experiences, knowledge, fantasies—such that they are materially satiated but socially starved. The professionalization of social care, with its growing dependence on state support and on experts, threatens to lead to a dangerous passivity and dependence, impoverishing the capacity for self-help. Good environments to grow up in would enable children to participate in community work, encourage the generations to cooperate, provide productive tasks for all, combat social rejection and isolation, fill adolescence with a reason for existence, create alternatives to the commercial leisure and culture industries, and promote a democracy of involvement. In the long term, caring work means de-professionalization and de-institutionalization. The "caring economy" of everyday life in local communities should be encouraged, because it is in this free, informal, economic sector where children and adolescents have productive functions. The many proposals to encourage caring production include reducing the social costs created by the market economy, reducing working hours for all employees in the market economy and public sector (enabling them to participate in caring work), productive tasks in the local community for all schoolchildren, greater school-community cooperation, greater educational emphasis on learning skills related to caring work, schoolchildren taking part in the practical work of their school (repairs, cleaning, decoration), a guaranteed right to employment for all young people, and aiding resettlement of the depopulated countryside by youth associations and cooperatives devoted to forestry or agriculture. [NOTE: An interesting critique that does not mention the umbrella concept of "national service," but nevertheless addresses a similar array of problems besetting modern youth, while concluding with proposals far broader than those proposed by the American advocates of national service. Also see **All Grown Up and No Place to Go: Teenagers in Crisis** by David Elkind (Addison-Wesley, 1984/$16.95;$8.95pb)]

(caring work for Swedish youth)

2457

A Robot Is After Your Job, Harley Shaiken (MIT), *The New York Times* (Op-Ed), Wed, Sept 3, 1980, A19.

The introduction of revolutionary new technologies such as robots (versatile computer-controlled mechanical arms) raises the painful possibility of sizable losses of jobs and of deterioration in the quality of working life. Such a socially destructive use of technology need not be inevitable. Jobs for workers displaced and improved working conditions for those who remain could be a condition for the introduction of robots. Productivity gains could translate into a shorter work week at the same pay, rather than into fewer jobs. And technology could be designed to enhance human skill and experience, rather than make people interchangeable with machines.

(avoiding socially destructive technology)

Electronic Mail and Computer Conferencing

2830

Electronic Mail in the 1980s. International Resource Development, Inc. Norwalk CT: IRD (30 High St), Dec 1979/ 233p/$895.00

As labor and fuel costs of traditional mail delivery continue to spiral upwards, interest grows in electronic message systems. The telegraph is one form of electronic mail. An enormous upsurge in the use of electronic mail systems and services is expected as a result of technological advances in satellite communications, semiconductor technology, computer message/packet switching, and non-impact printing. This report by the producers of the twice-monthly newsletter, *"Electronic Mail & Message Systems,"* examines how electronic mail services will be bought and sold, current US markets for these services, the Terminal-Based Electronic Mail offerings of more than a dozen vendors, developments in home information systems, the probable future of public electronic mail services, and strategies of more than 50 companies that offer products and services related to electronic mail and messages. Detailed ten-year market projections are provided, along with an assessment of the impact on the use of paper, envelopes, and other consumables.

(electronic mail in 1980s)

1460

Computer-Based Teleconferencing: Effects of Working Patterns, Robert Johansen and Robert DeGrasse (Institute for the Future, Menlo Park CA), *Journal of Communication,* 29:3, Summer 1979, 30-41.

Summarizes both documented and possible effects of computer conferencing on small-group communications. Possible effects include more international communication, greater geographic separation, information overload, more flexibility in working hours, longer working hours, more workplace variation, and a substitute for some mail and telephone usage. Several policy issues are also raised, e.g.: the high cost prohibits access by many people, the potential for violation of personal privacy, and the consideration that, although geographic decentralization is allowed, it does not necessarily follow that policymaking structures will be decentralized.

(effects of computer-based teleconferencing)

5373

Electronic Message Transfer and Its Implications. Alfred M. Lee (Cornell U Program on Science, Technology, and Society). Lexington MA: Lexington Books, Jan 1983/194p/$23.95.

The success of intracompany electronic message transfer systems has prompted various private vendors to offer new services to the public. Although these undertakings are intended primarily for the business community, one can easily envision the expansion of services to a more general public within a decade. Chapters are devoted to describing these new technologies in the context of an evolving information society, the traffic and use of message-transfer services, market organization issues (emphasizing the question of service provided by the US Postal Service), the impact on postal and office activities, and implications for liability and privacy. Concludes that it is difficult to assess whether such systems will yield net benefit or harm to society. The benefits could include productivity gains in the office and postal workplace, resource conservation, and balance of trade. Social costs can be mitigated by formulating policies that cope with labor, liability, and privacy issues, and by intelligent implementation policies.

(electronic message transfer)

5374

Implications of Electronic Mail and Message Systems for the U.S. Postal Service. U.S. Congress, Office of Technology Assessment. Washington DC: USGPO, Sept 1982/$5.50 (S/N 052-003-00885-8). Summary copies free from OTA.

Commercially offered electronic mail and message systems (EMS) and electronic funds transfer (EFT) systems will increasingly compete with portions of the traditional market of the US Postal Service. While there is disagreement on how fast EMS and EFT markets may develop, it seems clear that two-thirds or more of the current mailstream could be handled electronically, and that the volume of USPS-delivered mail is likely to peak and then fall below today's level sometime in the 1990s. A key policy issue is how USPS will participate in providing EMS services: doing so could cushion some of the effects of reduction in conventional mail volume and revenue. Regardless of the USPS role in EMS, improved postal worker productivity combined with eventual decline in conventional mail volume is expected to result in reductions from the present number of employees. The USPS labor force in 2000 is likely to be down by at least 20% to 25%, with some employee groups such as mail handlers down by 30% to 35%.

(electronic mail and US Postal Service)

Electronic Publishing

5372

The Birth of Electronic Publishing: Legal and Economic Issues in Telephone, Cable and Over-the-Air Teletext and Videotext. Richard M. Neustadt. White Plains NY: Knowledge Industry Publications, July 1982/160p/$32.95.

The marriage of telecommunications and computers is producing a new mass medium—electronic publishing. What rules will govern this business? How can the round pegs of such new technologies—videotext and teletext—fit into the square holes of such old legal classifications as broadcast, print, and common carriage? Neustadt, a communications lawyer and former White House assistant, explores such issues as: 1) how the regulatory structure will change as distinctions among broadcast, cable, and telephone blur; 2) the likely role of the FCC and Congress; 3) how privacy laws will be affected; 4) the effects of deregulation and the breakup of AT&T; 5) whether editorial content will be regulated, as in broadcasting, or not regulated, as in print publishing; 6) how advertising will be handled; 7) whether transmission companies such as AT&T should control content; 8) likely actions in regard to technical standards, copyrights, piracy, and retransmission.

(regulatory issues in electronic publishing)

1464

Videotex, Prestel, and Teletext: The Economics and Politics of Some Electronic Publishing Media, Michael Tyler (Communications Studies and Planning Ltd, London), *Telecommunications Policy,* 3:1, March 1979, 37-51.

Videotex, also known as "viewdata," describes some of the simple, low-cost electronic means of publishing text and graphics. The technology is expected to become widely available in the next five years. Tyler reviews some of the technical and managerial issues, impacts on various stakeholders (electronics manufacturers, the post office, the print media, and the unions), and policy problems involving editorial control, intellectual "property," competition, and telecommunications regulations and standardization. Unlike the situation in Europe, many institutional barriers stand in the way of any extensive implementation of Teletext in the US.

(effects of viewdata)

5371

The "Electrocution" of Print, Ithiel de Sola Pool (Prof of Political Science, MIT), *across the board,* 20:3, March 1983, 36-44. (Drawn from an essay in *Daedalus,* Fall 1982.)

In the near future, hardly anything will be published in print that is not typeset by computer. Both file retrieval and publishing will be done in editions of one, at the moment the reader wants the document. This may lead to the end of the canonical text, produced in thousands of uniform copies, and in some ways foreshadows a return to the individual style of hand-printed manuscripts and the ways of oral conversation. Electronic publishing with continuous modification will make referencing more ambiguous due to difficulties in identifying the original, official version. The implications of all this for copyright are horrendous.

(impact of electronic publishing)

2852

The Computer in Book Distribution: A Behind-the-Scenes Revolution in the Making, Publishers Weekly, Sept 12, 1980, 24-41.

The taken-for-granted areas of conventional product handling and management control promise to generate far-reaching change for the better for most book industry people. In the 1980s, electronic systems will vastly improve the information flow that surrounds the physical movement of books to market. Better management of physical handling will be enabled by electronic coordination of consolidated shipments, and selection of optimum delivery channels.

(computers and book distribution)

Education

5295

Information Technology and Its Impact on American Education. U.S. Congress, Office of Technology Assessment. Washington DC: USGPO, Nov 1982/ 269p/$8.00pb (S/N 052-003-00888-2). Summary copies free from OTA.

The information revolution is profoundly affecting US education and training—creating new demands for instructional services and new opportunities for improving and delivering such services. Further automation and the shift to an information economy will create a greater demand for basic literacy and an understanding of technology. Individuals will have to be continually educated and retrained, and lifelong education will become the norm. But many institutions traditionally responsible for educational services—public schools, libraries, and museums—may be unwilling or unable to adapt to these changing educational needs because of a decline in the resources at their disposal. New for-profit institutions are emerging to take advantage of the developing market for special educational services, but these services may not meet some national goals, and some educational benefits may become less accessible to all. Institutional barriers to the use of educational technology include high initial cost, the lack of high quality software, and the dearth of local personnel with adequate training. Congress could take a number of actions to affect the development, educational application, and distribution of information technologies, such as tax incentives for donations of computers to schools, funding teacher training programs, and encouraging high quality and economical curriculum software.

(educational technology)

Homes

2853

The Home Computer Terminal: Transforming the Household of Tomorrow, Hollis Vail (Audio Chairman, World Future Society), *The Futurist,* XIV:6, Dec 1980, 52-58.

Using a home computer terminal connected to an information utility, many people may soon be able to pay their bills, plan dinner menus, do homework, conduct business, make airline and theatre reservations, plan vacations, and converse with friends in distant cities. Over 450 data bases are now available, and competition among information utility companies is only starting. Home terminals will someday contain their own computer capabilities and memory storage, and it is likely that the 1980s will see terminals in some form added to the list of essential household items.

(information utilities; home terminals)

2828

Home Telecommunications in the 1980's. International Resource Development, Inc. Norwalk CT: IRD (30 High St), April 1980/196p/$1,285.00. [sic]

During the past 100 years, two large industries have grown up more or less separately to bring information into the home: the newspaper and broadcasting industry, and the telephone industry. The convergence of the telephone, video, and print industries is now at hand, bringing changes, disruption, threats, and opportunities to all of the major participants in these industries. Key catalysts in their convergence include the development of Viewdata and other technologies, continued growth in cable TV services, and partial deregulation of the telephone and cable TV industries. The IRD report examines recent developments in the US, Canada, Japan, and Europe, noting that developments in other countries will parallel and in some instances lead those in the US. Ten-year projections are provided for home telephone equipment markets, home terminals, video systems and earth stations, home telecom transmission services, and home information and transaction services. Estimates are provided on the supplier industry structure and the diversion of advertising revenues from newspapers, network TV, and magazines. Concludes that, by 1990, more than one-quarter of US homes will be equipped with various types of "intelligent" terminals capable of accessing and utilizing a whole range of new information and transaction services.

(home telecommunications)

Politics and Government

4314

Computers and Politics: High Technology in American Local Governments. James N. Danziger (U of California-Irvine) *et al.* NY: Columbia U Press, Nov 1981/320p/$22.50.

On questions of influence and control regarding decision-making and the application of computers in local government. The authors find that there is a general bias in the impact of computer technology: the politics related to the computer package have tended to benefit those who already have broad power and control of the organization. Concludes with an argument for reversing this pattern, and for "democratization" of computer technology in local governments.

(computers and local government)

84-492

Electronic 'Pollution' Plays Havoc With Modern Devices, John Holusha, *The New York Times,* Tuesday, 20 Dec 1983, C3.

A variety of incidents ranging from the ridiculous to the potentially tragic manifest the growing load on the radio frequency spectrum and the proliferation of sensitive microelectronic devices. Any time a material that conducts electricity meets an electromagnetic field, an electrical current is likely to be generated. The wires leading into electronic equipment can act like antennas in such cases, feeding in false signals unless precautions have been taken to screen them out. Left unshielded, the results can range from false readings on instruments to wrong commands from control units. And, as microprocessors and elecronic chips grow tinier and operate on smaller and smaller currents, weaker and weaker interfering signals can drive the devices amok. One area of growing concern is the automobile industry, where as much as 10% of the total cost of a vehicle by the end of the 1980s may be in electronics. Auto engineers have a three-fold problem of preventing one part of the vehicle from interfering with another, preventing emissions from the car from affecting things on the outside, and shielding the car from outside influences. Even if a small percentage of cars get into accidents because of electromagnetic interference, the product liability problems could be huge. [Also see *Electric 'Hash' New Menace of High-Tech Age,* U.S. News & World Report, 13 Feb 1984, which cites a maker of shields that block background interference as estimating a 50% annual increase in electronic "hash" or "noise."]

(electronic pollution)

The Future of Computer Data Security, Joseph F. Coates (J. F. Coates Inc, Washington), *Vital Speeches of the Day,* 48:9, Feb 15, 1982, 280-284.

There has been tremendous progress in the past eight years in developing the arts and crafts of safeguarding computer data. But the structural situation is far less satisfactory: the ways in which we conduct our business and our orientation toward personal and national affairs have latent within them the possibilities for unprecedented corporate and national disasters. The computer industry is so complacent, its buyers and users so beguiled by the equipment, and regulators so enchanted by the calm sea to date, that the nation needs its equivalent to a Hiroshima to be alerted to the enormous risks in the way we now organize our computer affairs. Computer systems are terribly vulnerable to both man-made and natural intrusions, but physical integrity of systems has received no significant public attention. The question of fake input into computer systems, which could distort or destroy someone's reputation, is virtually unspoken of. Privacy as a computer-related issue will always be an issue of the post-industrial society. A foreign agent hostile to the US could easily foul up the Electronic Funds Transfer system. Acts of terrorism directed at computers are quite likely to increase over the next decades. The endless linking together into a bigger and bigger system may be the single most pathological thing we can do.

Progress in computer security is inhibited by suppressing information about computer crime, apparently in the short-term interests of business and industry. There is no association, organization, or commission to look at the overall problem (a piecemeal approach that is sadly characteristic of current politics). There is little or no future orientation in government and industry. We have no positive model for privacy, and virtually no economics of knowledge. Suggestions for improving security include: 1) requiring computer manufacturers to carry insurance against system failures; 2) acknowledging error rates so that everyone realizes that there can be no foolproof system; this will help users to cost out potential risks and vulnerabilities; 3) designing portable records (e.g., one's medical history) so as to give the individual more control over personal information; 4) customizing information so that specific machines can be identified (e.g., by keys and typefaces), thus making it more difficult to counterfeit records, send illegal messages, etc.; 5) calling in all paper money and reissuing it with machine-readable codes on all bills to identify and trace the movement of large blocks of cash involved in illegal activities; 6) taxing information transfers so that banks and credit companies would be forced to keep records of their gross volume of information flow; and 7) monetizing information and privacy to give those who wish security some real choices (e.g., offering a subscription discount to magazine readers who permit their names to be included on mailing lists sold and circulated by the publisher).

(avoiding computer security disasters)

Health and Handicapped

2696

Medical Practice in the Twenty-First Century, Howard Lutz, M.D. (Director, Institute of Preventive Medicine,

Washington DC), *Technology Tomorrow* (World Future Society), 3:4, Aug 1980, pp1, 14-15.

The current medical scene is ridiculous, with its high-priced assembly line "preventive surgery," massive overuse of dangerous drugs, and irresponsible use of radioisotopes and other sources of diagnostic and therapeutic radiation. The clinical directions to develop initially will question the use of function-sustaining drugs and advocate the substitution of nontoxic therapies. When the causes of illness are addressed, tranquilizing drugs such as valium will eventually be used less rather than more. A prerequisite is to develop more sensitive means of diagnosing diseases that are now lumped together because they respond to one or another toxic drug. New research in measuring the magnetic fields of the human body will allow the development of diagnostic means that will validate Chinese medicine and chiropractic, homeopathic, and massage therapies. "Magnetodiagnostics" will result in many stress-reducing methods, while demonstrating the debilitating effects of pollution, chemicals, additives, and environmental allergies on health. To diagnose ourselves, we will use small appliances called "stress meters" to detect magnetic fields; they will be commonplace and no larger than a watch.

A minicomputer will help us choose food suited to our individual biochemical status. Hair follicle analysis will allow the correction of suspected mineral deficiencies (the single most prevalent health problem today). The blood tests of today—really serum tests—will be largely abandoned, with the part of the blood now thrown away (the red cells) becoming the exclusive test material. Through computerized testing of specific red cell biochemical pathways, stress reduction by eating foods of specific composition will be possible. X-rays will be abandoned for diagnostic purposes, and ultrasound, coherent light, thermography, and magnetic imaging will be used. **(new medical practices in 21st century)**

1413

Computers Work Toward Eyes for the Blind, Ears for the Deaf, Patricia E. Weil, *The New York Times*, Sunday, July 29, 1979, E20.

Electrical devices that could restore hearing and sight to the deaf and blind are finally becoming feasible. William H. Dobelle (U of Utah and Columbia U) describes a promising artificial vision device: a Teflon matrix containing 64 platinum electrodes, which is placed in the patient's visual cortex. Eventually, Dobelle hopes to put a micro-miniature TV camera in a glass eye attached to the eye muscles, although the best vision that can be hoped for will approximate the blurry black-and-white TV images of early television. Parallel experiments in artificial hearing are also taking place at the U of Utah, using auditory electrodes placed in the patient's inner ear. Dobelle estimates that these visual and auditory prostheses could be produced for $3000 to $5000 each. The problems of rehabilitation may be harder to solve than the technical difficulties of developing the devices, since major readjustments in the patient's emotional and vocational lives would be inevitable. **(electrical devices for deaf and blind)**

Networks

4308

Many-to-Many Communication Through Inquiry Networking, Chandler Harrison Stevens (Participation Systems, Winchester MA), *World Future Society Bulletin*, XIV:6, Nov-Dec 1980, 31-34.

Advances in computer-assisted communications still tend to emulate older forms of information exchange such as letters or face-to-face conferences. A new technique will allow participants to selectively access and exchange information simultaneously with many people at different degrees of interaction, depending on depth of interest. This "inquiry networking" is an extension of electronic mail and computer conferencing, using the computer's fundamental capability of branching to allow many-to-many communication to take place without producing information overload. Such networking can decrease duplication of effort and increase productivity in certain situations, if there is some similarity among the interests of those involved, standards as to what types of inquiries and responses are preferred, and facilitators to help develop such standards.

(inquiry networking; many-to-many communication)

4307

Computer-Based National Information Systems: Technology and Public Policy Issues. U. S. Congress, Office of Technology Assessment. Washington DC: USGPO, Oct 1981/ $6.50. S/N 052-003-00852-1. A 27-page summary (OTA-CIT-147) is available free from OTA.

The development and use of computer-based national information systems—such as those already integral to air traffic control, military command and control, and electronic funds transfer—will be accelerated by major continuing advances in microelectronics, computer programming, and data communication. Small computers will become common in the home and business. Corporations will compete intensively to provide information services. The number and size of computer networks linking users and data bases anywhere in the US or the world will expand dramatically. But these information systems are generating policy issues at a rate outstripping the ability of government to respond. The US appears to lack a coherent information policy to guide the updating of numerous laws and regulations, some overlapping and some potentially or actually conflicting, that affect system operators and users. New applications—such as an automated securities exchange, in-home information services, electronic publishing, and electronic mail—may introduce policy issues over secondary use of personal information, surveillance, and protection of individual privacy. The increasingly complicated systems now being designed and built will magnify the need for adequate protection of Federal information systems and vital non-Federal systems, and for developing improved data security. Large-scale information systems may also affect Federal decision-making, constitutional rights, computer-related crime, regulatory boundaries and definitions, and negotiations over the international flow of information.

(implications of computer-based information systems)

2826

Everything You Always Wanted To Know May Soon Be On-Line, Walter Kiechel III (Associate Editor), *Fortune*, May 5, 1980, 226-240.

A new industry is growing up around on-line data bases: huge banks of information that are processed, stored, and delivered electronically. What the new businesses provide is not so much new information, but a radical improvement in the ease with which information can be retrieved. Many companies are elbowing each other to enter the business or enlarge their stake in it. There are now some 450 data banks on-line, with 50 new data bases offered in the last quarter of 1979 alone. Industry sales are still small (probably less than $500 million), but revenues are increasing at more than 30% per year. The challenge is to package the data so that users can get it quicker and more cheaply than they could through old-fashioned information-gathering techniques. About 80% of the customers are businessmen, economists, lawyers, and people in finance. The remaining 20% of the industry involves bibliographic data directed to information specialists. As end users become more confident of their ability to summon what they require from a terminal, there might also be a reduction in corporate staffs and in the use of consultants. In the heaven imagined by data base pioneers, managers will be transfigured from narrow-minded specialists into generalists.

(on-line data base industry)

Artificial Intelligence

5360

The Fifth Generation: Artificial Intelligence and Japan's Computer Challenge to the World. Edward A. Feigenbaum (Prof of Computer Science, Stanford U) and Pamela McCorduck (NYC). Reading MA: Addison-Wesley, May 1983/237p/$15.55. [NOTE: The price appears to emphasize the book title!].

A pioneer in artificial intelligence and a science writer warn that the computer revolution has barely begun. Japanese planners view the computer industry as vital to their nation's economic future, and have made it a national goal to become number one in the industry by the late 1990s. To implement this vision, they have avoided head-on competition with dominant US firms and found an arena of great economic potential now overlooked by the more shortsighted and perhaps complacent US firms. The tactics are set forth in a major national plan on Fifth Generation Computer Systems implementing in April 1982 a ten-year R&D program on Knowledge Information Processing Systems (KIPS). This new generation of computers will be more powerful than any other by orders of magnitude. The power will lie not in their processing speed, but in their capacity to reason with enormous amounts of information constantly selected, interpreted, updated, and adapted. Users will be able to speak with these new computers in everyday conversational language, or show pictures to or transmit messages by keyboard or handwriting. They will require no special expertise or knowledge of programming languages, and the machines will be inexpensive and reliable enough to be used everywhere in offices, factories, shops, farms, and homes. The Japanese expect these machines to be the core computers by the 1990s—those most generally in use worldwide. They aim not only to dominate the traditional forms of the computer industry, but to establish a "knowledge industry" where knowledge itself becomes the new wealth of nations. The options open to Americans are: 1) to maintain the status quo, and continue short-term R&D spurred only by market considerations; 2) form industrial consortiums to meet the Japanese challenge; 3) enter a major joint venture with the Japanese; 4) forget about producing the machines and specialize in producing only the software; 5) prepare to become the first great agrarian postindustrial society; 6) form a Los Alamos-type national laboratory for the promotion of knowledge technology. The authors favor the final option: a large-scale concentrated project that is seen as essential to the national interest and national defense. Such a national center would serve as insurance in a world where other nations have already perceived the centrality of knowledge to their self-interest and are acting upon it. [Also see *The Race to Build a Supercomputer," Newsweek* (Cover Story), 4 July 1983, 58-64, which describes how the US is taking on Japan for control of the advanced technologies that will dominate computing in the 1990s. There is no indication whether the "three huge new programs" now getting underway in the US are the equivalent of the large-scale project recommended above.]

(Japan's Fifth Generation computers)

5361

Artificial Intelligence: The Second Computer Age Begins, *Business Week,* 8 March 1982, 66-75.

Cover story on the new technology that is changing the computer from a fast calculating machine to a device that mimics human thought processes. Some computer scientists see the coming commercialization of AI—a field in which the US presently leads in development—as the most significant advance in computer science since the invention of the computer. Early applications of AI include computerized consultants, artificial senses, and diagnosis of diseases.

(artificial intelligence changing computer use)

*84-500

Machines Built to Emulate Human Experts' Reasoning, Robert Reinhold, *The New York Times*, Thurs. 29 March 1984, p1.

A new kind of engineering may ultimately exert as profound an influence on the workplace as factory automation did decades ago. The aim of "knowledge engineering" is to interview leading experts in science, medicine, business, and other endeavors to find out how they make judgments that are the core of their expertise. This knowledge is then codified so that computers can make similar decisions by emulating human inferential reasoning. The knowledge engineer does this by reducing the expert's wisdom to a series of interconnected generalized rules or "knowledge base." A separate computer program or "inferential engine" is then used to search this knowledge base and draw judgments when confronted with evidence from a particular case. While knowledge engineering is still a primitive art, it has already been used with some success in prospecting for minerals, diagnosing disease, analyzing chemicals, selecting antibiotics, and configuring computers. The promise has led hundreds of US companies to look into the possibility of using expert systems to perform such tasks as evaluating casualty insurance risks, making commercial credit decisions, and controlling oil well drilling. Some critics view knowledge engineering (a branch of "artificial intelligence") as the vanguard of an Orwellian future in which thinking machines take control. They also argue that expert systems cannot perform a key function of the human brain—learning from experience—and that they are largely limited to cases in which knowledge lends itself to classification of facts into neat categories. The knowledge engineers respond that they are trying to demystify expertise and that the new expertise is merely advisory. On the other hand, the possibility of aggregating the knowledge and insights of several experts in the same field opens the prospect of computer-aided decisions based on more wisdom than any one person can contain. [NOTE: What will they think of next?] **(knowledge engineering)**

Future Prospects

1471

The March of the Japanese Micro, Gene Gregory (Visiting Prof, Sophia U-Tokyo), *New Scientist,* 84:1186, Oct 11, 1979, 98-101.

Microelectronics are important because they will be the basis of the industrial system for the next 25 years. US semiconductor manufacturers still hold more than 60% of the world market, compared with 24% for Japanese producers. But the Japanese semiconductor industry now has better techniques and more advanced automated equipment than its US counterpart, and the Japanese have recently attained technological parity with leaders of the US industry. With the examples of steel, autos, and television sets in mind, US manufacturers in California's "Silicon Valley" are convinced that they will be faced with similar devastating competition in the 1980s. European firms feel that they should do something, but the cost of catching up with the US and Japanese industries promises to be staggering.

(**microelectronics industry—Japan and US**)

1472

Integrated Circuits: The Coming Battle, I. M. Mackintosh (Chairman, Mackintosh Consultants, London UK), *Long Range Planning,* 12:3, June 1979, 28-37.

Examines the impact of changing computer technology on the computer manufacturing industry. These changes will affect both the distribution of technology and economic power. The US has heretofore dominated the integrated circuits industry due to government support, good management, and large markets. But in the new era of complex large-scale integration projects, the balance of advantage is now beginning to swing away from the US. The most probable prognosis is that US domination will be replaced by a condition of approximate parity with Japan, possibly joined somewhat later by Europe. (**world computer industry**)

1473

Proceedings of the Sixth Annual Telecommunications Policy Research Conference. Edited by Herbert S. Dordick (USC and MIT). Lexington MA: Lexington Books, Sept 1979/ 475p/$21.95.

The 33 essays derived from a 1978 Airlie House conference are arranged in four sections: the social effects of television and resulting policy issues, computer-communications networks and the emerging information economy, spectrum allocation, and the economics of regulation and of pricing telecommunications services. A few of the specific topics include personal computer networks, regulatory barriers to home information services, policy implications of US Postal Service use of telecommunications technology, issues in advertising policy, and economic effects of state regulation of cable television. (**communications policy**)

4305

And Now—the Biochip, Stephanie Yanchinski, *New Scientist,* Jan 14, 1982, 68-71.

The electronics industry is on the brink of a new era in which electronic chips no bigger than large molecules will be able to enter a human cell to do repairs. Research on fashioning electronic chips from organic molecules is also described, as well as the possibility of designing a chip as a three-dimensional array so as to imitate, in a very small way, the complexity of the human brain. (**biochips**)

1454

Information: The Ultimate Frontier, Lewis M. Branscomb (Vice President and Chief Scientist, IBM, Armonk NY), *Science,* Vol 203, Jan 12, 1979, 143-147.

An attempt to assess what will happen to information technology in the next 100 years. The key element is the computer, and recent developments in circuitry and memory are surveyed. Extrapolating present trends, the computer of 2078 will contain the data memory equivalent of 16,000 human brains, and will be relatively low cost. It will respond to speech (a capability that will be realized in a decade or so), and there will be a new ability to write symbols, using display screens and nonimpact printers. Various information technologies such as typewriters, television, telephones, records, and movies will all be interchangeable. The computer will overcome the deficiencies of the industrial revolution by enabling articles such as shoes to be made on a mass basis, with each one fitting specific requirements of the intended end user. In general, the computer will be better integrated into our future communication patterns, leading to profound changes in education, politics, and other social institutions. (**information technology; computers**)

Critical Issues

2824

Is Human Memory Obsolete? W. K. Estes (Prof of Psychology, Harvard U), *American Scientist,* 68:1, Jan-Feb 1980, 62-69.

Comparison of computer memory with the picture of human memory emerging from psychological research suggests basic differences in modes of operation, with little likelihood that one can replace the other. Although the efficiency of modern digital computers in storing and retrieving information is awe-inspiring, the idea of a race between man and computer is inappropriate. Humans have considerable capability of retaining large amounts of relatively imprecise information regarding past experiences, although the capability is less than optimal for the special purposes of calculations and logical operations. Any serious consideration of the possibility that computers could soon take over important functions of human memory seems premature. However, a long-term goal of research on human memory is to develop ways of remedying failures of the human memory system, perhaps with the development of "mental prosthetics" in which computers take over some functions of the human system.

(**computers and human memory**)

5363

Micro Man: Computers and the Evolution of Consciousness. Gordon Pask (Prof of Cybernetics, Brunel U) with Susan Curran (Norwich UK). NY: Macmillan, Dec 1982/222p/$14.75.

On the developing relationship between humans and computers, and whether it will be one of antagonism or cooperation. The authors hope and believe that the two species will cooperate, leading to a transformation of the human mind and the nature of computing. Just as the boundary between living and non-living things is becoming increasingly blurred, so the distinction between human and machine thought is becoming untenable. We could even evolve to a single species or mind, which may reside in one or many people or machines. Chapters dwell on the history of computers, threats posed by the computer, computers and consciousness, populations of computers, language and knowledge, data structures and knowledge structures, applications of the microprocessor, maverick machines that deviate from the mainstream of computer development, computers and education, and the information environment. Concludes with positive and negative views of the year 2000. In the former, work is no longer essential, a negative income tax assures all of a basic income, and society is classless. Negative visions consider microfreak societies, anthill cultures, and a togetherness cult. [NOTE: The scenarios of the future are skimpy and naive, but otherwise a useful introduction helped by 150 photographs, half of them in color.]

(introduction to computers)

84-499
Human Evolution in the Age of the Intelligent Machine, William I. McLaughlin (Jet Propulsion Laboratory, California Institute of Technology), *Interdisciplinary Science Reviews,* 8:4, Dec 1983, 307-319.

The future evolution of man can no longer be restricted to the domain of biology, but requires a systems analysis which considers, at least, the disciplines of exobiology and artificial intelligence. The life stuff of the universe is seen as composed of three subsystems: man, intelligent machines, and intelligent extraterrestrial organisms. Each subsystem is assigned a designation of success or failure: man can decline or flourish, the machine can stay dumb or become intelligent, and extraterrestrial intelligence may exist or not exist. The relative lack of integration among brain components makes man a weak evolutionary contestant compared to machines, which should become dominant on earth within 100 years, probably by means of continuing development of existing man-machine systems. Advanced forms of extraterrestrial intelligence may exist, but are too difficult to observe.

(machines to dominate earth in 100 years)

4320
Computer Control and Human Alienation, Thomas B. Sheridan (Man-Machine Systems Lab, MIT), *Technology Review,* 83:1, Oct 1980, 60-73.

As we enter the age of computers, we will have to strive to preserve human dignity and values. The new technology of computer control can be put to many good uses. But these large-scale control systems are alienating because: 1) people unfairly compare themselves with computers and worry about their inferiority and obsolescence (people do have poor memories and are slow, but unlike computers they are adaptive and creative); 2) computer control tends to make human operators remote from their ultimate task; centralized control creates spatial distance; 3) skilled personnel are often "promoted" to become button pushers and machine tenders; 4) the technologically illiterate majority feels increasingly at the mercy of the technical elite; 5) the mystification of a computer-control panacea seldom reveals computer limitations; and 6) phylogenesis is feared: the real or perceived threat that the race of intelligent machines is becoming more powerful than humans. To insure that the human-machine interaction offers humanity and dignity, we must strive to celebrate those things human that computers can never be. We must affirm the role of subjective input into computer-aided decisions and control processes. Operators and other skilled professionals must be introduced to new and constructive tasks that trans-

cend button pushing. And, in education, we must prepare future generations to become active participants in a computerized society. [Also see **Being Human in a Technological Age,** edited by Donald M. Borchert and David Stewart. Athens, OH: Ohio U Press, Dec 1979/168p/$12.00;$4.95pb.]

(human dignity in an age of computers)

85-189
Six Grave Doubts About Computers, Jerry Mander (Public Media Center, San Francisco), *Whole Earth Review* (formerly *Co-Evolution Quarterly*), No 44, Jan 1985, 10-20.

Author of **Four Arguments for the Elimination of Television** (Morrow, 1978) argues that the first waves of news about a technology are invariably positive, even utopian, because the information comes from corporations and scientists who stand to gain from a favorable view. By the time we begin to notice problems, the technologies have advanced to a point where it is difficult to do anything about them. Some perspectives are offered that are not found in the computer ads. 1) The computer industry has a high incidence of occupational illness (more than three times the average for the manufacturing industry), and it produces environmental side effects. 2) "Information" is increasingly defined in terms of what can be collected and processed through machines; thus a certain sort of knowledge will dominate, while other more subtle forms recede. As computer programs replace teachers, a great degree of uniformity will likely emerge. 3) Automation and computation will eliminate many jobs, especially among the middle class. 4) Computers make possible a high degree of military centralization and enhance the possibility of annihilating the world by minimizing the time available for human decision-making at critical moments. 5) Slow is beautiful, and computers speed up processes and accelerate our nervous systems. 6) Computers help large institutions and work against small, decentralized institutions.

(computers questioned)

*85-190
Mythinformation, Langdon Winner (U of California-Santa Cruz), *Whole Earth Review,* No 44, Jan 1985, 22-28.

According to some visionaries, industrial society is being supplanted by a society in which information services will enable all the people of the world to satisfy their economic and social needs. According to Winner, author of **Autonomous Technology** (MIT Press, 1977), these beliefs taken as a whole are "mythinformation": the almost religious conviction that a widespread adoption of computers and communications systems, along with broad access to electronic information, will produce a better world. It is common for the advent of a new technology to provide occasion for flights of utopian fancy. But even within the great tradition of optimistic technophilia, current dreams of a computer age stand out as exaggerated. The arguments of computer romantics draw on four false assumptions: 1) people are bereft of information; 2) information is knowledge, and speed conquers quantity; 3) knowledge is power; 4) increased access to information enhances democracy and equalizes social power. The long-term consequences of computerization will be quite different, and will require rethinking of many fundamental conditions and institutions. Three areas of concern seem paramount: the growing technical ability to monitor various human activities, the elimination of social layers that were previously needed, and the basic structure of the political order. Concludes that, rather than being guided by new wonders in artificial intelligence, the present course of the computer revolution is influenced by something much more familiar: the absent mind. **(computer romanticism questioned)**

EDUCATION

Education in the Information Society

The information revolution is creating new demands for education and training—demands that the U.S. educational system as it is now structured and operating is largely failing to meet, according to a report from the U.S. Office of Technology Assessment.

"The so-called *information revolution*, driven by rapid advances in communication and computer technology, is profoundly affecting American education," says OTA director John H. Gibbons. "It is changing the nature of what needs to be learned, who needs to learn it, who will provide it, and how it will be provided and paid for."

The emerging information technologies may also be the major tool for responding to the very challenges that they create, OTA found in a two-year study called *Informational Technology and Its Impact on American Education*. As Gibbons writes in the report's foreword, "Information technology can potentially improve and enrich the educational services that traditional educational institutions provide, distribute education and training into new environments such as the home and office, reach new clients such as handicapped or homebound persons, and teach job-related skills in the use of technology."

OTA found that technology can aid and extend education in several ways:

TED SPIEGEL © 1982/U.S. OFFICE OF TECHNOLOGY ASSESSMENT

Computers in the classroom are making many new demands on education—and providing some solutions. A U.S. Office of Technology Assessment study found that information technology is changing what needs to be learned, who needs to learn it, and how it can be taught.

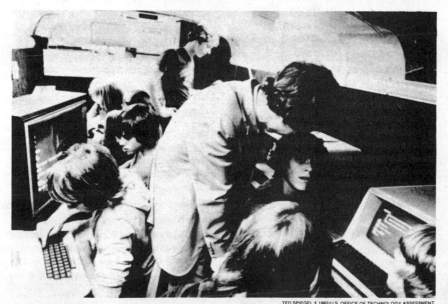

TED SPIEGEL © 1982/U.S. OFFICE OF TECHNOLOGY ASSESSMENT

Computer programs are "bused" to schools throughout the Oxford (Massachusetts) School District. Informational technologies can provide education in a number of nontraditional ways, according to a report by the U.S. Office of Technology Assessment.

• **Basic skills.** Computers can assist in providing individualized instruction in reading, writing, mathematics, and other skills that require repetition and drilling.

• **Distribution of educational services.** Information technologies can provide education and training services in the home, at work, in a hospital, or in any other location where and when they may be needed. Lifelong learning can also be emphasized.

• **Instruction management.** Computer-managed instruction can raise teachers' efficiency at administrative tasks such as testing, scoring, and managing student records, thus freeing teachers to devote more time to developing creative teaching strategies.

• **Technological literacy.** Computers used to aid in teaching basic skills also compel students to become technologically literate. Computers teach new ways of thinking and problem solving that may be more appropriate to the information age.

The importance to students, teachers, and society of taking advantage of information technologies is also being examined in Canada.

April 1983

Stuart L. Smith, chairman of the Science Council of Canada, recently told a workshop of the Canadian Education Association that computers can overcome a primary obstacle to education by "removing the need to teach all students the same material, in the same way, at the same time."

Smith points out that a subtle effect of individualized computer instruction is that students who do not understand a particular point may have less anxiety about repeating their questions to a computer than risking disapproval of their peers or teacher. Students who grasp the material quickly can move on rather than become bored or restless; education can thus be tension-free and stimulating for all learners.

The OTA study found that the widespread use of the information technologies does have its dangers, however. For example, while a human teacher can call out to a student who is not paying attention, computers are infinitely patient and cannot tell when the student is daydreaming. Thus, in some cases, replacing teachers with new technology-based methods might shorten students' attention spans and reduce the effectiveness of learning.

Another possibly negative consequence is loss of social interaction when students can only "discuss" course material with a computer and not with other students.

For the information technologies to fulfill their educational potential, several barriers must be overcome:

• **Institutional barriers.** New educational technology must be designed that can be easily integrated into the schools and other educational institutions that will use it. These institutions will have to make some adaptations in curricula, schedules, and classroom organization.

• **Teacher training.** Widespread use of information technologies will require teachers that are proficient both in their use and in the production of good curriculum materials. Too few teachers are so qualified today, and there is little evidence that teacher training colleges in the United States are providing adequate instruction to new teachers in the use of information technologies.

• **Lack of adequate software.** OTA found that the quality of currently available courseware—curriculum material designed for educational technology—generally is not very good. Educators must learn how to use the new technologies to be able to tell producers of the software what they need.

• **Cost.** Although computer hardware and communication service costs are dropping, educational technology still represents a substantial investment by schools that are already facing higher costs and reduced tax support.

OTA concludes that meeting the educational needs of an information society will involve all individuals, groups, and institutions. It will require the use of a full range of educational approaches and technologies.

Stuart Smith of the Science Council of Canada agrees that the information age requires vast changes in society and in its educational services:

When information is available at the touch of a finger to a keyboard, the important skills for individuals are those that enable them to *use* that information to *solve* specific problems, *to criticize, assess,* and *manipulate* data to form new conclusions. We try, with difficulty, to teach these skills today; the computer may finally free us to do those tasks effectively. If we, and our institutions, are truly open to *change* and don't simply try to ensnare the computer in our existing system, the rewards are likely to be great even beyond our present comprehension or prediction. Change requires courage and skill—I trust we will not be found lacking.

For more information, see *Informational Technology and Its Impact on American Education* (Office of Technology Assessment, November 1982, 269 pages; for sale by the Superintendent of Documents, U.S. Government Printing Office, Washington, D.C. 20402) or contact Stuart L. Smith, chairman, Science Council of Canada, 100 Metcalfe, Ottawa, Ontario, Canada K1P 5M1.

VALUES

Computer Ethics

The computer is creating many new ethical problems, reports Douglas W. Johnson, executive director of the Institute for Church Development, Inc. For example, while most people would not dream of breaking into their neighbor's home, they might see no harm in tapping into someone else's data base.

In a new book, *Computer Ethics: A Guide for the New Age,* Johnson offers these examples of ethical problems involving computers:

• Invasion of privacy by hackers invading other people's computers.

• Copyright violation, or "piracy."

• Alienation from family and friends and isolation from other sources of human gratification. ("Computer widows" may now be as numerous as "golf widows.")

- False advertising and the lack of integrity of computer manufacturers and vendors.
- Transmission of pornographic illustrations or stories.
- Widening of the gap between the "haves" and "have-nots."

So far, only invasion of privacy and copyright violation have received much attention. Even so, the extension of privacy and copyright laws to include home and business computer operations has not been seen as necessary or feasible.

Computer-ethics questions now are urgent because the offenders are so numerous, and the law cannot invade people's homes in seeking computer programs that have been illegally copied.

"Codes of conduct are more important than laws when so many individuals are involved," says Johnson. "Ethics is essential to a computer-based society, not because the phenomenon of computers is new, but because the number of individuals who use them has increased manyfold."

Johnson offers the following suggestions for beginning constructive discussion and action for providing an ethic for the computer-dependent society. The ethic must:

- **Be adaptable.** Ethical behavior must be adapted to changing situations, such as new skills for which the computer will be used and the advent of artificial intelligence.
- **Outline users' rights.** Individuals should have the right to monitor information about themselves, and to have access to data that are vital to their work. They should have the opportunity to examine and make corrections when information is inaccurate and the right to authorize or deny the use of their personal data by corporations and others, but no right to unauthorized access to the data stored in any computer.
- **Allow equal access.** The ethic must face the fact that there will be

Thou Shalt Not Covet Thy Neighbor's Data Base

groups of people who cannot use and will not have access to a computer. Providing people equal access to computers is an ethical task that has not been adequately explored.

- **Be based on existing laws.** Consumer laws, such as those that prohibit the selling of shoddy merchandise, strengthen manufacturers' warranties, and outlaw misleading advertising, should be adapted to the needs of a computer-dependent society. Laws governing information would protect the confidentiality of data that corporations and government have stored in computers, and they would protect copyright holders.
- **Place time limits on use.** People tend to spend too much time with the computer. A warning sticker, "Computer Use May Be Harmful to Your Personal and Social Life," might be placed on every personal computer sold.
- **Provide guidelines for use.** Personal-computer purchasers and users should be given guidelines on what is and is not a proper use of the computer. For example, the computer should not be used for transmitting pornographic pictures or stories, duplicating copyrighted materials, or other illegal activities.
- **Outline manufacturers' responsibilities.** Makers, vendors, and trainers should be responsible

for warning purchasers about potential problems. Prospective customers should be told several times what the computer can do and what it does best.

- **Exact penalties.** An ethic, to be effective, must have the power to exact meaningful penalties from those who transgress. Stronger surveillance and better security for computer systems are necessary. And, since stealing by computer affects everyone, each person would be responsible to keep watch and report wrongdoings.

An ethic for a computer-dependent society would be concerned with guaranteeing individual integrity by keeping a minimum of data about any person in computers. Each person would be allowed an annual opportunity to correct personal data held in any computer. All people would have access to and knowledge of how to use a computer. In addition, the ethic would stress the privacy of information and the protection of products people create through an expanded copyright law. Finally, the ethic would remind us that people make decisions while computers process data.

For more information, see *Computer Ethics: A Guide for the New Age* by Douglas W. Johnson. Brethren Press, 1451 Dundee Avenue, Elgin, Illinois 60120. 1984. 120 pages. Paperback. $6.95.

Take an Active Part in Building Tomorrow...
... Join the World Future Society Today

Join the 30,000 people from all over the world who want to make sense out of today's rapidly changing world. The World Future Society is unique. Since its founding in 1966, the Society has served as a neutral clearinghouse for people at the forefront of social and technological change. Through local chapters, seminars and conferences, and its many publications, the Society reaches out to those who want to explore the alternatives for tomorrow.

As a member of the World Future Society, you will receive:

THE FUTURIST
—the Society's bimonthly magazine of forecasts, trends, and ideas about the future. The latest in technological developments, trend tidbits, interviews, and in-depth articles give members a comprehensive look into tomorrow.

CONFERENCES
—Special rates at all assemblies and conferences. The Society sponsors and organizes meetings to bring together futurists from all around the world.

RESOURCES CENTER
—Discounts on books, cassette tapes, films, educational games, and learning kits that deal with the future. The Society also publishes a wide range of books.

LOCAL CHAPTERS
—Access to your local chapter. Over 100 cities in the United States and abroad have chapters for grass-roots support for future studies. They provide a way for members to get involved in their local communities through workshops, discussion groups, and speakers.

JOIN NOW!
For only $25 a year, you can become a regular member of the World Future Society. Just fill out and mail the attached form to receive all the benefits of a Society member.

The World Future Society is a non-profit, non-partisan organization. Headquarters are at 4916 St. Elmo Avenue, Bethesda, MD 20814, (301) 656-8274.

☐ **Yes!** I want to take part in building tomorrow...today. Enclosed is my $25 check or money order for the first year's dues. I understand I'll receive a one-year (six bimonthly issues) subscription to THE FUTURIST, discounts from the Society's Resource Center, and special invitations to General Assemblies and other meetings sponsored by the Society. I may also join the local chapter in my area.

☐ Please charge $25 annual dues to my
   ☐ MasterCard ☐ Visa ☐ American Express Account

Acct.# _____ Exp. Date_____

Name _____

Address _____

City _____ State _____ Zip _____

8033

Mail to:
World Future Society
4916 St. Elmo Avenue
Bethesda, MD 20814
U.S.A.